T0320305

ROUTLEDGE LIBRARY EDITIONS:
INEQUALITY

Volume 5

ECONOMIC EQUALITY
IN THE CO-OPERATIVE
COMMONWEALTH

ECONOMIC EQUALITY IN THE CO-OPERATIVE COMMONWEALTH

H. STANLEY JEVONS

Routledge
Taylor & Francis Group

LONDON AND NEW YORK

First published in 1933 by Methuen & Co. Ltd

This edition first published in 2023
by Routledge
4 Park Square, Milton Park, Abingdon, Oxon OX14 4RN

and by Routledge
605 Third Avenue, New York, NY 10158

Routledge is an imprint of the Taylor & Francis Group, an informa business

British Library Cataloguing in Publication Data
A catalogue record for this book is available from the British Library

ISBN: 978-1-032-43329-5 (Set)
ISBN: 978-1-032-43453-7 (Volume 5) (hbk)
ISBN: 978-1-032-43683-8 (Volume 5) (pbk)
ISBN: 978-1-003-36841-0 (Volume 5) (ebk)

DOI: 10.4324/9781003368410

Publisher's Note
The publisher has gone to great lengths to ensure the quality of this reprint but points out that some imperfections in the original copies may be apparent.

Disclaimer
The publisher has made every effort to trace copyright holders and would welcome correspondence from those they have been unable to trace.

ECONOMIC EQUALITY IN THE CO-OPERATIVE COMMONWEALTH

BY

H. STANLEY JEVONS
M.A., B.Sc., F.G.S., F.S.S.

METHUEN & CO. LTD.
36 ESSEX STREET W.C.
LONDON

First Published in 1933

PRINTED IN GREAT BRITAIN

CONTENTS

v

PART III

REALIZATION

PREFACE

THE present severe depression of trade has features which distinguish it from all those previously experienced and lead thoughtful people to wonder whether the prevailing economic system of competitive production and international trade is not breaking down from its own inherent weaknesses. There are many grounds for thinking that its days are numbered ; though there is likely to be a recovery from the present depression, to be followed in a few years by another collapse. Invention has been applied too fast and too universally for the competitive economic system to absorb its results and distribute the benefits. In recent years the introduction of highly efficient labour-saving machines in agriculture and in the getting of all raw materials has caused a break of prices which leaves no buying power to farmers and all primary producers in every part of the world. Mass production has similarly disorganized many manufacturing industries. Production is being restricted, however, at the present time. Demand will recover ; and business will again function normally, at least for a time. But at what a cost in suffering is normality reached !

Indeed we are not yet far removed from nature, when we await the survival of the fittest as the means of progress, instead of adopting a deliberately planned co-operative organization. Advance by the survival of the fittest involves the destruction of economic and human values in times of peace ; and war, in modern times, we may remember, is almost wholly the product of commercial rivalry ; of the imperative need to extend foreign markets and control sources of raw materials— ' imperative ' because the price system prevents the absorption of surplus production by the home market however much the poor may be in want.

It is coming to be realized that the capitalist competitive system will not permit of rapid progress in the welfare of the people. An ingenious engineer addressing the Royal Society of Arts called it ' the Leaky Tank System '. ' One can visualize the whole process,' he said, ' in terms of a leaky tank into which one group of people pump water unceasingly and at an ever increasing rate, while another group hidden in the background unceasingly create new leaks so that the level of the water shall not rise.'[1] That is a picturesque way of stating what economists well know : that the installation of labour-saving equipment in competitive industries, whilst usually profitable, and ultimately socially beneficial, is accompanied by appalling social wastes. Progress is only achieved by the wrecking of businesses and destruction of capital rendered useless by new inventions, or by the development of a capacity for production in excess of the demand, and by ruining the lives of workers whose only asset, their skill, is suddenly replaced by machines. Any extensive saving of labour in industries is for some years offset by an equivalent commercial waste in the form of unemployment. The group of engineers in America who have constituted themselves the pioneers of Technocracy are producing authoritative statistics which, it is asserted, prove the impossibility of the continuance of the competitive price system.

The desire for a new and orderly economic system which shall realize social justice is becoming widespread in this country ; and it is by no means confined to the ranks of labour. In the teaching profession, amongst ministers of religion, and in professions like engineering and architecture are many who in their writings, speeches, and conversations proclaim the need of a just and stabilized system of production and distribution, and some who have made tentative efforts at planning a new system. They realize that the malady is too deep-seated for any plan of currency reform, however drastic, to establish an economic system which would provide an equitable distribution of wealth, and treat all with justice. Seeking the same end in another way are thousands of members of co-operative societies eagerly discussing the Co-operative Commonwealth and how to bring it into being.

Social reformers and economists of the orthodox school are shy, however, of giving any support to socialist doctrines, for the good reason that they are not convinced that socialism would work. It appears to postulate an altruism which is not

---

[1] *Journ. Royal Soc. of Arts*, Vol. LXXX (1932), p. 335.

observable in human nature as we know it, and, it is assumed, would involve the creation of an immense bureaucracy extending its deadening hand over our industries. The intelligent middle classes form their opinion of socialism from numerous writers expressing such views, quite as much as from the spokesmen of business interests. On the other hand, it is fashionable amongst a section of socialists to declaim against the *bourgeoisie* as being dominated by capitalist mentality, mostly from self-interest, but partly in imitation of their social superiors. It is said or implied that middle-class people have no sympathy with the poor ; or, if they have, that their class interest prevents them from forming an unbiased opinion about the only possible permanent remedy for social injustice.

Probably these accusations against the middle class are less true of England than of any other country. Englishmen have not lost their independence of thought gained by centuries of struggle ; and, if conscious that it were threatened, would suffer much to retain it. I believe that the middle classes, in forming their opinion about socialism, are swayed quite as much by reason as by self-interest. Many of them are honestly convinced that the country would go to the dogs quickly under socialism as they understand it ; and conceive it their duty as patriotic citizens to oppose the spread of what seems to them a pernicious doctrine.

That the working classes, in the sense of persons engaged in manual labour, must eventually enter into control by sheer force of numbers is even clearer to-day than it was in the time of Karl Marx. Whether their entry shall be by way of the ballot-box or the barricade is the question to which every member of the aristocratic and middle classes in England should give his earnest attention. A peaceful transition to a state of economic equality depends more upon the attitude of the middle classes than upon anything else ; and the middle classes ought, therefore, to take the initiative in establishing an economic system acceptable to all. But reason forbids even a first step in the dark. Hence the necessity of devising a clear-cut scheme of co-operative socialism, based ultimately on economic equality, which will commend itself to the intellectual middle class as satisfying three essential conditions : firstly, that it shall be workable ; secondly, that it shall enhance the welfare of the people ; and thirdly, that it shall facilitate the maintenance of defensive military power at whatever strength may prove necessary. It will be agreed, I think, that the scheme of society outlined in this book does satisfy these three conditions.

To initiate a scientific investigation of the working of a stable society planned upon a basis of co-operation rather than competition was the chief task I set myself ; and I venture to think that any one who considers carefully what is written in Chapters VI to XIII will be inclined to agree that the common prejudices against any such scheme rest on an insecure foundation, when the assumption is that the population is educated ; and will agree further that a case has been made out for extensive research as to the possibilities of such a society. On the difficult question of the steps by which a peaceful transition to the new system may by realized, many opinions are possible ; and I do not claim finality even as regards my own. The importance of this book lies, as I see it, in the indication it gives of a vast new field of study and research, which should be directed to discovering the possibilities of a functional society in which the whole country would be organized permanently as an economic unit on the basis of economic equality. This form of society must be investigated, because it is the only form which can fully realize social justice ; and only a society which is just to all can be permanent when all are educated. The world is adventuring light-heartedly on a wholly new era, because education, and the desire for a higher standard of living, have been extended to all. The consequences of this in the economic and other spheres need to be most carefully thought out beforehand.

This book falls naturally into three parts. The first is devoted to general principles, explains the origin of differences between men, gives a brief account of the economic theory of the capitalist system and its decline, and investigates the economics of the growing demand for social and economic equality. The second part is an exposition of the economic organization devised by the author as likely to be the most efficient in providing for and safeguarding the welfare of the population organized co-operatively on the basis of equality, followed by a discussion of the economic principles involved in price-fixing and foreign trade ; whilst the third part is devoted to the means and stages by which the proposed society of equality may be actually realized in this country. The general tenor of the book will perhaps be understood best if its substance be outlined briefly here in advance.

It is shown first that in human evolution in its later stages group selection had become more important than individual survival ; and that the progress of civilization consists mainly in the alteration of the moral tradition and in the accumulation of knowledge—scientific, technical, and cultural—and of the capital and skill needed for applying it to promote human welfare. There are marked differences between different individuals as regards temperament, intellectual ability, and other inborn tendencies. These are mainly the result of occupational selection, of different factors having contributed to the survival of different tribes and races, and of the subsequent mixing of races. Early education and environment add their effects and largely determine character. Consequently the differences between individual persons are to a very small extent due to their own efforts. Those who succeed and those who fail in the present economic struggle do so largely on account of their innate qualities and early environment. Egoistically disposed persons with ' push ' and determination gain large incomes, and generously minded persons who may work as hard remain poor ; but this is no proof that the former are in any absolute sense cleverer, or have greater power of ministering to the real welfare of the community. It should be realized that the existing inequality of earnings is largely accidental, and could be greatly reduced, perhaps almost abolished, in the present money economy. The State could provide unlimited free education, with maintenance stipends, if necessary, for entrants to all the highly remunerated professions and kinds of business activity, until the remuneration in each occupation had been lowered to a pre-arranged figure. Economic inequality cannot be justified by any principle of abstract theory or justice. In practice it will not be possible to maintain it for many more decades ; but it is not here advocated as something to be forcibly established by the wage-earning classes. Rather it should be planned as a gift by those who are strong under the present system to those who are weak, when the justice of the demand has become recognized. The grant of votes to women is perhaps a precedent which indicates how this great change may come about.

The proposition of this book is that, after due investigation and preparation, the nation will step by step abolish the competitive system, and organize itself on the basis of co-operation and production for use rather than for private profit. To establish the society of equality outlined in this book by a sudden measure of reform is impracticable. A preliminary stage is the realization of socialism, in the sense that land and all the means of production will be owned by co-operative societies, philanthropic institutions, and the State or public authorities. Money would still be in circulation and inequality of incomes would persist, though greatly lessened. Industries would be controlled and planned on a national scale by the State, or under its authority; but operated partly by private enterprise, co-operatively or philanthropically controlled, and partly by public boards, in all cases on a basis of paying only fixed interest on capital.

Extensive research work meanwhile would develop plans for the complete co-ordination of all production and of the distribution of goods, and define more accurately the ultimate social objective. The realization of the society of equality, which had been fully studied and become widely desired, would follow as the logical outcome and end of this complete co-ordination. A great increase of the national dividend having already been achieved by technical progress and the abolition of the wastes of competition, a higher and still increasing standard of living for all would render practicable the realization of economic equality without hardship to any one. Thus a large majority of the electorate would favour the change, and realization would soon follow.

The organization and working of the scheme of society which it is anticipated would be thus established is examined in some detail in the middle part of the book. Every adult man and woman would have individually his or her rights as a citizen of the country, and corresponding obligations. The former would include receiving all the necessaries of life from public sources and the enjoyment of a credit income (equal for every

adult) for purchasing comforts and luxuries at the stores of
each town or suburb. The obligation consists mainly in offering
himself or herself for work of an approved kind according to
general rules laid down for all. There can be no doubt that
after the first few years people would be able to choose their
occupations as freely as they can now ; whilst the hours of
work would be much shorter than now, or holidays and periods
of leave would be much longer.

Apart from work, there need be no contact with officials,
other than representatives of local committees. Government
finance would be replaced by the simple plan of allocating the
necessary number of workers directly to the army, police, and
the civil administration. The only official who would keep a
watchful eye on people, like the income-tax collector does now,
would be the 'registrar of occupations', whose business it
would be to see that every one was employed in some authorized manner. Foreign travel and emigration would be facilitated ; and immigration restricted as now. No form of society
could be devised in which *all* the people would have greater
freedom of thought and speech and action than now ; but the
majority would have greater freedom. Being a stable form
of society, and the people having leisure, art in all its varied
forms would come to a new and true life, as William Morris
foresaw.

The economic organization of the country would require a
carefully thought out plan for the whole, with adequate checks
and balances, as between the different authorities. It is suggested that a Legislative Assembly for Economic Affairs and a
Supreme Economic Council will be the ultimate legislative
and executive authorities. Under the latter there would be
councils in general control of national economy, of industrial
production, of plant and equipment, of industrial welfare, of
occupations, and of professions, of the distribution of goods, and
of foreign trade. These controlling councils would consist for
the most part of specialists of the industries, with representatives elected by consumers and workers. The universities
would be self-governing ; and so would the guilds or associations
of professional workers, excepting only as regards the number
of persons admitted to the profession. Private trade would
be unnecessary, and also illegal, because the profit incentive

must be wholly removed from the social organization ; for
backsliding would always be possible until the newly accepted
incentives became firmly established by habit and custom.
Saving for investment would be impossible, and also unnecessary, since the provision of capital for industries would be made
by simply allotting sufficient labour to the industries making
machinery and other plant.

The method of inquiry which has resulted in this book is,
I think, in itself of some importance ; and the reader will gain
most if he understands it and tries to adopt the attitude of
mind which it involves. There being no society of equality in
existence it was necessary to proceed by deduction from general
principles based upon observation of man as he is. I began
therefore by trying to divest myself of every preconceived
idea, and by accepting no theory about human nature whatever.
I determined also, in every question that arose, to go straight
to the most fundamental ideas and facts—those of which often
we are so little conscious in our daily controversies on social
and economic questions. Furthermore, it seemed reasonable
to assume that all theories and doctrines which at any time
have gained public expression are in part true, or had some
aspect of truth or rightness at the time they were formulated.
If many people believed them, this must be so. Then, when I
had gathered many ideas and general principles, it became
evident that an eclectic synthesis was needed to build a consistent and workable economic system on the new basis. In
framing this I proceeded always with certain dominant ideas
before me : economic equality ; the abolition of money with
its stimulus to self-interest ; the necessity for making the whole
country the economic unit ; the human desires for freedom and
variety ; and the tendency to take the line of least resistance.
From the first I have had in view the necessity, which has
been insisted on by Mr. Bertrand Russell,[1] of placing myself in
my own thoughts, not as an administrator with authority, but
as a common citizen. This has made me see how essentially
democratic the whole system must be. In industries it will be
necessary to have appointments made by bodies of experts ;
but for all manner of purposes connected with people's

[1] *The Prospects of Industrial Civilization*, p. 154.

activities as workers and as consumers there must be national and divisional councils and local committees, of an *ad hoc* character.

It has been helpful to fancy myself doing various things in such a society, as if I were writing a story of the future ; and, again, to imagine how I would be doing in the future the things that I am doing now. For instance, on going a railway journey, I have thought of the incidents which would occur on a journey in the future ; no bother with heavy luggage, which would be ' expressed ' through (as the Americans say) to the house address at my destination ; of having to remember to bring my 1,000-mile ticket, issued to every one at the beginning of each year ; of there being no tips ; of simply going into the dining-car or a refreshment-room and having anything plain to eat and having nothing to pay or sign, food being an incident of travel.

A difficulty in writing this book was the choice of a name for the economic system it describes. The scheme proposed has much in common with the rather vague project frequently referred to as the ' co-operative commonwealth '. It is also a development of what is termed by some authors ' a functional society '. A system closely similar to it has been called in America ' integral co-operation '. Bellamy writes of ' universal co-operation ' as the basis of the economic system he describes in *Looking Backward* : but he avoids giving it a definite name.

The earliest and most widely accepted term for an economic system of this kind is *communism* ; and, if this book had been written before 1917 I should have adopted it without hesitation. At the present time, however, ' communism ' means for the vast majority of newspaper readers the creed of the Communist Party of Russia, including the class war and the dictatorship of the proletariat. Hence it was only after much hesitation that I decided to adopt the word ' communism ' for the society of economic equality here foreshadowed and described. This decision was forced upon me by the imperative need of a single word by which to name the system in writing and speech. Projects of economic equality must sooner or later become the subjects of research, propaganda, and controversy ; and this progressive work, particularly the educative propaganda, will be hindered if there is not a single easily remembered word to describe the system.

The word ' communism ' has been in use in England for nearly a century. Of the classical economists, John Stuart Mill alone paid serious attention to communism ; and his views are of considerable interest at the present day. He begins by distinguishing between communism and socialism thus : ' The assailants of the principle of individual property may be divided into two classes : those whose scheme implies absolute equality in the distribution of the physical means of life and enjoyment, and those who admit inequality, but grounded on some principle, or supposed principle, of justice or general expediency, and not, like so many of the existing social inequalities, dependent on accident alone. At the head of the first class, as the earliest of those belonging to the present generation, must be placed Mr. Owen and his followers. M. Louis Blanc and M. Cabet have more recently become conspicuous as apostles of similar doctrines (though the former advocates equality of distribution only as a transition to a still higher standard of justice, that all should work according to their capacity, and receive according to their wants). The characteristic name for this economical system is Communism, a word of continental origin, only of late introduced into this country. The word Socialism, which originated amongst the English Communists, and was assumed by them as a name to designate their own doctrine, is now [1849] on the Continent, employed in a larger sense ; not necessarily implying communism, or the entire abolition of private property, but applied to any system which requires that the land and the instruments of production should be the property, not of individuals, but of communities or associations, or of the government.'[1] Soon after the revised edition of Mill's treatise was published [1849] this meaning became attached to the word ' socialism ' in England also.

It is to be hoped that the term ' communism ' will gradually lose its extension to connote the class war and dictatorship of the proletariat, which the Russian revolution, following Karl Marx, with some degree of misunderstanding, has given it. It should be needless to add, as any one who reads this book, even the preface, will realize, that I personally am entirely and

---

[1] J. S. Mill, *Principles of Political Economy*, 4th edn., Book II, Chap. i, § 2.

absolutely opposed to propaganda advocating the class war and dictatorship of the proletariat as the only means of attaining communism. A violent uprising is much more likely to damage all classes and destroy the progress of a generation. The purpose of this book is just the opposite ; to point a constitutional way of realizing the legitimate aspirations of the people for social, and hence economic, equality in a system of democratic communism.

There is a larger literature in English bearing closely on the subjects treated in this book than is commonly realized. I am not aware of the existence of any other book devoted to a special study of economic equality as a practical proposition for adoption in a particular country within a few decades ; but utopias presupposing some form of communism, and other schemes of social reconstruction proposing the elimination of competition, are numerous. There are besides many well-known works on socialism ; and the ' literature of approach ', as it may be called, is growing rapidly. The subject on which I have written is so novel, and so extensive in its ramifications, that I cannot hope that my words alone will bring conviction to many readers. But I feel positive that, if the unconvinced will devote time to the study of the subject and follow the same course of reading as I have done, they will come back to the present book to find a better understanding and readier acceptance of its statements and proposals.

With this hope in view a classified bibliography of books— mainly those which have given me ideas for the present work— is added as Appendix III. I think the bibliography taken with references in the footnotes represents fairly all the sources on which I have drawn. Most of the chapters of this book were written consecutively during the years 1924 to 1927 ; and unfortunately some recent books appeared, or came into my hands, after the corresponding part of this book was written. This is especially true of Chapter V, on the Defects of the Capitalist System, which I salved from an abortive book written by me in 1919.[1] Its argument could have been strengthened

[1] In that year I set myself the task of writing a book which should be an exposition of the organization of society in a régime of socialism, justified by economic analysis. The conviction was forced upon me, after writing half the book, that neither socialism nor guild socialism would work, in the sense of being a stable and permanent form of society, for reasons which will be found in Chapter VI (pp. 106–7) of this book.

considerably had I used *The Decay of Capitalist Civilisation* by Sidney and Beatrice Webb, and some American works on waste.

More's *Utopia* should be read by every one, and the social writings of William Morris. For myself, however, I feel that I have gained more from Bellamy than from any single author. He deserves more attention from economists than he has received. The casting of his message in the form of a story, his acceptance of middle-class values—delight in the splendour of marble halls and the triumphs of mechanical devices—his industrial army, with its captains and lieutenants, are to many social thinkers repulsive features of his scheme. Yet he had a remarkable prevision of the mechanical and electrical progress of the twentieth century, for he describes television and the broadcasting of music by telephone, and mentions travel by air. Perhaps in the social sphere his forecasts may not be less accurate. The economic system he outlines does stand a rigid examination for workability in its essential features. It may be that in the United States and New Zealand even his idea of the industrial army will be realized. Physical drill and military training are compulsory on all students in many universities and colleges of those countries. Some populations like military discipline. The English do not ; and I do not think they will need it when service in disagreeable tasks is counted honourable.

PART I

IDEAS AND IDEALS

ECONOMIC EQUALITY IN THE CO-OPERATIVE COMMONWEALTH

CHAPTER I

PRESENT AND FUTURE

RECENT PROGRESS

THE past thirty years have seen more changes and events of the first magnitude than any similar period in the world's history. This apparently bold assertion is amply justified by consideration of the facts and their significance. Since 1900 the motor-car has been adapted to all purposes, and has gone far to revolutionize land transport ; for the first time in history man has mastered the air ; and wireless telephony has been not merely invented, but has already created a new industry, which, with television, will soon rival in importance the cinematograph industry, itself the product of the same period. On the political side, the most colossal war has destroyed great empires, and completed the organization of Europe as a family of nation States, at the same time that the League of Nations—dream of the past two centuries—has been officially established as mediator of the world's peace. At home and abroad the franchise has been extended to women ; and they now sit in Parliament. At the same time there has been a decay of the prestige of the organized churches, comparable only with the fall of the Roman Church from supremacy over all men's minds at the time of the Reformation.

As if these inventions, events and movements were not enough to be crowded into three decades, there has been also a profound change in the mechanical equipment and organization of industries and in the status of labour ; and these I regard as being possibly more significant for the future of this country and the world than any of the great changes just enumerated.

The design and manufacture of motor-cars provided a field free from prejudices and vested interests to which the results of scientific research and refined mechanical engineering were applied with surprising success, leading the way for the development of the aeroplane. The universal demand for motor-vehicles facilitated that organization of mass production, and later the extraordinary development of machine tools, which has been an important factor in the reduction of cost. Mass production, standardization and scientific management are essentially American contributions to the evolution of industrial methods, the movement for systematizing production having begun in the United States seventy years ago. Of recent years these ideas centring round mass production and scientific control have spread to all the newer industries in the leading industrial countries and to some extent in the older industries, causing bankruptcies of existing concerns by sudden reduction of manufacturing costs, and resulting in extensive unemployment through the displacement of skilled labour by semi-skilled men and women.

The progressive improvement of the organization of labour has combined scattered unions into nation-wide societies or federations ; and with this closer organization has come the power of national strikes. Since the first great miners' strike in 1912, the railwaymen, miners, engineers and transport workers have given ample proof of the power which they wield on account of their loyalty to their fellows and their perfected organization. Employers being also organized on a national basis in opposition to the men, their power of resistance has increased ; so that industrial struggles, other than those in the export industries, are developing into a pressure on the public, which, so far as the voicing of opinion is concerned, means the middle class. The Government is thus forced to act as mediator, and tries, often successfully, to persuade the employers to accept terms which otherwise they would have stood out against.

The improved organization of labour has extended to the political sphere, and a Labour Government has held office for the second time. Before another decade has passed we may expect a Labour Government to be returned to power with a substantial majority over all other parties. Strikes on a national scale may then become additionally effective, for, the men being assured of the sympathy of the Government (assuming the trade union has officially approved the strike), legislation may be undertaken to secure the greater part of their demands, and so avert a general strike. The tendency, already evident in 1926, will be for Government to become, not merely the arbitrator, but the paramount director and controller of the great industries. This seems likely to lead eventually to nationalization of the mining industry and the railways and land transport generally, as avoiding the complexities of a triple control by employers, workmen and the State.

A PERIOD OF CHANGE

Throughout history periods of rapid change have alternated with periods of stagnation or slow and steady progress. Possibly now we are in the early phase of one of the greatest periods of rapid change. Certainly the indications are that we are not likely to reach a position of stability in so short a time as ten or fifteen years.

This becomes obvious when we consider that for a century there has been no considerable change in English social or political organization ; and this in spite of immense colonial expansion, the remarkable progress of discovery, the huge growth of industry and trade, the monopolistic power of the aggregation of capital, and the advance of the Labour movement. The social classes of England—the landed aristocracy, the wealthy business class, the middle class (business and professional), the artisan and labouring classes—stand in their serried ranks now much as they did a hundred years ago. Some decay of the first and expansion of the second is all the change we can notice ; except the advance of all in education and economic well-being. Similarly, since the time of the younger Pitt there has been relatively little change in the English Constitution. The franchise has been extended, the power of the House of Lords has been clipped a little further, there has been some growth of an ' inner cabinet ', the larger colonies have obtained full self-government, and

Ireland has won Home Rule. Compared with the great alteration of the material aspects of life, this is equivalent to standing
still.

Not for these reasons alone is it clear that changes of our
political and social structure are to be expected. There is
everywhere a feeling of unrest : a discontent, a conviction that
things are not right—that drastic reforms have got to come.
Such a general feeling of unrest always portends change ; and
it is accompanied by fear—dread of what the unknown future
has in store for men of substance, their women and children.
And fear generates hate ; hence the Fascist movements in various
continental countries, which find a slight echo in our own.

No difficult analysis is needed to understand this unrest.
It was accentuated by the War ; but the symptoms were
evident enough before 1914, and expressed themselves in ways
economic, social and political. During the twenty-five years
1873 to 1898 the cost of living fell relatively to money earnings,
so that there was a substantial increase of the *real* wages of
skilled workers (i.e. in terms of goods which could be purchased);
and consequently there was a considerable improvement of
the standard of living of the working classes. From 1898 to
1914, however, wages on the average rose but little, if at all,
faster than the cost of living ; and in some industries workers
had a struggle to maintain their standard of living. At the
same time the wants of the younger generation were increasing
—the standard of living desired was rising, on account of the
general diffusion of education.

During the forty years following 1873 there was an expansion
of the middle class in numbers, and a distinct improvement
of their standard of comfort. Yet little or no increase of
happiness seems to have attended this growth of material
prosperity, which, moreover, received a set-back from war
taxation and high prices. Possibly men, and certainly women,
are enjoying greater freedom ; but in all minds to-day there
is doubt, dissatisfaction, anxiety, when not despair. Some
might lay the blame upon the War and the recent unexampled
collapse and depression of trade. I think the cause lies deeper,
however, and must be traced largely to the decay of religious
life, and with it the disappearance of much of the spiritual
comfort and moral restraint on worry and discontent. Thus

the economic difficulties or heavy taxation and high prices relatively to income are not borne philosophically as in the past; and the loss of spiritual consolation is itself a loss of happiness.

It may well be argued, however, that the disappearance of religious conviction may be traced to more fundamental causes, chiefly intellectual and social. These have not, in the main, made people less religiously inclined, but have destroyed their faith in the old doctrines, the old forms of devotion, and in the organized churches. Two movements seem to have been of overwhelming importance in bringing about this result: firstly, the diffusion of the spirit of free inquiry, and, secondly, the spread of education.

Complete freedom in the diffusion of ideas is an innovation of our own time—at least since the decay of Roman civilization. The publication of the results of scientific research was penalized by the Church in the seventeenth century, banned to its members in the eighteenth century, and only tolerated in the nineteenth century because science had ' made good ', and had proved its utility to mankind. But the extension of the scientific method to subjects other than the natural sciences, and the general acceptance of Darwinian thought, characteristic of the past half-century, has so weakened the position of ecclesiastical dogma that doctrinal authority now counts for little, at any rate outside parts of the United States and a few countries, mainly Roman Catholic. The application of observational and inductive methods to historical research, and throughout the social sciences, in psychology, and even in philosophy, is having the most far-reaching results on all our thought and ideas. Even morality, that last exclusive field of church dispensation, is gradually freeing itself; and we look for a new science of ethics which will give us a new moral code capable of variation in consonance with the needs of social and political progress.

Compulsory general education came into effect in this country in 1871, and I venture to predict that historians of the future will regard that as the turning point between the old and the new civilizations. To us now compulsory education is a commonplace necessity. We have forgotten how revolutionary it seemed to the generation who took the fateful step:

we quite fail, even now, to grasp its full significance for the future. The consequences of this reform will be revolutionary ; and this book is mainly devoted to an investigation of its social and economic effects, and as to how the profound changes which are inevitable may best be guided and controlled towards a safe and happy objective.

COMPULSORY GENERAL EDUCATION

Until the early nineteenth century the world had never seriously thought of educating the mass of the people. Plato, in his *Republic*, would educate all except slaves, who would be numerous. Sir Thomas More came nearer in writing *Utopia* (in 1515), because there all were educated, except presumably those bondmen who came from foreign countries, and would be relatively few in number. The watchwords of the French Revolution—' Liberty, Equality, Fraternity '—gave a new value to the life of the common man. The English humanitarian movement, whilst freeing slaves throughout the British dominions, and reforming conditions of labour in mines and factories, taught men to think of elevating the masses. The humanitarians not only thought : they acted. The growth of voluntary schools and mechanics' institutes from about 1810 onwards was a quiet movement, which may be regarded as having been of greater importance than even free trade and the reform of the parliamentary franchise. State aid was demanded for the support of voluntary schools when private resources failed to meet the growing need ; and once this practice was well established, nothing could prevent the growth of the movement into general compulsory education, at the cost, wherever necessary, of public funds.

The acceptance by Parliament of this reform, and its actual execution, marks the commencement of a wholly new standard and tradition in the moral aspect of our civilization. We hold now that every man born an Englishman, in his own interests, and in the interests of the community at large, must be educated up to a certain standard ; and we hold further that every English boy and girl is entitled to the opportunity of such further education as his or her innate abilities permit. The endeavour is to guarantee to every person equal opportunity of advancement and of culture to the full extent which the resources of the State permit.

This new embodiment of the conception of the equality of man is by no means a hypocritical ' sop to the working man ' ; nor yet an ' opiate ', such as the doctrine of the Greek or Roman Churches. On the contrary, general education is a leaven that stirs men to new ideas and activities. Already it is beginning to make the masses realize and believe in the equality of men. The leaven has only just begun to work. We may well believe that it will go on fermenting until the dough has ' risen '—that is, until, as we shall see later, equality comes to prevail in the economic as well as in the political and social spheres.

A little consideration shows that the economic effects of general education have been already as striking as its social and political results. Education and travel are the two principal causes of people developing new wants. The arousing of new desires, such as for better food, neat, if not showy, clothes for evenings and Sundays, better house accommodation and furniture, and amusements, creates what is called a higher standard of living. This also involves the wish for more leisure. The higher standard of wages and reduced working hours following the War enabled the fulfilment of the desires formed by the new interests which education awakened, partly by its tendency to stimulate imitation of the well-to-do classes. A higher standard of living once experienced for a year or two becomes a habit ; and the reduction of wages to a level which makes it no longer possible to maintain the new habitual standard of living causes widespread discontent amongst the workmen in all the industries so affected.

Many reformers regard the discontent caused by education with complacency, for they say, ' Is not a divine discontent the mainspring of progress ? ' Assuming the way forward is known, and an orderly progress assured, most of us would agree with them. The trouble is that at present there are so many people advising different roads, that the nation cannot make up its mind to any one of them. The hesitation is leading to exasperation amongst the more energetic of the discontented who join the Communist Party ; and to apathy and acceptance

of capitalist newspapers and films by the majority. Again we
see the necessity for frank and scientific discussion of the
ultimate social objective, and the way towards it.

It is almost impossible for persons of the propertied, business
and professional classes to realize the outlook of the average
working man, who feels himself one of the great proletariat.
Modern facilities of locomotion have created a class consciousness amongst the working classes of all industries ; and it
would be folly, merely because the term has been bandied
about in revolutionary socialist propaganda, to ignore the
reality and continuance of the growth of class consciousness.
Call it an instance of ' group consciousness ', and you are at
once in accord with the terminology of the modern school of
psychologists.

Now there cannot be a group consciousness unless there is
some antithesis, some other array of people in which the group
recognizes or imagines a difference of thought, desires and
policy, such desires and policy being inconsistent with its own.
There cannot be a cohesive political party if there is no party
with a definite program opposed to it. The cause of the
class consciousness of the workers is that they see everywhere
the well-to-do classes living in a pleasanter and more costly
manner, enjoying prestige and privilege and freedom of which
the workers may have an occasional taste, sufficient to whet
their appetite, but which they are generally denied. Some of
the men and most of the women in the comfortable class are
idle, or appear to be so ; though the worker will admit that
some of them make for themselves a great deal of work in
raising money by bazaars to relieve the necessity of those
amongst the proletariat who are down and out, and who, being
respectable citizens, would never have been crushed if the
social system had been just. But those well-to-do men and
women who are earning their incomes do so apparently under
pleasant conditions and with ease, for the burden of mental
effort and nervous strain is not obvious.

The more the class consciousness of the workers grows, the
less ready are they to take any account of sub-groups amongst

their opposite—the well-to-do. Hence all the trials, discouragements and losses from which the working man suffers through no fault of his own are ascribed more and more to the heartlessness of the ruling classes, who in effect are the rich and the middle class. It is for this reason that the demand for the rectification of what are distinctly economic grievances —dependence on employer's will, risk of unemployment, and so forth—is called a demand for *social* justice.

The working man of to-day is conscious that he and his kind in many ways are not regarded as inferior to the propertied and professional classes. The workers and their families are all expected to be educated, and not a few of them are conscious of being better educated than some wealthy grocers or successful contractors. Moreover, the law of the land regards them as being the equals of the propertied classes for political purposes. The residence vote of a labourer at a colliery is as good as that of a millionaire coal king ; and an able seaman can balance the vote of the chairman of a great steamship company. Only by translation to the House of Lords do the successful attain a higher political status according to law !

Even more significant than equality of voting power is the change of social status which has come about in the last thirty years. The manual workers are no longer regarded as a lower caste with whom gentlemen would never associate on equal terms. It depends now upon education and manners. Any man who has gained a high office in his union, or some public position, finds himself invited to social functions at the houses of the well-to-do. Royalty in this century has been careful to make no distinction on the ground of a man's occupation. When King Edward went to open a new dock at Cardiff, a Labour alderman, by trade a carpenter, was Lord Mayor, and he was duly knighted according to the usual custom. Our present King, when the first MacDonald Government came into power, made no distinction whatever against Labour men on social grounds ; and the democratic sympathies of the Prince of Wales are well known, and are the basis of his immense popularity.

The first effect of this social acceptance of Labour men was to cause unrest amongst the rank and file who believed, and perhaps not without cause, that mixing with the middle classes

as social equals tended to weaken the fighting zeal of their
leaders. They came to see things from the middle-class point
of view, and in some cases might, more or less unconsciously,
hesitate to take that action which might lose them new and
agreeable social contacts. But a new and totally different
effect upon the rank and file seems to be following; though
it has had but little conscious expression so far. If working
men with suitable education and opportunities are afforded
social intercourse on equal terms with aristocrats and the
middle class, is this not at last the *proof* that, *given similar
advantages*, the working class *are as good as* any other class ?
Then why should equal opportunities be denied any longer ?

This brings the argument to the economic sphere, where
equality most certainly does not reign. The skilled mechanic
is carried away by his feelings, and his thoughts run somewhat
as follows : ' The boss who, at any rate if he is a Member of
Parliament, will ask me to a party at his house, will any day
turn me, and the likes of me, into the street to starve, if he
finds orders have fallen off. He calls that business. I call it
a damned shame, especially when his money runs into six
figures.' The workman hates the insecurity and indignity of
his position. He objects almost as much to the big profits
when prices are rising, which seem to be a gift from heaven,
because he gets little, if any, share of them. Yet when prices
begin to fall again, the majority of employers immediately cry
out that wages must be reduced. Having spent their big
profits, they declare, often with truth, that they will fall into
financial difficulties unless wages be reduced.

With the increasingly large scale on which businesses are
conducted, with the great increase of amalgamations and
combinations of industrial concerns, and the organization of
employers' associations, the personal relation between employer
and employed has been disappearing more and more completely
from British industry. The phalanx of capitalist employers
seems to stand solid like a wall. The workman has no chance
of making a personal bargain : he must accept what terms are
offered. His range of choice as between different employers
and different terms of work has been steadily narrowed from
year to year. Thus the skilled manual worker, whilst increasing
his real wages, has lost something particularly dear to an

Englishman—his sense of freedom. With an improving standard of education, and the recognition of political equality, and to a large extent, of social equality also, the manual worker has developed a self-respect, which was rarely to be found amongst former generations of workers. This self-respect is outraged by the growing feeling of dependence on the will of an impersonal capitalist employer—usually a company—represented by its managers and foremen. Some of the latter have most objectionable manners, which wound the pride of the modern young workman, whereas his grandfather was obliged to accept insults as if he were a soldier at drill, and thought no more about it.

At the same time that owners have achieved more or less of a monopoly, and power of fixing prices, in their industry, unemployment has grown. A trade union can secure a standard wage for its members, but it cannot secure employment for those of its members who are out of work, unless it be willing to sacrifice its standard wage. Displacement of workers by labour-saving machinery, the so-called 'technological unemployment', is an even greater problem. So unemployment remains the greatest bugbear of the workman, his greatest grievance against the capitalist system. He demands that society shall not sacrifice individuals, so as to have a convenient reserve of labour for busy times. The Labour Party has constantly agitated this question, but without achieving anything more than State insurance against unemployment. For several consecutive years (1907 to 1912) a 'Right to Work' Bill was introduced in the House of Commons on behalf of the Labour Party—varied a little in form from time to time. The principle underlying these Bills was that the Government should be responsible for providing, itself or through local authorities, suitable work for all ablebodied unemployed, paid at trade union rates of wages. 'Suitable work' means work of the kind in which the unemployed worker is normally engaged, and paid at the same rate. This would involve public authorities in a whole series of industrial undertakings. Any such provision of work would be entirely artificial in the capitalist competitive system of industry, and would be financially impracticable. Morally it would be far better for the workman than our present system of doles without requiring work, but at present we can do no better. The 'right to work' is an idea which belongs to a wholly different economic system.

The demand for social justice resolves itself into a demand for a new status for the worker in industry : that his opportunities and conditions of employment should not be determined by the exigencies of employers competing for profit ; that safety in coal-mines and other dangerous employments shall not be prejudiced by the employers' continual search for means of cutting down expenses, that the workman should have opportunities of initiative, and be treated with respect as an educated man, and that large profits due to exceptional circumstances should be treated as belonging of right more to the workers than to the capitalists—an idea which is strengthened by the practice of paying only a fixed rate of interest on capital in all co-operative undertakings.

It is important to note that the demand is for *social* justice and not for *economic* justice. As was pointed out above, the group consciousness of the worker arises from a feeling of opposition to the whole of the well-to-do classes in all their ways of life. There is no clear separation in their minds between the economic sphere of life and the social and political spheres. Society welcomes him in the political sphere, accords him more and more recognition in social ways ; but, by maintaining the capitalist employer, degrades him in the economic sphere. He demands that society shall alter the system of employment.

RADICAL AND SOCIALIST REFORMS MERE PALLIATIVES

The point of view of the restless workmen of to-day has perhaps been sufficiently indicated. It is useless to discuss arbitration and conciliation boards, Whitley Councils, and other policies for securing co-operation between workmen and employers. Everybody agrees that such co-operation would be most beneficial, and that both employers and workmen might do more towards achieving it. There are strong forces working against it, however, namely, the supposed, and often real, clashing of economic interests as regards the immediate future, and the growing and continued opposition of class feeling. It is only in the long run, and provided that nearly all workmen increase their efforts and efficiency, that they will benefit by a true co-operation with their employers. The men of each shop, mine or mill think, and rightly, that with the present competitive system, their particular employer will be tempted to give away to the consumer in lower prices the results of their increased labours. The object of the workman is the same as that of the business man : to sell his labour for the highest price he can get. As he can be given no real security that if he increases his rate of output his rate of remuneration *per unit of work done* will not be reduced, owing to his employer having to reduce the price so as to sell the increased output, he prefers to secure a high remuneration per unit of work by doing as little work for his wage as the normal employer will stand. The trade unions of the great industries, with their immense power, tacitly permit, if they do not actively support, this policy. This is the great waste of the capitalist system, and its mortal sickness.

Present-day English publicists are like people who rush about with buckets full of water when a city is on fire. The palliatives of conciliation, profit-sharing, unemployment insurance, and so forth, count only for a few gallons of water each. They may help to prevent the situation from getting rapidly worse ; but they cannot stop the blaze. Investigators who have the ability and opportunity to study economic and social questions more deeply should put aside questions of the near future, and concern themselves with the fundamental conditions of human progress.

This book is an attempt to search out the deep undercurrents of evolution which are causing present economic disturbances, to forecast the probable future changes in social and economic organization which the continuance of the same causes may be expected to bring about, and to discover a stable form of society to which the forces of change may be consciously directed. Economists, and even socialists, neglect too much questions of individual and mass psychology. I shall show that the innate qualities of men, and the moral tradition and civilization, including education, of the people, are determining factors of the economic organization, and that the latter adapts itself to those determining factors and the physical conditions of the country. Physical conditions become of decreasing importance, however, as civilization advances.

No sufficient analysis of the economics of a country organized in accordance with the doctrines of socialism, whether State socialism or a system of national guilds, seems to have been made as yet. In 1919, stimulated by the general hopefulness and unrest, and the socialization actually proceeding in Russia and Hungary, I set out to examine the economics of a socialized state, having, as regards industries, special reference to England. The result was that I could not complete my book, which had been planned to show the advantages of a socialist state as. commonly advocated. Study and reflection for another five years convinced me that a socialist régime as now generally conceived, based on the price system, with money in circulation, is impracticable, because it would be unstable. It would be little more than a jumble of super-palliatives. Causes of friction would be innumerable, and the fabric would collapse sooner or later as surely as the individualistic order will do so, as I shall show in a later chapter.

A better, and a stable, order of society can only be achieved by changes much more fundamental, which fully recognize in the economic sphere the altered human values which our moral sentiments acclaim and which in other spheres are slowly being realized. We no longer follow the *laissez-faire* school and admire self-interest as the force supposed to conduce to the greatest good of the greatest number. Self-interest has always needed to be checked by other motives ; and the era during which it can usefully be the supreme motive in industry is coming to a close. In our hearts we admire self-sacrifice and devotion to duty, and the doing of work voluntarily for the nation. We demand self-sacrifice and devotion to duty of our sailors daily, and of all men to whom we entrust our lives. In war-time we expect all men to be actuated by no other motives.

ANTICIPATION

The argument which I shall develop is that a stable order of society, consisting entirely of educated men and women having political equality, cannot be founded on self-interest, but can be built up only by reliance on the highest motives

in work as well as in public service. In fact, all industrial
work will become public service, organized locally or nationally
according to its nature. Every man and woman will be
required to work in some industry or service, the rearing of
children being accounted a social service ; and in respect of
such work faithfully done to the best of a man's ability every
man and woman will receive an equal income. All the instruments of production, and all considerable property, such as
houses, will belong to the people collectively, usually under
local, but sometimes central, administration. Private property
will be limited to a man's personal and household belongings
in reasonable quantity.

To most readers a society organized on such a basis must
appear merely a Utopian dream ; but I assure them that it is
not so, and that it is capable of being realized in England
within fifty years, if so the nation wills. Nor is the proposal
a novel one. The system I propose to examine is in effect a
kind of limited communism. It was thought out in some detail
by Edward Bellamy when he wrote his *Looking Backward*,
though perhaps he gave undue stress to the mechanical advantages, which are merely incidental. The Russian Communist
Party made a gallant, but foolish, attempt to establish a system
based on the same principles, which was a most tragic failure ;
and necessarily so. Russia had experienced crushing defeats,
and a political revolution followed by an agrarian revolution,
which was the greatest upheaval of the country's history.
Then followed the attempt to impose upon the country, already
in a state of chaos, a new economic system which it did not
understand and did not want. Obviously it could only add
to the calamity ; and a reversion to the economic system
suitable to Russia's present stage of moral and educational
development was inevitable.

When England adopts communism, as I believe she will, it
can be only after a substantial majority of the whole adult
population desires it. It will be adopted by general consent
as the outcome of a desire for the extension of voluntary co-
operation according to a scheme planned by the State. Only
after many years of patient education and preparation can the
fateful step be taken safely.

Is the labour of preparation worth while ? I hope to show

that it will be abundantly worth while. Money will be completely abolished, and its deleterious moral effects will automatically disappear. There will be no tax-collectors, because there will be no taxes to collect. All will receive gratuitously the necessaries of life ; and every man and woman will be allotted a credit income for comforts and luxuries. Any person who refuses to work, and fails to reach the standard demanded by public opinion, will, after due trial, be ejected from the commonwealth, and will be looked after in a colony by a body specially appointed for the purpose. A study of the enormous wastes of the present system—the wastes of duplication, of advertising, of failures of businesses, all inseparable from competitive trade, of the vast army of book-keepers employed by the Government, banks and business firms, who will become unnecessary, except cost accountants and stock-keepers—will show that a large section of the population can be freed for productive work. This fact, and the economies of large-scale production, and increased use of labour-saving machinery, welcomed by the workmen, instead of being opposed, as now, will lead in a few years to a great and growing expansion of the national dividend. This will enable all to enjoy a standard of living at least thrice as good as that of the skilled workman of to-day ; which will be rapidly improved to the standard enjoyed by the professional, intellectual, and medium employer classes of to-day.

To most of us the greatest relief would be the complete absence of the petty worries, anxieties and enmities of life, inseparable from the earning and spending of a money income with fluctuating prices. There would be a freedom and expansiveness which would allow all life to rise to a higher plane. Amongst all advantages I place highest the spiritual and moral elevation, which would be the necessary accompaniment of the change, and its permanent endowment. No longer would men be degraded by the struggle for money ; no longer would they be constantly assailed by the temptation to allow base motives to overcome the just and generous. Always the thought to render service and co-operate with others would be uppermost ; and every man would find his work more valued, and value it more himself. To-day we are torn, as in no previous period of the world's history, by conflicting emotions, duties and desires. We want more than any earlier generation to be just, to do the right and kind thing. And our whole economic system is organized so that we have to do the unkind, sometimes the cruel, deed, or suffer unduly ourselves. The Sermon on the Mount cannot be literally applied whilst we continue bound in an antiquated economic and social system ; but a new order can be devised and worked which itself embodies the teachings of Jesus Christ. Those are the eternal principles of human goodness and happiness ; and mistake is impossible if we work conscientiously and consistently in preparation for the establishment of a new state of society founded upon equality and generosity, and using to the full the highest powers of man's intellect.

CHAPTER II

HUMAN EVOLUTION

THE STUDY OF PROGRESS

NO fruitful discussion of a radical improvement of the social order is possible without a clear comprehension of the nature of progress. We have to understand its causes in the past, and the ways in which it may occur in the future, or may be deliberately obtained. One of the distinguishing features of the twentieth century, as compared with all preceding time, is likely to be the acceptance by mankind of the idea and practice of planning for the progress of the race. Until the eighteenth century the very idea of progress as a continuous process of advance to a better and better state hardly existed. It was not until the nineteenth century that the results of the agricultural and industrial revolutions, the great expansion of trade and population which they initiated, and the extension of scientific thought, led all men to expect that such growth would continue indefinitely. So we still believe, though our reasons might not stand a rigorous examination. I shall show, however, that if we consciously set about finding out what measures must be taken to secure progress, the probability is that it can be realized continuously and rapidly.

Ideas derived from the investigation of heredity and the processes of evolution of animals and plants have been applied in recent years by sociologists and psychologists to elucidate the conditions and causes of progress so strikingly exhibited by the peoples of European origin, and by Japan ; to find out why the civilization of other peoples has remained stationary ; and the reasons for racial differences. There have been brought to light many facts and principles of supreme importance, which it is the business of every one seeking to reform the social condition of his country at least to understand.

In the present chapter I propose to give a brief connected

account of human evolution in its early and later stages, so that we may gain some idea of how racial qualities, and also the innate differences between individuals, have arisen. This will lead to a consideration of how far the existing capitalist system, with its money economy, has tended to perpetuate itself by economic and social selection. Succeeding chapters will be devoted to the question how a far-reaching and beneficial development of our social and economic organization may be stimulated and directed consciously towards an end acceptable to the great majority of the people ; and this without danger of violent revolution.

THE SURVIVAL OF THE FITTEST

Amongst the primitive ancestors of man progress was doubtless the result mainly of natural selection, as was the evolution of every species of animal. Individuals varied in all directions from the normal—possibly a larger proportion of individuals in some directions than others—and the individuals most fitted to survive in the environment of the place and time escaped destruction. They would survive, at any rate, in larger proportion than variants less fitted to their surroundings ; and the characters possessed by the majority would be transmitted to their progeny, so that with each generation there would be a smaller and smaller proportion of individuals born unfitted to survive. The race would thus become more and more adapted to a given environment, assuming the latter to remain long without substantial change. The evolution of brain-power was almost certainly the principal factor of survival in primitive man, enabling him not merely to elude dangerous enemies, human and animal, but to hunt and trap intelligently, and eventually to use primitive weapons and tools. The discovery that edible seeds could be planted and would reproduce themselves in abundance was made in some favourable environment ; and the tribes which learnt this art multiplied in numbers, because, within limits, the food-supply could be expanded thus with far less labour than by searching in forests or wild grasslands, or by hunting or fishing. Other tribes must have discovered they could catch wild animals most easily at certain seasons, and were led to the idea of rounding up a number and keeping them closely guarded until needed for food. They would pasture them, and discover that the animals would breed in captivity, and thus the domestication of animals arose, and the pastoral tribes.

It is important to remember that the environment includes everything which can react on man's senses—the climate, food-supply, dangers from wild animals and poisonous snakes or plants, his fellow-human beings, and all the forces of nature. The beginnings of civilization—the practice of agriculture, the domestication of animals, the discovery of fire and cooking, the invention of tools, and finally the smelting of metals, the use of animals for carrying burdens and then for drawing sleds, and the use of wheeled carts derived from rollers, and canoes from hollowed trees—meant so many successive changes in the environment. The warming of huts by fire, and the use of skins, made northern climates habitable ; and so, from age to age, man has gone on modifying the environment in his favour, until the triumphs of the nineteenth century in the control of disease, the construction of vast irrigation canals, and the transport of food by rail and water from the ends of the earth, have nearly defeated natural forces and united the whole world's food-supply.

GROUP SELECTION

It will be remembered that some species of animals live as isolated individuals or families, each at war more or less with all others of the same species, as well as with many other species ; and that other animals live in herds, the members of which act together in fleeing from danger or in defending themselves. In a few cases, like a pack of wolves, they even co-operate in obtaining food-supply. Such animals have a gregarious instinct, and are happier in company with their fellows. It is obvious this instinct has a survival value, because any individual which strayed from the herd would be more liable to perish. In man, too, the gregarious instinct would be a factor of survival, except perhaps in the case of hunters in wild places where game was scarce. Thus the great majority of men at a very early stage formed themselves into tribes.

A new and very important factor of survival then developed, namely, the co-operation of persons composing the tribe in obtaining food, and in offence and defence. As numbers increased relatively to the area providing food-supply, different tribes would come into competition and conflict. Evolution would then proceed by elimination of whole tribes, namely, those which had least cohesion and intelligence in the use of weapons and of animals. Fleetness of foot and mere physical strength, so important for survival of isolated individuals, would become of secondary importance in a conflict between groups. Thus consciousness of kind, which may be defined as knowing and bearing active goodwill to members of one's own tribe or group, and disliking or hating individuals of any other, would make for cohesion ; and a disposition to mutual aid—a willingness to make personal sacrifices of comfort, and actually to face danger, in the interests of other members of the tribe, individually and collectively—would tend to the survival of the group.

The surviving tribes of the Eurasian continent have produced all the great races of mankind ; so we have fixed in us in varying degrees an innate consciousness of kind. To these fundamental characteristics of our nature must be ascribed, on the one hand, in part at least, the terrible problems of race conflict and discrimination, which are creating even now more and more difficult political problems. A white man in the tropics will always rush to the assistance of another white man in need or danger ; but he must have a strong moral conviction and self-control, if he is to rush equally quickly to the aid of a black man. On the other hand, we see the altruistic tendency towards our own kind expressing itself nowadays in patriotism, in voluntary public service of all kinds, and in certain forms of charity. Perhaps acts of personal charity to persons known to us are due mainly to an extension of the parental instinct ; but the larger charity—a desire to assist all less fortunately situated than ourselves, which in many people is over-borne by other tendencies—is probably directly connected with consciousness of kind. Altruistic action has been enormously extended and systematized by religious and moral tradition.

THE IMPORTANCE OF TRADITION

The efficiency of a tribe in warfare is enhanced by two habits of mind and action : submission to a leader and conformity with certain generally accepted rules of conduct. A tribe composed of persons all determined to do things their own way, and refusing obedience to any one, must rapidly disintegrate and be annihilated in warfare. The majority appreciate very early what kind of conduct is advantageous to the tribe as a whole, and public opinion rigorously insists on submission to an accepted leader, and obedience to the custom of the tribe. Aberrant independent men are either ejected from the tribe or killed in quarrels.

There is to be seen in the accepted chieftain of the tribe or clan, and in the men he selects to act as his assistants in leadership when the tribe grows large, the beginning of the emergence of a military caste or class, which eventually becomes definitely separated in the case of a people which settles down to agriculture. In the code of conduct, usually very detailed and exacting, we see the beginning of a system of law and of social conventions as we know them now.

When we consider all the stages which have been passed through from a primitive tribal organization to a European nation of to-day, it becomes evident that civilization has three principal aspects, in each of which it is capable of change, to some extent independently, and each of which can be further sub-divided. The first embraces the growth of classes or castes ; the structure of government, whether it be a feudal system, or an autocratic king with ministers and grades of officials, or a republic ; the whole complex of rules of conduct —statute and common law, by-laws, trade customs and social conventions ; and the national institutions and ceremonies. All these are grouped together under one heading and called the *social organization* of that people or nation.

Secondly, there is the whole body of *tradition of skill and of knowledge*, including the methods of thought and acquirement of new ideas and principles, in other words, research. There are obviously two branches : on the one hand, all the accumulated knowledge and skill in the arts and crafts, in all trades and industries, engineering, navigation, and the technical sciences generally ; and, on the other hand, the great body of literature, philosophy, historical knowledge, the natural sciences, and pure science generally, including political philosophy and sociology. These two branches, originally distinct, are coming more and more to influence one another, which is mainly the result of changing social organization, which leads to industrial technologists being no longer despised by men of science. The whole body of skill and knowledge in these two branches may be called conveniently the *intellectual tradition*.

Thirdly, we have the *moral tradition*. The growth of this has been intimately connected with religion. The immense importance in the interests of survival of the community of securing conformity with the accepted code of conduct has led to the military or ruling caste from the earliest times seeking the aid of the priests to give a supernatural sanction to certain rules ; whereupon the priestly caste have adopted this as one of their special functions in society ; and have defined, and to a large extent stereotyped, those rules which had the general approbation of the more thoughtful portion of the population. Fear of everlasting torment in a future life or lives has been the main instrument for securing obedience for the past four thousand years, with the addition in many religions of the reward of perpetual bliss for the good. No State religion, or any sect, ever secures conformity to all its precepts by the mass of the people. There are always some persons whose moral code and practice are in advance of the general level, and some who fall behind and break the rules, and who are treated with social or legal restraint or revenge. Thoughtful individuals, like the Stoics of Greece and Rome, have at all times had their own individual standards of morality ; but there is at any one time a clearly recognized convention of proper conduct, supported both by organized religion and secular law. Sidgwick has called this body of rules, supported by the prevalent opinion, the *positive morality* of the community [1] ; and I shall adopt the term in this sense. At any one time there is a positive morality characteristic of each people or country, which is the moral tradition modified by the recent emotional, intellectual and economic movements, especially by contact with other nations or peoples having different positive moralities.

[1] *Elements of Politics*, 4th ed., 1919, pp. 23 and 204-6.

The evolution of positive morality is by no means always an advance, judged from the point of view of social welfare, or even of the survival of the nation. There have been in history many periods of degeneration. On the whole, the tendency of morality in Europe has been an improvement to levels more beneficial socially and individually. The individual benefit has arisen not only directly, but also through the greater freedom which social organization has permitted in response to an advancing standard of positive morality. Christianity is responsible, of course, for an enormous moral advance ; but under the aegis of an established church, or as a result of war, or of commercial prosperity producing a class of idle rich, there have been times of backsliding.

Formerly many authors were of opinion that the enormous advance of Western civilization, especially in comparison with the stagnation of the ancient civilized peoples of Asia, could be accounted for only on the assumption of an improvement of the innate (that is to say, inherited) intellectual powers of the white races. It was supposed that by a process of selection, natural or social, evolution had brought about in the long course of history an enhancement of the average intellectual capacity of the European people, and possibly also an evolution of a higher innate moral capacity. Modern authorities[1] hold the contrary view—that the evidence is in favour of there having been little or no advance in the innate intellectual ability, taking the average of the population of Western countries, and certainly no advance in innate moral qualities. This does not preclude the possibility of an improvement of intellectual leadership, in other words, an increase of the proportion of persons with innate intellectual ability much above the average ; and a considerable increase of the actual number of men of great mental capacity—a question which will be discussed later in referring to the social classes.

The progress of modern civilization consists, therefore, mainly in the alteration and accumulation of the moral and intellectual traditions. The wide diffusion of the latter amongst the people (especially in its branches of skill and invention), and the accumulation of capital, may be regarded as the special features of the progress of the nineteenth century, compared

---

[1] e.g., McDougall, Carr-Saunders, Giddings.

with which the progress in positive morality, though distinct, was small. The inborn (i.e. innate) differences of individuals from one another are considerable in all the characters of the mind as well as in physical features ; and, just as some races are dark and others almost exclusively fair, so also there seem to be differences between races as regards their average innate disposition. The French as a whole compared with the English have a different emotional quality, and perhaps a slightly different intellectual tendency. Action upon abstract reasoning and logical deduction is common in France, but is obnoxious to the average Englishman.

Although such innate differences exist, it is a great mistake to attribute to them too great an influence in creating the observed differences between individuals and between nations. The intellectual, and especially the moral, tradition is enormously powerful in shaping every individual, and hence the nation. All Europe has a common tradition, differing immensely from that of India or China ; there are lesser differences between the European nations, and still smaller differences between the social classes within each nation. Every person has been born into some family, which is a member of some religious community, say, the Methodists, and belongs to a class, say, the commercial middle class of a provincial town. And he is brought up as an English boy, with the outlook of an Englishman. Our thought, our conduct, our manners are all intimately the product of our social class and our country ; and possibly we modern adults owe more to tradition than to inherited qualities.

VARIATIONS OF INDIVIDUALS

Nevertheless, the inborn differences between individuals are of great importance in certain social questions, and they deserve careful study. We are all the product of the operation of natural selection in the earliest prehistoric ages, and of group and social selection in the prehistoric and historic periods. Individuals differ greatly in disposition and temperament, which are inborn characters, the former exclusively so. The causes of these differences are, as above described, the selective action of the natural and human environment on a population of individuals varying from the normal in many different respects. To understand these differences we must know what are the impulses prompting men's actions ; and many of these may be traced right back to the instincts which man has in common with the animals.

In his *Social Psychology* McDougall recognizes seven instincts, each having a corresponding primary emotion. These are : the instinct of flight and emotion of fear ; the instinct of repulsion, with its emotion of disgust ; the instinct of curiosity and emotion of wonder ; the instinct of pugnacity and emotion of anger ; the instinct of self-abasement and emotion of subjection ; the instinct of self-assertion or self-display and emotion of elation ; the parental instinct and the tender emotion.

There is, of course, the instinct of reproduction, or sexual attraction, with its varying and complex emotions ; and there is an instinct of acquisition, which leads children to collect shells or stamps, and adult men pottery, furniture or trophies of the chase. An instinct of construction is also recognized, which comes out powerfully in many children, and in adults with a bent for building, mechanical work or hobbies, or for planning. The instinct of gregariousness was mentioned above, and is best exemplified by the way people delight in flocking together in great crowds—for example, at football matches. McDougall is curiously silent on the subject ; but I think we must recognize an instinct of co-operation, or of mutual aid, as Giddings calls it. Amongst men there is an instant impulse ' to help the other fellow ', and without thought of reward, if some help given for a few minutes seems likely to be welcome.

Besides the instincts, McDougall recognizes certain general *innate tendencies*, which are quite as much inborn and primitive as instincts, but are general rather than specific in the emotions and actions which they produce. There are the tendencies to imitation and to play, both strongly manifested by children, and by adults too, more than we are apt to think. The tendency to suggestion is highly important ; and the opinions of most of us are formed by suggestion by word of mouth or in print rather than by reasoning. There is also sympathy, a tendency apt to be misunderstood. It leads to the emotion of the observer being stirred by expressions of emotion on the part of some other person whom he sees or hears. A cry of pain from an invisible child, or the sight of an emaciated and obviously starving woman, instantly arouses sympathetic emotion ; but we must avoid assuming that action in relief of the suffering automatically follows. There are persons who suffer exquisitely at the sight of distress on the part of other people, and this merely leads them to avoid the sight of suffering. Persons who can ' pass by on the other side ' when their help is really needed are not necessarily devoid of sympathy, but must be weak in the parental or protective instinct, and their education must be below the prevailing standard of positive morality.

Now the various instincts and the general innate tendencies are developed to different relative strengths in different individuals. Some persons tend naturally to self-assertion, others to self-abasement. The instinct of curiosity is very strong in some, leading them on to scientific research ; and pugnacity is prominent in others. The tender emotion and parental or protective instinct is strong in the great majority of women, and in a good few men. As we shall see later the predominant instinct often determines a man's occupation. Here it is important to note that the sum total of the instincts and innate tendencies to which a person is subject in varying degrees is called his *disposition*. The differences of strength of the instincts and tendencies are largely inborn, but may be accentuated by use. A person may be of a tender, or timid, or acquisitive disposition. The last is the kind of person who collects and piles things in his house without end, or the man who pursues money long after he has made all he needs for enjoyment or power, and in former times would have become a miser, hoarding actual coin rather than making investments.

Temperament must be distinguished from disposition and from character. It may be optimistic or gloomy, quick in response or slow. These are mainly innate differences of nervous and organic constitution, but may be affected by disease. Here should probably be classed also those innate differences of mental endowment, such as whether a man is musical, humorous, good at mathematics, or has any other marked mental character. A broad distinction may be drawn, dividing all persons into two classes : those whose keener sense is sight or hearing respectively, and whose memory and imagination are mainly visual or auditory accordingly. The latter are good at languages.

Character is the complex result of the whole effect of environment on the disposition and temperament. It consists of a person's habits of thought and action, partly the result of formal education, especially if definite moral instruction has been given; but also very largely the result of imitation of older persons in the home, in the school, and in the first business of earning his living. Character is thus partly inborn, partly the result of education and of the person's own efforts at self-improvement, and partly an absorption of the positive morality of his social class.

ALTRUISTS AND EGOISTS

For the purpose of this book one particular classification of persons according to character is highly important. There are certain virtues which constitute a strong character : honesty, courage, self-control, power of self-denial, industriousness, prudence. The want of, or opposites, of these give a weak character. From another point of view, persons of both strong and weak character present themselves as being predominantly either altruists or egoists. These terms are not to be understood here as having any implications other than those of the definitions which follow.

Only a few of our actions are wholly instinctive ; most are either wholly deliberate, like going out to one's work in the morning and to the theatre in the evening, or they are partly instinctive, in the sense that a deliberate decision is influenced by an emotion due to an instinct. The primary motive of most economic actions in the world as we find it is to obtain either things which will ward off pain or discomfort, or the means of experiencing pleasure by the satisfaction of the appetites, or by refined enjoyment. There is disagreeable or painful effort in work prolonged beyond a short spell, which we undergo, to obtain the means of enjoyment or of avoiding discomfort in the future. Under the existing economic system, most of our actions are necessarily selfish, or we perish ; but there are many daily actions also which are solely for the benefit of others, especially for our own children and other members of the family.

It is an indubitable fact that some persons have a tendency to generous actions for the benefit of others who are not of their family ; and it is equally true that many persons unostentatiously give much of their time and of their resources to the service of some group or community, or of the public at large, from the love of benefiting others, or from a sense of duty. The tendency to give is of two distinct kinds : giving out of pity, which becomes the best kind of charity, as nowadays understood, when there is no public acknowledgment expected ; and giving from a pure feeling of generosity, as some people do whenever they see a chance of being of real service to a friend or fellow-worker, or in fulfilment—and most people would say pedantic fulfilment—of some real or fancied obligation. By ' giving ' I do not mean chiefly the gift of money or things, but the gift of service, the taking of trouble for another. People whose tendency is to offer their goods or their services out of pity or pure generosity, sometimes to an extent limited only by their own absolute needs, are altruists.

The egoists, on the other hand, are the persons most of whose actions, in relation to others outside their family, are instinctively or unconsciously selfish, and the remainder calculated to be sooner or later to their own advantage. We all know the various types of egoists ; the strong-charactered man determined to get on, who weighs big things most prudently to his own advantage, and can afford to appear generous in little things ; the man who does not so much ' get on ' as merely pile up money—honest maybe, but always a hard bargainer, and his charity only such as will bring him credit ; verging to the worst type, who is selfish and mean in everything. There is, of course, no hard and fast line between types. In every man there are tendencies to altruism and to selfishness. We must classify people according to the tendency which prevails in their normal moods. There is a considerable part of the population in which altruistic and egoistic motives roughly balance in ordinary circumstances, and these I shall term *neutral* persons in this connexion. A great national emergency like war leads in many neutrals and even egoists to the arousal and predominance of altruistic actions ; and immediately the emergency is terminated a reaction sets in, leading perhaps to egoistic motives predominating more than ever, at any rate temporarily.

The causes of these differences must lie partly in differences of innate disposition and partly in acquired character due to the social and economic environment. The altruist has probably the parental or the co-operative instinct strongly developed, or both. By education, and absorption of the moral tradition of his class and the special moral tone of a group in which he grows up in the formative years—his family, his school, his church, his university or a society—these instincts come to have a greatly extended application, to all people of his village or town, to all the working classes of his country, or to all peoples of the world. Moreover, he acquires, by imitation, by instruction, and by his own self-discipline, applied as the result of an ordered conception of life, a sentiment of duty, which in the course of years produces a habit of altruistic thoughts and actions. So do innate tendencies in the altruistic direction become extended, developed and fixed in a person who has had the right moral guidance in youth.

The egoist, on the other hand, is probably usually a person in whose disposition instincts and innate tendencies of a self-preserving nature were initially strong, whilst his education and moral contacts have not overlaid them with acquired habits of altruistic conduct. The reverse, in fact, has often occurred : the moral contacts, and even education, may have developed the innate tendencies to self-preservation. All men have inherited animal nature to a greater or less extent ; and selfishness, except in relation to offspring, is a strong factor of race survival, when every family of a species is at war with every other. Only when the species has adopted a herd or tribal mode of life do the gregarious and co-operative instincts become highly important factors of survival. Physiologists have shown that all life-sustaining and propagating actions are associated with pleasurable emotions, and that unpleasant emotion and actions are devitalizing ; and this must obviously be the result of natural selection. We come, therefore, not merely to desire food to stave off hunger, and clothing to keep out the cold, that is, for the avoidance of discomfort (unpleasant feeling), but to desire pleasure, that is, the pleasant state of feeling, for its own sake. Special activities (recreations) are undertaken to produce it. The particular activity, bodily or mental, which conduces most to pleasant feeling varies with each individual, and for him according to time and place. Some persons find their highest pleasure in the approbation of their kind ; others, failing that, find it in self-approbation.

It is impossible to present briefly and in popular language the complexities of the psychological reactions of civilized life. It will suffice for the purpose of this book to understand that in the dispositions of some persons the innate egoistic tendencies are relatively strong, and that in the dispositions of other persons the altruistic tendencies are relatively strong. The education and moral environment of the individual will tend to accentuate or repress instincts and innate tendencies having either an egoistic or altruistic nature, so that the character of a person innately egoistic may become partly altruistic or vice versa.

CHAPTER III

COMPOSITION OF THE PEOPLE

OCCUPATIONAL SELECTION IN PRIMITIVE TIMES

IF we study the peoples of the British Isles we find that English, Welsh, Scotch and Irish have clearly defined racial characters, both physical and mental. The differences of the normal temperament and disposition are well known ; and in intellectual qualities there is some difference of kind, the Welsh being imaginative, the Scotch and north-country English being quick and methodical but unimaginative, and so on. It has been suggested that Ireland owes her troubles mainly to an imperfect mixture of races having different characteristics, e.g. the landlords and Ulstermen being mainly of mixed English and Scotch blood, whilst the well-to-do farmer class are said to have innate characters distinct from the proletariat. When we examine the people of England alone we find endless individual variations in disposition, temperament and innate intellectual qualities ; and such differences, when we recognize them, are more striking than the variations of complexion and physical features. These differences have arisen doubtless by two main processes : (1) occupational selection and (2) successive waves and streams of immigration from different sources.

Climatic conditions and the available mineral resources have determined the industries of Great Britain to a larger extent than most people imagine ; but the progress of invention and the accumulation of capital has emancipated us from immediate dependence on nature and the vagaries of the rainfall. Primitive man, on the other hand, must accommodate himself absolutely to the natural conditions of his environment. In dense forests he may live by trapping animals and birds, and by collecting fruits, berries and roots. On open grass-lands he can pasture cattle, being obliged in many regions to migrate between the plains, which give winter pasture, and the hills, which are freed from snow when the plains are burnt up with

32

drought. On upland and rocky pasture, too rough for cattle, sheep will thrive ; and in the hills will be the stream-beds and veins where gold, silver, lead and copper may be found, and sometimes masses of iron-ore. On the rivers men occupy themselves with fishing and the carriage of goods and persons ; whilst along the sea-coasts good fishing may be practised here and there, and a coastal carrying trade may be developed if storms are not too violent. Primitive agriculture must have begun, as we see it to-day in backward countries, on the lower grass-lands in areas of sufficient rainfall, and in clearings in the forest. At first it was ' extensive ' agriculture, fresh land being broken up each year ; but, as population increased, the difficulty of finding land led to the discovery of the rotation of crops and the use of manure. So the peasant cultivator emerged, with primitive implements, but having to plan the best use of his fields at least three years ahead.

In all these primitive occupations a selective tendency operates which, after the lapse of several generations, or even centuries, will have left the inhabitants of each district with a particular temperament and disposition predominant. Consider the hunter, who must follow his quarry for miles through trackless forests. He lives on the meat of the animals he catches, and by bartering skins. For days together he may be unsuccessful, but must bear up against hunger and fatigue, or he dies. Fleetness of foot and power of endurance are physical qualities which will lead to success ; but equally important are mental qualities—an absence of the gregarious instinct, so that he does not abhor solitude watching alone for his prey ; a large measure of fearlessness ; perseverance ; self-confidence. It is fairly obvious that persons to whom the labour by which they live is irksome or distasteful will on the average survive in less numbers than the persons to whom the labour is pleasing, because the former individuals will frequently delay taking the necessary steps to provide themselves and their dependents with food, and sometimes disastrously so, for the opportunity will have slipped. In primitive conditions, and later, as in Medieval England, the work in which a man follows his father and his grandfather is usually the pleasantest kind of work to him. Thus it is that the hunter born of generations of hunters takes a delight in the chase and in killing. Tender emotion and

3

the protective instinct would merely handicap him ; for even as regards his own children, he rarely sees them—merely leaves their mother behind in some safe place and returns with food.

Turn now to the shepherd : what qualities does he need for success ? Obviously his first business is to save life. His flock are his children. He must face the blizzard over the high moors to fetch them in ; he must tend the newborn lambs and their mothers. In him, therefore, there must be a strong development of the parental or protective instinct : he is innately an altruist.

Again, take the peasant cultivator : what should be his inborn propensities ? He must be industrious, patient, thrifty, and intelligent enough to gather experience and knowledge of land and crops. He must have foresight to make it seem worth while to plan for years ahead ; and he needs the instinct of construction, not only to build his hut and sheds, but to lay out and improve the little farm and for planning the use of his fields. Sea-fishermen, on the other hand, unlike the cultivator, require the instinct of co-operation. They work as a crew, from five to ten in number, under a captain. They need high courage, and an instinct of self-abasement (for obedience), but, also, some of them, the power of command and leadership of men. Winter storms soon eliminate captain and crew if they have not these qualities, on which instant concerted action depend.

RACIAL QUALITIES AND MIXTURES

Wherever the physical features of a country are on a fairly large scale, we find that the population of every part has become adapted in its innate mental characters to the occupations which necessarily prevail according to the physical character of each region. This adaptation has occurred partly by what is called lethal selection—the death by starvation, accident or disease of persons unsuited to the environment— and partly by migration. Thus variants from a tribe of shepherds may feel inclined to try cultivation, and will wander to lower lands in search of cultivable waste ground. Not all the children of sea-fishermen will be born with the innate qualities which enable them to take to the occupation like a duck to water. After going for a few months in his father's boat, the boy may decide he wants to be a carpenter or a gardener, and goes inland to seek his fortune. In prehistoric times a large proportion of a tribe, or of a group of tribes, would migrate, leaving behind the less enterprising members. Thus the whole coastal region of Western Europe from Scandinavia to the Bay of Biscay came to be peopled with enterprising emigrants from Eastern Europe and the Mediterranean. The later comers necessarily had been victorious in battle with the earlier inhabitants, and had been subjected thus to military selection also.

The Anglo-Saxons, Danes and Normans were probably all derived from one stock, upon which the physical environment impressed their peculiar qualities of enterprise and daring. Fair-haired immigrants from Eastern Europe settled along the shores of the Baltic, on the Scandinavian coasts and in Denmark. The Norsemen, as we may call those who settled mainly along the coast of Norway, lived by fishing in the fiords, and carried on a little cultivation where the shores permitted, the labour for which was probably provided largely by the women. The cultivable land consisted only of small areas at the feet of the mountains, and was strictly limited. When such land became fully occupied, the younger sons were obliged to venture forth beyond the Norwegian coast. Some became pirates in the North Sea ; others deliberately set out not merely to raid the coasts, but to conquer and to stay. They settled along the north coast of Germany, and maintained their peculiar social custom of primogeniture, which later they introduced to England. Generally, as in the east of England, they drove away or exterminated the inhabitants, and became cultivators themselves. In other parts, especially Normandy, they preserved the population and became feudal chiefs. England received successive invasions of these Norsemen : from their original home, from the North German coast, from Denmark, and finally from Normandy. The people of Great Britain have in their veins the blood of numerous races : Iberian, Keltic, Roman, Gallic (Mediterranean race), in small degree, and Norse. The second and last are predominant : the Keltic especially in the west, the Norse in the east.

Sociologists believe that race mixture tends to produce a

population superior to either stock, so long as the difference between the races is not too great—as between European and negro. The mixture by intermarriage of the Norse with the Keltic (including Romano-Keltic) may conceivably not have proceeded far until late in the Middle Ages ; for not until after the Wars of the Roses had the common people any opportunity of movement, except for a few years after the Black Death. So perhaps the full benefits of race mixture have only been accruing since Henry VII's time. The admixture of foreign blood by no means stopped with the Norman Conquest. Skilled artisans from Holland, Flanders and France were many times encouraged to settle permanently in England ; and England has always been the home of political refugees. In the seventeenth century came the Huguenots, including some of the finest Norse blood of France ; later some of the aristocracy of France ; and in the past hundred years Jews and Slavs, not yet absorbed.

The original inhabitants of France are believed to have been a group of pastoral tribes who migrated westwards across Europe and settled down to agriculture in the plains of France, because they could get no farther west. Hence the patriarchal system of the French family law and custom. Large accessions of Norse blood at various times gave the people variety of temperament and disposition. In so far as the Norse element held itself aloof from the mass of the population of France, however, an appreciable part of it was eventually lost. The Norse peoples, with their spirit of independence, are almost exclusively Protestant ; and it was this element of the population which suffered death and exile in the persecutions of Protestants. It is believed that after the Revocation of the Edict of Nantes some hundreds of thousands of French Protestants emigrated to Prussia, England, America and elsewhere. The Revolution and the wars of Napoleon must have further drained France of this enterprising stock. It is interesting to observe that the French people have apparently the innate disposition and temperament noted above as characteristic of an agricultural population. The peasantry are notorious for their thrift and foresight, and the genius of the French in civil engineering and architecture may be the outcome of a strong, inherited instinct of construction. It is no wonder that the

English, on the other hand, excel in leadership and enterprise, the former including power of organization and command over men, the latter the readiness to venture to the ends of the earth in exploration, trade and colonization, and the willingness to risk the loss of capital in mining and industrial undertakings at home and abroad. The English people seem to be endowed in an unusual measure with men capable of organizing industry on a large scale, and willing to take the risks which were inseparable from industrial enterprises during the nineteenth century. Is this perhaps due to the Viking ancestry, and to the continued schooling in British sea-fisheries ? It would be an interesting line of inquiry how far the twentieth-century movement for the elimination of risk by trade combinations leading to monopoly may be due to a different type of man, the cautious financier, coming into control, as a result of the extension of joint-stock organization and the great concentration of facilities in the London money market. A further selection of enterprising settlers has endowed America with a still larger proportion of men capable of leadership in large industries.

Innate racial qualities should be understood to mean those characteristics which are predominant, and any which are important in comparison with other races in the existing social and political conditions. Obviously every race must have a multitude of innate qualities, and must differ from every other race in respect of the proportions in which they occur. The importance of these characters is, however, entirely relative to the social organization, and the intellectual and moral tradition prevailing at the time. There is no abstract standard of good or bad racial qualities. Thus the latent enterprise, industry and intelligent daring of the Englishman could find no scope under the feudal system. The qualities of the French peasant, on the other hand, made France a rich and powerful country whilst feudalism still prevailed. It was not until other nations had invented the mariner's compass and learnt how to build ocean-going ships : not until the Genoese, the Portuguese, and the Spaniards and the Dutch had established a new tradition of long voyages, trade with India and the Far East, and had discovered new lands and founded colonies, that Englishmen began to take an interest in these things. Once they understood the opportunities that were open, and could raise capital, their special racial qualities began to tell, and led quickly to success.

The most remarkable case of this kind surely is Japan. Under the rule of isolation maintained by the Shoguns, European culture scarcely touched the ideas of the people. After the enlightened revolution a new social and political organization soon freed the common people, particularly in the towns, and education was extended. Foreign trade was encouraged and the Japanese travelled. They brought home the European intellectual tradition, and modified their own moral tradition. A similar introduction of foreign trade, education, and the European intellectual tradition to India, Burma, Siam, and French Indo-China has not had similar results. Only on the west coast of India, where the population has a proportion of Persian and Arab immigrants who came *across the seas*, and has a sprinkling of hillmen from the north, who came as an invading host across the deserts, do we find that enterprise and leadership of men which has been an important factor in the industrialization of Bombay and other western cities. Successful establishment of large-scale industries elsewhere in India has been under the management of Europeans.

We may conclude, therefore, that the importance of racial qualities lies in the question how far a particular social organization, in harmony with the world tradition of the time, intellectual and moral, will give scope for the innate qualities of the race to express themselves. In other words, a nation advances, and all its people are suffused with hope and energy, when there is harmony between the social organization, the positive morality, and the stronger racial characteristics, whether operative or latent. The social organization includes, of course, the economic organization. Certainly, in England at the present time, there is a growing want of harmony between the social organization and the positive morality, which is rapidly advancing. The unrest of the times, which we all feel more or less, is due to this. The question to which an answer must be found is whether a new social organization, in harmony with a new positive morality, which requires a real equality of social and economic status for all men composing the nation, will also be in harmony with the outstanding innate racial qualities of England.

The ideas presented in this section being somewhat new, it is as well to state that my views here expressed have been largely formed by, and are in general agreement with, the opinions recorded by Carr-Saunders in his well-known book, *The Population Problem*. Many authors have pointed out how the great body of moral and intellectual tradition is handed on from generation to generation ; and for the past five hundred years the tradition of civilization has been evolving with constantly accelerating pace. Carr-Saunders emphasizes the effect which physical environment formerly had in the evolution of tradition in each country ; but the cheapening of printing and paper in the nineteenth century has tended towards unifying tradition in all countries. In one sense tradition may be more widespread than racial groups ; and it may develop in a way unfavourable to the innate qualities of a particular section of the population. These either oppose the Government, and are imprisoned or executed, or they emigrate. ' Men are favoured in so far as they are innately adapted to the chief features of the tradition,' as Carr-Saunders [1] puts it. Thus the *average* innate qualities of the people may be altered to some extent by a change of tradition, and a consequent change of social organization. The last great change of that kind has been the expulsion from Russia of monarchists and all obstructers of the Bolshevik revolution.

MODERN OCCUPATIONAL SELECTION

There seems no reason to suppose that occupational selection, whilst strong in the conditions of primitive life, ceases to operate as the economic system develops and occupations become more numerous and specialized. In so far as different occupations requiring different qualities of character and skill are segregated in separate districts, the populations of those districts must gradually become modified accordingly as regards innate qualities. There is very little lethal selection, though persons of slow nervous reaction and low intelligence may be more subject to industrial accidents. In the main selection takes places by migration. Persons innately least adapted to the prevailing industry of the district will be

[1] *The Population Problem*, p. 454.

frequently out of work, or will find the work disagreeable and tiring. To be successful will require a greater effort of will than is needed by persons innately adapted. Hence they seek other work, more congenial, more remunerative, and with less risk of unemployment ; and this usually means going to another town. There may also be a slight effect of selection through such ill-adapted persons marrying later, so that, as a group, their fertility will be slightly less than that of persons well adapted and consequently regularly employed.

In towns and districts where there is a number of different industries carried on, and no one of them greatly predominant, the chances are that there will be some occupation to suit almost every type of mental endowment ; and, though there will always be misfits and migrations, the results of inter-marriage between persons whose ancestors were in different occupations will be to maintain approximately the same average innate qualities.

Examples of highly localized industries of long standing are coal-mining, cotton-spinning in Lancashire, woollen- and worsted-spinning in Yorkshire, and the pottery manufacture. Of these, coal-mining undoubtedly selects men of courage, intelligence and alertness ; and proof is given by the splendid record of the miners' battalions in Flanders. In cotton-spinning and weaving, deftness of the fingers in piecing threads, quickness and keen eyesight are innate qualities on which skill depends ; whilst resistance to nervous fatigue from noise and continuous attention must be additional factors of selection. It is to be hoped that experimental data may be collected to determine the extent of such selection ; but it is not an undue stretch of the imagination to assume that the innate qualities of the population of Lancashire, and perhaps more particularly of the women, have been, and are being, modified, so that they can more easily develop the necessary skill than the average population of other towns. Lancashire is always spinning finer and finer counts of yarn, and thus holds its place as the greatest cotton-spinning centre of the world in spite of cotton mills springing up in America, Japan, India and other countries, in spite of the manufacture tending to move, as in other indus-tries, towards the source of the raw material. Such a founda-tion of innate skill is a national asset, and will persist, along with the great technical tradition of Lancashire, whatever the form of industrial organization. The importance for an industry of innate capacity of the resident population as the result of selection should not be over-emphasized ; in the cases of most industries the tradition of technique, handed on from generation to generation of managers and workpeople is more important.

OCCUPATIONS OF WOMEN

Occupational selection may occur through the employments of women as well as of men. The husband may follow some trade which can be practised in any town ; and the fact that his wife can earn good money at knitting fine hosiery might, for example, determine their residing in Leicester. From remote ages women have taken part in cultivation, and in many countries of the East they may be seen at the present day regularly doing the lighter work in the village agriculture, and in some districts heavy work as coolies. Motherhood does not absorb the whole of a woman's time, especially where it is the custom to send children to school at an early age. Consequently in most races women have become adapted to other functions in society as well. As was pointed out to me by the late Professor Sir Patrick Geddes, it is the wife's function to save, and store the grain or hide the money ; and it is the woman's business too to organize the home and its daily tasks, which in many countries extends to running the dairy and farmyard also. Obviously those peoples amongst whom it is the custom for women to take their part in productive work have an advantage as against those who seclude their women, or permit them no tasks outside the house. Assuming the physical conditions of agriculture and industries to be equally favourable in the two cases, the former peoples will probably have a greater production per head, and either a greater density of population or a higher standard of living, if the birthrate be restrained, both of which are factors of race survival.

There are many facts which suggest that reproductive selection in the early stages of civilization has impressed an instinct of acquisition and hoarding on the women more than the men, this being evident amongst certain peoples at the present day, e.g. the French, the Burmese, and some other

European and Asiatic peoples in less degree. We are coming to realize, too, that amongst ourselves many women have in high degree the talent for organization ; and it is conceivable that, owing to the ordering of the home being a primary function with survival value in a primitive peasant population, women may be found to have organizing power more frequently than men, who are more endowed with powers of leadership and command. The conditions of industry are changing fundamentally. The qualities of the military commander and the ship's captain were needed pre-eminently in the early days of large engineering and industrial undertakings. With the willing and highly educated workmen of the present day the old-fashioned ' military ' discipline is out of date, and efficiency is realized by careful planning and regulation of work—a ready co-operation between the men and the controlling staff. An opening for the employment of talented women having the necessary training in the planning of industrial processes and buildings is thus created. Already a number of women have become highly trained as mechanical and electrical engineers, and are organized in the Women's Engineering Society, established twelve years ago.

The tradition of our civilization imposes upon women a limited outlook on life and a restricted range of occupations. Every social contact from earliest infancy, in accordance with deeply rooted custom, stamps the characters of women with the qualities demanded by the social organization of the time. It is extremely difficult to say, therefore, whether the innate mental qualities of women are different from those of men in the same population or not. There is, of course, a difference of physical characters, though much less marked than in many species of animals. *A priori* we seem to be justified in assuming some innate difference in mental characters : in temperament and disposition, and possibly in the bent of intellectual activity. Individuals differ enormously, of course, and some women are endowed with masculine characteristics, and some men with feminine characteristics, in varying degrees ; but investigation might reveal a difference of the average mental constitution. Any such difference would probably be to some extent complementary in character, as seems to be the case amongst some primitive agricultural peoples.

Social custom, far more than maternal duties, has prevented women from obtaining the training and experience necessary to participate in the direction of industry. With labour-saving appliances in the home, and school for the children, women can have time to devote to nationally productive work after marriage as well as before ; and it will surely be to the advantage of the community if ample opportunities are given to enable those having the innate capacity to fit themselves for the higher posts. Whatever innate average difference there may be between men and women must tend to the occupations in which men and women respectively could attain greatest efficiency being to some extent complementary. In a properly organized society, therefore, there will be an appropriate place for every woman in some industrial or socially useful occupation, according to her capacity and education ; and when the nation attains a collective consciousness as to its greatest advantage, it will encourage women to give all that they will to the work of the country.

EFFECTS OF OCCUPATION ON CHARACTER

Whilst any given occupation tends to select from the mass of the people those having innate qualities most suited therefore, the occupation itself usually has a retroactive effect upon the character of the person. This effect is usually insensible and gradual, and naturally varies much in degree in different persons, though not in the kind of result. In general we may say that the occupation affects the habits as to prevailing motives to action, and that the habit as to motives produces a moral result. It is clear also that a person's occupation affects his habits of thought, and may thus have important intellectual results. It is generally believed that a man employed in killing animals is thereby rendered callous as regards the sufferings of human beings also. On the other hand, the tending of animals makes men kindhearted. The constant driving of a motor-car may tend to make a man self-assertive and intolerant. The professed teacher becomes didactic, perhaps dogmatic.

Uncertainty of results, as, for example, a highly speculative business, has a demoralizing effect on the majority of persons ; and men, such as commercial travellers, when paid mainly by commission, sometimes become morally undone when business is bad, and give way to gambling or drink. The effect of casual employment, such as prevailed formerly more extensively than now at the docks of all our port towns, in undermining a man's character, and turning him into a shiftless wastrel, is well understood. Turn again to business men, and consider the moral effect of constantly seeking profits for themselves or for their employers. Those who have an egoistic bias must be thereby confirmed therein ; and neutrals, and altruists even, must, if the onus of securing the profits falls on them, develop a somewhat selfish attitude of mind towards all strangers and the public in general. In bygone days, when an established local business seemed almost to run itself, there may have been less of this tendency than there is now when competition is so much keener.

The intellectual effects of a man's employment are no less striking than the moral results. What the lawyer gains in being able to see both sides of the question he often loses in intellectual honesty. His views are decided by his own or his class interests, and he is hardly capable of constructive thinking. As a politician it is his second nature to catch the public ear with pleasant phrases, to play off against one another those who cannot be beguiled. On the other hand, the engineer or architect or town-planner is a constructive thinker in many other lines as well, and hates the methods of the lawyer. The manual occupations too have their intellectual influence. The woodman engaged in felling trees, and the miner ceaselessly labouring and devising ways to bring down the face of coal, have purely a destructive outlook. It is amongst men so engaged that syndicalism finds the majority of its supporters : a policy of revolution in industry with no clear future beyond. On the other hand, carpenters, turners, and fitters, and most workers in the engineering trades, have naturally a constructive habit of mind. They want to know what life is going to be like when socialism is adopted ; hence the cautious attitude and waiting for intellectual conversion.

In the actual reorganization of society upon a new basis the moral aspects of employments will obviously require the most careful attention. It is impossible to establish communism until positive morality has been advanced to the necessary standard ; and the stability of the system will depend upon the elimination of all causes predisposing to moral degeneration. The intellectual effects of occupations might have very important political bearings as regards the assignment of power to representatives of industries, and so are worthy of close study.

CHAPTER IV

THE SOCIAL CLASSES

NATIONS AND CLASSES

A NATION is a group of people inhabiting a particular area and possessing a group self-consciousness. The area is usually well defined geographically by physical features. The self-consciousness is due to the growth of a cultural tradition widely spread amongst the people, who are distinguished in language or other respects from neighbouring peoples. An individual becomes conscious of himself as distinct from other persons, and learns to know himself—his mental and moral equipment, his strong and weak points—by comparison with his friends and business associates and great men about whom he reads. The population of some territory, in somewhat similar manner, gradually comes to be conscious of itself as an entity, and to know itself. Such consciousness proceeds from contact with other peoples, which reveals their differences ; the knowledge comes by comparisons with them which require and stimulate self-examination. The first stage is when the people inhabiting a territory becomes interested in itself as an entity, and this seems to require a certain level of cultural and economic advance. The elementary ' consciousness of kind ' then receives a spiritual and intellectual extension. There follows some ' introspection ', or discussion by the people of its own condition, and comparisons with other peoples. As such interest and knowledge extend amongst the population so does it become welded into a nation. The process may be greatly stimulated by actual domination by a foreign power or by threat of invasion.

Patriotism is a sentiment growing from the idea of nationhood, and is a fertile source of altruistic effort. It has called forth the most noble devotion and sacrifice from millions of men in many countries. ' My country right or wrong ! ' is regarded as a Jingo cry ; nevertheless it is the effusion of a very real and deep emotion—one which might be most powerful in the service of man in peaceful progress, could it be diverted thereto. And such diversion is possible when it is proposed to make the nation in all things the economic unit, and to put every person into direct relation with it. Patriotism can be called to the aid of social progress by seeking to establish communism on a national basis.

Probably the chief obstacle to social progress receiving an impetus from patriotism and national pride lies in class distinctions. In the emergency of a great war, class interests are subordinated to the country's service ; but immediately the fighting is over class barriers are re-erected, because our economic and social organization is such as to create and even require the well-to-do and leisured classes. No discussion of the social objective could be thorough which did not take account of the origin of the classes and their present functions, and consider by what means class distinctions can be abolished.

Within each class and sub-class there is a strong group consciousness ; and this cuts across the national consciousness and prevents the existence of a feeling of unity amongst the people as a whole—rich and poor, clever and dull. Class and caste feeling may be, or become, so strong as to predominate over consciousness of nationality, or prevent its being attained. Poland was weakened for centuries by class dissensions ; and Spain would seem to be a modern example. India cannot become a nation until the rigid caste system of the Hindus is dissolved, and the religious antagonisms are allayed. Communism requires an immense development of the national self-consciousness ; and patriotism must be exalted to twenty times its present strength. Then Englishmen will in fact regard all men born in their own country as brothers ; then they will be ashamed to belong to a country which cannot provide honest work for all its citizens and educate all to efficiency in production and to refined enjoyment of leisure.

PRIMITIVE REGULATION OF POPULATION

Primitive peoples have always been faced with the inevitable tendency for population to grow faster than the means of subsistence. The great majority of tribes seem to have reduced the growth of population by the practice of infanticide, chiefly of deformed and female children, whilst abortion and abstention from intercourse were also common, if we may judge from the analogy of many primitive races in modern times and some remarks of classical authors.[1] It would appear, however, that tribes which were repeatedly successful in warfare began to look upon the permanent conquest of adjoining territory, and not mere raiding, as normally desirable. They either drove out or exterminated the inhabitants, or enslaved them; or they merely settled as a ruling caste, leaving the indigenous population to work as a proletariat of cultivators and labourers. Whatever became of the original inhabitants, the conquering tribe or group of tribes had room to grow in numbers. Infanticide and all practices tending to restrict the birth-rate became antisocial amongst the conquerors. Public opinion turned against such customs, and social rules and even laws would be made against them, especially when the group of tribes became a people under a king having imperial ambitions. Where the tendency was to annex territory and settle as a ruling caste, it is obvious that the strong instinct of race survival would lead the public opinion of that ruling caste to favour the utmost possible fertility. In fact, it would seem that polygamy, based on the ruling caste taking numerous women of the conquered people, would be likely to be favoured, so that a large number of children might be brought up in the religion and tradition of the rulers. This may be the reason for Mohammedanism, the religion of a conquering people, countenancing polygamy. It would seem that a noble and spiritual religion was obliged to embrace a social organization which was adapted to the continued ascendancy of a group of militant tribes.

It is interesting to notice that in all ages the ruling class have desired to increase the numbers of the people, for therein would lie the strength of the empire or kingdom in war. We are ourselves unconsciously influenced by a tradition of the benefit of a large population, dating at least from Elizabethan times, if not earlier; and doubtless, as the German military writers said before 1914, numbers will always ultimately tell. From the earliest historic times a ruling caste has always wanted to increase its own numbers and the numbers of

[1] Carr-Saunders, *The Population Problem*, Chaps. VII, VIII, IX, and X.

submissive persons under its dominance. Religions, with the exception of Christianity and Buddhism in their early stages, have been largely moulded by the needs of the ruling class, especially as regards moral teaching and sanctions. Hence infanticide and restrictive practices have been made illegal by temporal law, and have been discountenanced by all the great religions. The Hindus venerate the generative function, perhaps because such doctrine suited the early Aryan conquerors ; and Buddhists teach that life may not be taken, including that of the unborn babe. The most densely populated parts of the world are those where the religion of the people discountenances practices limiting the natural increase of the population. Amongst Christian peoples the need for some restriction of increase has been felt at various times. The Christian Fathers, from the fifth century, advocated continence and celibacy ; and it has been suggested that the consciousness of the advantage of restricting the growth of population was a factor in gaining acceptance of these precepts. In the Middle Ages we find various measures enforced by custom to prevent early marriages.

ORIGIN OF CASTE IN SOCIAL FUNCTION

In tribes leading a primitive pastoral or agricultural life there are no class distinctions. The chieftain may have much wealth and many wives ; but amongst the rest a rigorous equality is usually insisted on, not excepting the elders of the tribe and the village headmen. The accumulation of property is discouraged ; in fact, in the absence of money, social disapproval only reinforces an actual physical difficulty of storing accumulated property, mostly liable to deterioration. The very idea of private property scarcely extends beyond a man's few odds and ends of household possessions and his weapons. The land is regarded as common property to be portioned out according to need, and a man who has plough-oxen must help to plough the land of others. Many examples of primitive tribal life can be found to-day in tropical Africa and the hill countries of South and Central Asia. There is abundant evidence too that similar customs formerly prevailed amongst peoples now more or less civilized. We know, for instance, that

4

some tribes conducted their agriculture on a co-operative plan, each family having an area of land corresponding with the number to be fed, and the whole village being responsible to get the ploughing, sowing and harvesting done. There existed a kind of primitive communism ; and it was doubtless the tradition of this, as having been the original condition of the people, which made communism popular in Sparta, and a familiar idea amongst the Greek proletariat generally.

A ruling military caste appears sometimes to have arisen within a tribe by the chief selecting courageous and intelligent young men as a fighting force to protect the tribe from raids, and to preserve order internally ; but more often, probably, its origin was from without by conquest and settlement as rulers. A priestly caste has usually arisen as the interpreter of the mysteries of life and nature ; and at all times has gained its means of livelihood mainly by inspiring fear and selling either absolution from sins or prognostications of the future. The power which an organized priesthood gains over the people has led the ruling military caste to give it special honour and protection. Sometimes the priesthood has gained the upper hand and has made and unmade princes and kings.

The most fundamental classification of men, according to Comte, distinguishes them according to their function in society, which depends mainly upon innate qualities of temperament and intellect. There are three classes with distinctive qualities, which are of peculiar importance although they form but a small proportion of the population, namely, the ' chiefs ', the ' intellectuals ', and the ' emotionals '. The remainder, numbering probably from 90 to 95 per cent of the whole, may be called the ' people '. The *chiefs* are the rulers and military leaders, able to command men and organize. The *intellectuals* are the thinkers, philosophers and theologians ; the humbler ones are teachers. The *emotionals*, until modern times, have usually been village priests or wizards, or leaders of popular revolt. They are fluent speakers, emotional and even passionate, and logic does not appeal to them.

Professor Patrick Geddes has shown [1] how in every stage of

----

[1] *Ideas at War*, by Patrick Geddes and Gilbert Slater, 1917, pp. 23–6, and 129. See also *The Coming Polity*, by Geddes and Branford, Chap. II. These two books deserve careful reading by any one who would understand the play of social forces in our present civilization and its historical background.

civilization throughout Europe these three classes have played essential parts in the life of the time. In the Medieval Age, for instance, the chiefs were the feudal barons and squires, the intellectuals the members of the monastic orders, the emotionals were the village priests and the mendicant friars, with here and there a village malcontent. The same classes appear amongst all peoples. For instance, in India, there has always been the Kshatrya, or warrior caste, perhaps represented nowadays mainly amongst the Rajputs and Sikhs, who were chiefs until the Mohammedan conquests, and remained so in parts until the British adopted that function. The pundits are the intellectuals ; and the *sadhus* (and *fakirs*), that is to say, wandering priests and religious beggars and ascetics, are the emotionals. The same classes appear amongst Mohammedan peoples. At the present day in England these same classes can be recognized ; but their occupations have become diversified with the increasing complexity of social organization. The chiefs comprise the ancient English landed nobility : military officers who instinctively chose the army as a career ; ' captains ' and managers of industry ; officers of the navy and merchant marine ; and all who command the labour of men in large bodies. The intellectuals are represented typically by university professors and higher grades of school-teachers ; by the larger part of the clergymen of the Church of England ; by some authors, lawyers, and so forth. The emotionals are to be found in many Nonconformist pulpits, including the Salvation Army ; as labour leaders of the type who appeal with passionate speech to mass meetings ; as journalists of the popular and yellow Press ; as faddists of various kinds. It would seem that the proportion of emotionals is larger amongst women than men.

Incomplete as this enumeration is, it indicates one highly important classification of the majority of persons who stand out from the mass of the people on account of innate qualities. These innate qualities, as we shall see, have now ' economic value ' in varying degrees, according to education, above the qualities common amongst the people at large. The three classes will presumably always exist in every country : the born ' chief ' loving power and being a capable leader of men ; the ' intellectual ' instinctively thinking out problems, advancing

knowledge and teaching it ; the ' emotional ' holding forth to
rouse the people by word of mouth or in print, to carry on a
propaganda for good as he sees it.

There are of course other innate qualities of disposition and
temperament, which may occur in combinations such as to
predispose the person to excellence in callings belonging to a
more developed state of society. The acquisitive intellectual
becomes a merchant or financier ; the intellectual with strong
parental instinct extended becomes a doctor ; the intellectual
with strong constructive instinct becomes a trained civil or
mechanical engineer or architect. Emotionals who tend naturally to auditory or visual expression tend to become musicians
or creative artists.

In the earlier stages of civilization persons exercising any
function in society—as chief, intellectual, emotional, or as
merchant, barber, etc.—tended to become a separate social
class, or even caste, very largely hereditary. In India these
castes became peculiarly crystallized, their rigidity and
exclusiveness being maintained by the prohibition of inter-
marriage between castes, which may have been a rule initiated
by the Aryan conquerors to maintain their own blood pure,
subsequently imitated by the lower classes. The rapid change
of modern society and the multiplication of occupations of a
highly skilled character has to a large extent broken down class
exclusiveness as between persons in the various intellectual and
highly remunerated occupations, though ' snobbishness ' may
be regarded as a relic thereof. The idea of function in society
was the distinguishing feature of class or caste in Europe in
the Middle Ages ; at the present time wealth and education
define a man's class, with little reference to his occupation.
Tracing this change will lead us to understand the classes as
they are now.

INCOMES OF ABILITY SCARCE IN RELATION TO DEMAND

From the earliest times different occupations have com-
manded very different incomes. Our consideration of cases
in which the whole or part of the income arises from ownership
or rights over land or capital may be deferred ; it is sufficient
here to have in view the remuneration for work done or services

rendered. We need to take account, however, only of such kinds of work or service as have an earning power, for there are many activities, from gathering acorns to comforting the sick, writing poetry, or pursuing scientific inquiries in a new direction, for which no one is willing to pay. In general it may be said that no class or caste of persons can exist, excepting by heritable rights of property, or by theft, unless it is exercising some function in society, or at least offering some service which some people *want*, irrespective of whether the service be in reality for their immediate or ultimate good or not. No distinction need be drawn, for the present purpose, as to the manner in which the service reaches the consumer. A cook who bakes a pie for her mistress renders a service to society at large which need not be distinguished from the service of a cook who bakes a pie for a catering firm which sells it from a shop.

Broadly speaking, the remuneration of every service rendered to the community—manual or intellectual labour, spiritual ministrations, or the finding of a market for goods— is governed by demand and supply. In the long run this is always true, though divergencies may be caused for periods of several years by custom, by long contracts, or by monopolistic combinations, such as trade unions or rings of sellers or buyers. An illustrative example will help to make the relations of demand and supply clear. In the medical profession ordinary practitioners earn anything, say, from £700 to £2,000 a year. There are two ways in which their earnings might be reduced to the level of a skilled manual worker or a school-teacher, say, £150 to £300; either the demand might fall off, the supply remaining unchanged, or the supply might be increased, the demand remaining unchanged. Let us suppose that rules of hygienic living, as to diet, clothing, avoiding contagion, etc., were to be rapidly and very widely diffused through the Press and the schools, and that people attended to them seriously. Very soon the doctors would find themselves with very little employment, and be obliged to charge lower fees in order to attract business. On the other hand, we might assume that, the demand remaining the same, the supply of doctors' services was greatly increased by stimulating the education of a much larger number of men and women as medical students. This would be possible by establishing a number of new medical colleges, charging no fees, and offering stipends for the maintenance of all needy students. Thus the profession would soon become overcrowded and the average earnings very much reduced.

The well-to-do classes, in so far as their incomes were earned, have always consisted of persons having some kind of ability which was scarce in relation to the demand for such services. In primitive times, for example, the chiefs offered protection of life and property to all who lived in their territory or would come and settle there. Peaceably disposed cultivators of the soil have no greater need than such protection, and willingly they gave presents or rendered services to their lord ; and so arose in most countries the feudal system in one form or another. Feudal barons rendered a real service to society prior to the establishment of a strong central government, which took over their functions of preserving law and order. But Henry VII in England, and Louis XIV in France, could never have established a dominant central Government, nor could the British in India, if they had tried to strip the barons of their rights of income, on account of their services as governors being no longer required. Guaranteeing them permanent incomes from land was in effect the price paid for the creation of centralized national government. That price has long ago been paid ; and in countries where the landlords did not render a social service in promoting the improvement of agriculture, as they did in England, they have been eliminated—in France and Russia by violence, in Denmark, Ireland and parts of Italy and Central Europe by State-aided purchase.

The incomes of intellectuals have generally averaged less than those of chiefs, the apparent exceptions in the cases of the wealthy cardinals and abbots of the late Middle Ages being probably cases of men who by nature were intellectually disposed chiefs, and to whom opportunity offered only an ecclesiastical career. Other exceptions, such as wealthy lawyers and merchants, who made their mark in the intellectual world, owed their wealth to an innate acquisitive tendency, which we shall consider in connexion with property. On the whole, intellectuals have usually been able to live in comfort, though not in luxury. Not so the emotionals, who, even more than the intellectuals, are apt to occupy themselves, not with what the public demands, but with what they think it ought to want, and hence are generally poor, often earning, in spite of good education, hardly the wage of a skilled craftsman. The true emotional is an altruist, and has no acquisitive tendency. Only the imitators, clever rascals sometimes, have that.

INCOMES DEPENDENT ON PROPERTY

Every one will agree that all the wealthy and well-to-do, except a minute fraction, owe their large incomes to the institution of private property and the laws which safeguard it. It is commonly maintained that, without the rights of property as we know them, these men who now get rich would not work, or at any rate would exert themselves much less. That is a question which will be considered in a later chapter. Here we are concerned only with knowing what types of men constitute the well-to-do class, and how they have come by their wealth and their abnormal earning power.

A simple classification of the propertied class divides them first into two main groups : those living on rents and the interest on capital, the property having been either inherited or accumulated by saving during their lifetime ; and those who utilize their capital or land, or the greater part of it, for some business in which they are active workers. The first group have no work except to collect the income or see that it is done for them ; but some of them occupy their time in public service or in other ways socially useful, as in the pursuit of science or art. They are spoken of as ' the leisured class ', and in England and some other countries have undoubtedly done much at certain periods to maintain a high level of culture. The second group are conveniently termed ' the rich workers ', and we may subdivide them roughly into four sub-groups : landlords, merchants, financiers, and industrialists (that is, manufacturers and directors of industrial concerns).

The majority of landlords belong to the leisured class, and live on the rents of agricultural or urban lands or mining royalties. There are a certain number, however, who devote much time to managing their estates themselves. This does not mean merely collecting their rents or royalties, which a clerk will do, but looking after the upkeep of the property and its development.

The merchant exercises a very useful function in bringing goods from the producer to the consumer. It is by no means easy for a producer to find consumers for his goods, nor for a shopkeeper to find out foreign sources of supply of things known to be wanted. In primitive times the merchant was always a traveller, who actually took with him a cargo or caravan of goods : jewels, ornaments, fine cloths, spices, sugar, salt, articles of useful metals, and so forth. As methods of transport improved and security was established, the business of carrying became a separate trade, and the merchant had to travel only occasionally to seek new markets or appoint new agents. Having then a permanent headquarters, he could build a warehouse and keep stores of various goods. He became the wholesale merchant supplying shopkeepers in towns and villages. Until the nineteenth century shopkeepers never became wealthy, for there were no great emporiums or chain stores. The wholesale merchant, on the other hand, became wealthy in Roman times, and again from the fifteenth century on in Venice and Holland and from Elizabethan times in England. With the great development of navigation and foreign trade the merchant class became the big capitalists, and some of them shipowners. Very rarely have they become manufacturers, though they used to advance capital to manufacturers. That, however, merely means exercising the function of financier. The qualities which make a good merchant are intelligence, acquisitiveness, thrift, prudence, foresight and patience. Knowledge and experience, combined with these, provide him with good judgment.

The financier is much older in the world's history than the manufacturer, using the term in its modern sense. Probably he branched off the retail shopkeeper in his form of village money-lender, just as the capitalist financier was first a merchant, or came of a merchant family. In every country having a peasant population the village shopkeeper was accustomed to make advances of grain, even before money came into general circulation. As soon as money transactions became general, the shopkeeper would not only advance grain as before, but occasionally advance money also to his agricultural customers to meet their payments of rent and taxes. Eventually, with growing population, some men came to specialize in lending money, and gave up the troublesome business of keeping stocks of grain. By charging the highest rates their clients could bear, and living in the most parsimonious manner, such money-lenders enlarged their capital from year to year.

In the towns there arose from very early times ordinary money-lenders, on the one hand, and bill-brokers, on the other hand, who financed exports of local produce, such as grain and cloth, and sold bills to importers. Such bill-brokers augmented their own capital by taking loans from merchants, landlords and others having money to deposit for fixed terms. The goldsmiths and silversmiths at times took to money-lending of the pawnbroking description, and accepted deposits of money. From the bill-brokers and goldsmiths developed the private bankers, who prevailed universally a century ago. During the nineteenth century banking gradually came into the hands of the big joint-stock companies ; stock- and share-brokers grew in number, and a new class of financiers emerged— those engaged in attracting new investments from the public, recruited probably mainly from the old bankers, the stock-brokers, and some high-class money-lenders.

The innate qualities leading to success in all these lines of finance would seem to be the same : acquisitiveness, thrift, foresight, intelligence, prudence and cautiousness based on a rather pessimistic temperament ; and combined with these a ready insight into, and experience of, human nature, and some mathematical capacity, or at least a facility in making rapid mental approximate calculations. The big financier of modern times must have imagination, and an extensive knowledge of commerce and industry, so that he may know where to get reliable facts ; and his pessimism must be subject to reason.

Manufacturers and industrialists as a class are quite distinct from any of the foregoing. Their business is to organize the work of a large number of men in one place for the production of some commodity. Whether the work be the mining of coal, smelting of iron-ore, rolling of steel plates, weaving of cloth, making biscuits or furniture or building ships, the same qualities of character are needed. The employer ought to have primarily a ready human interest and sympathy, and a sense of justice. He must have a good memory for faces and things, immense patience, tireless industry and obstinate perseverance, good health and a well-balanced temperament. Combine with these a thorough knowledge of the technique of his trade, alertness in discovering improvements of methods, and honesty in all his dealings with customers and employees, and you have the type of man who has made England the industrial country it is. Acquisitiveness the successful manufacturer has in moderate degree ; if too strong, he may be good in buying and selling, but his staff will consist mainly of third-rate and discontented men. In buying and selling many manufacturers lose what they make by good organization or cheap labour ; and the great industrial companies of the present day employ specialists for buying and selling, presumably usually men with more of the merchant's bent.

CONDITIONS OF GROWTH OF THE PROPERTIED CLASSES

No social phenomenon of the present can be fully understood without reference to its history. Social evolution is proceeding faster than at any previous period ; but always the tradition of the past constitutes the most part of the present, and exercises a moulding influence on the path of progress. Hence in our study of the social classes it is essential to trace, at least in outline, their historical emergence.

In all countries having a peasant population carrying on a more or less primitive agriculture the same social classes are found, whether we go back to antiquity, survey Russia, India or China of the nineteenth century, or take Europe in feudal times. Wherever the land was fertile and yielded to labour, according to the accustomed methods, a surplus above the peasant's minimum needs for subsistence, there a landlord class arose : sometimes from amongst the people, but usually by appropriation of territorial rights by conquerors. Fertile land pays taxes to a ruling prince and rent to a landlord ; but unfertile land, such as hills or sandy plain, pays only a light tax to the ruling prince. As soon as taxes and rent have to be paid in money, trade is stimulated ; trading towns grow up, and a class of traders emerges who dispose of the agricultural products and provide the luxuries of the landlord and the few simple goods from afar which the peasant must have. In the fertile tracts money-lenders find much opportunity for profitable business. Wherever the seasons are uncertain (as in India), or the tenure is insecure, the money-lender becomes an indispensable part of the social fabric. The uncertainty of income leads, however, to the majority of the peasants being thriftless. The money-lender preys on them, and skins them of all that the landlord leaves, so that the great majority never have more than the bare means of subsistence left. On the other hand, the money-lender keeps them alive after a failure of the crops until the next crop. The opinion that character is largely determined by economic conditions receives much support from observations that the peasants of the Asiatic countries are as a whole thriftless where the results of months of labour are liable to be annihilated by drought, flood, or locusts ; and that wherever rainfall is adequate and secure, and the land fertile, grasping landlords arise, particularly in tropical countries under European rule, which protect the landlords' property rights and largely fail in their efforts to protect the tenants. Wherever, as in most of Europe, the peasants have freed themselves from landlordism, and the climate gives a sure return to labour, the peasantry become thrifty, and even progressive.

A free peasantry, except in hill tracts, is, however, a phenomenon of the nineteenth and twentieth centuries. The characteristic classes of primitive agricultural countries, like Europe in the Middle Ages, are : the landlords (chiefs), the priests (both intellectuals and emotionals), the merchants and bill-brokers, the shopkeepers and petty money-lenders, the peasants in serfdom or tenancy, labourers holding an acre or less of land for their own cultivation, and landless labourers, some of whom become wanderers and thieves. Artisans, such as carpenters, blacksmiths, and weavers, are to be found in the larger villages ; and, in the towns, besides these, there are the craftsmen of various luxury trades. This would describe Russia in 1850 and most of India at the present day.

In a primitive agricultural country before trade is developed the landlords are the only wealthy class. They are essentially fighters, and spenders of money. They have not the merchant's qualities of prudence and thrift, but have always tended to build great houses and live nearly up to their incomes. The accumulation of capital did not begin till security was established by a strong central government (in England by the Tudors) and the means of communication improved—as by the adoption of the mariner's compass and larger ships, and on land by the improvement of rivers and roads. Thus was trade developed in volume, and traders began to accumulate wealth. Commerce had been extensive in the Roman Empire, and merchants then grew very wealthy; but the process had to be repeated in most of Europe in the fifteenth and sixteenth centuries. By the end of the latter century the merchants and financiers had become numerous, and constituted the nucleus of an educated middle class, which did not exist previously.

The conditions which led to the growth of the complex middle class as we know it to-day are decidedly interesting. Just as the merchant and financier class developed with the extension of security and communications (ultimately worldwide in extent) so every other constituent of the middle class has resulted primarily from discoveries and inventions, and from the progress of science and of the art of organization in conjunction with the ever-growing accumulation of capital. The manufacturers, for instance, with their powers of leadership and organization and their understanding of men, could never have come to control the labour of thousands of men, and derive great wealth therefrom, had it not been for the invention of the steam-engine and a great series of labour-saving machines which could only be driven by power. Men having the innate qualities of successful manufacturers, including industrialists of all kinds, doubtless existed in the population two hundred years ago in much the same proportion as they did a hundred years later (say in 1833). In the meantime the industrial revolution created opportunities for them to exercise their full capacity, and with ever-increasing scope a class of wealthy manufacturers arose. I would hazard the opinion too that inventive genius was not suddenly born into the English people in the eighteenth century, but that persons with inventive capacity existed in former centuries. It was the expansion of trade, growth of workshop manufactures, and of accumulations of capital which stimulated ingenious persons to invent, and gave them the opportunity of putting their ideas into effect. Similarly, the immense progress of medical science has increased the number of doctors, so that they have become a not inconsiderable fraction of the well-to-do class. Engineers, and all kinds of technical experts, have been called into existence by the progress of science and of the industrial arts. All such occupations demand highly educated men of intellectual ability, and the demand having increased faster than the supply they are usually well-paid members of the middle class. The growth of the professional classes has, of course, at the same time been dependent on the general increase of the national wealth and the expansion of trade, without which there could not be the demand for their services. The invention of the new occupation is the first essential ; but unless the people are well enough off to be able to pay for the new service, as, e.g., wireless telephony, and there is capital forthcoming to set up the plant, a new profession cannot arise.

The financier could not develop great earning power until property had been vastly multiplied by foreign trade and shipping, and by large-scale industries, and until the middle class had become familiarized with investing in joint-stock companies and the law had protected investors. Lawyers multiplied and became wealthy concurrently with the increasing complexity of the laws of property and the growth of commerce ; and at the present time, as a class, they are reaping even further benefit by the complicated laws which have become necessary to protect the public from the power of capital and vested interests.

In brief, we may say that all the rich and well-to-do workers are people who have taken advantage of opportunities socially created. They had innate qualities suiting them for occupations which progress rendered remunerative ; their early home-training and experience gave them the necessary strength of character. They received a good education, and applied themselves to learning and hard work, and conducted themselves generally with a prudent eye to getting on. Those who failed in any of these essentials did not get on. They were excluded by competition from the occupation to which they aspired, and either emigrated or sank back into some poorly-paid employment.

The idle rich, on the other hand, are the product of anti-quated laws of property, which once served a socially useful purpose, but whose utility is almost, if not wholly, exhausted.

THE SOCIAL LADDER

In view of the fact that the political power of the rich and middle classes combined is still predominant, and likely to be so for many years, it is of special interest to consider the composition of those classes according to personal capacity and character. As was stated above, the rich and the middle class are composed of persons following a great number of different occupations, all, however, being alike in that the supply of competent persons does not equal the demand for persons capable of giving such special services except at a rate of earnings much higher than the average earnings of skilled artisans. The deficient supply—deficiency being inferred from a high rate of remuneration—is due to the high cost of the education and experience necessary, quite as much as (probably more than) to any absolute paucity of persons with the requisite innate capacity. It does, however, happen that more persons prepare themselves to follow certain professions, e.g. as doctors, architects, lawyers, and so forth, than ultimately find employment therein, the most probable reason being the allurement of the very high earnings of the most successful members of the professions. Consequently there is keen competition for the available salaried posts and for the available practice. This competition seems to have a threefold result : (1) it reduces the average earnings of the existing members of the profession, (2) it weeds out the most incompetent amongst the competitors, (3) it puts a premium on personal qualities other than pure competence in the profession in question. The first two effects will be readily admitted ; the last needs a little explanation.

When the Civil Service examination is being held for appointments to the Home and Indian Civil Services all candidates must be of good character and health, but the competition is purely intellectual. The method of selection is such that ' push ', and cleverness in ' wangling ', have no influence. Hence, among the appointees there is no bias in the direction of selecting persons skilful in these arts ; in other words, egoists and altruists are probably in the same proportion amongst the selected as amongst the candidates. In the entrance to a profession or business, however, after the passing of a qualifying test, there are few restrictions as to the methods of competition, other than common honesty. Hence the egoistic young man ready in intrigue and in clever, though not blatant, self-adver-tisement, not scrupling to belittle his rival behind his back, is the man who gets on. His ingratiating manner easily deceives the public, and he may be clever enough to deceive experienced employers into preferring him to a competitor really more competent, but anxious to be perfectly straightforward and deceive no one. Men of the highest ability make good in the profession, whether egoists or altruists ; but amongst the men of second- and third-rate ability the great majority of the altruists go to the wall. Ultimately they become discouraged and seek some other occupation, probably less remunerative, being prevented mainly by professional etiquette—really a kind of trade union *esprit de corps*—from undercutting prevailing rates of remuneration in the occupation for which they have trained.[1]

The conclusion to be drawn is that the competition for entry into all well-paid occupations, other than Government service, leads to a higher proportion of egoists amongst the successful than amongst the competitors. The process of selection among the men who enter and succeed in rising in mercantile

[1] After this chapter was written I came across a brief note in a newspaper, entitled ' Intelligence versus " Push ",' which puts so forcibly what I wanted to say that I reproduce it below in full. I regret that I carelessly neglected to make a note of the source.

' We all know people of ability far greater than the average who fail to get on. They are in every profession, every trade—the steady pioneers and the clever bankrupts of life. Men of less than a tithe of their parts outstrip them every time, while they go on plodding, or uncomplaining or grumbling go to the wall. Why ?

' The answer is, that the successful fellows push, asserts a doctor. Whatever their abilities may be they are abundantly conscious of them. They have a quality which the failures, for all their intelligence, lack—a conceit of them-selves which makes for success.

' From time to time these hopelessly clever people astonish us with flashes of their genius. From time to time the plodding ones show what they can really do. But they lack the steady drive of self-assertion. " Get on or get out " is the slogan of the times ; and bare intelligence without drive gets out.

' Indeed, it would almost seem that intelligence, beyond a certain point, is a positive bar to success, unless it is strongly compensated for by character qualities of the assertive kind. For the more a man knows the more clearly he realizes his ignorance.'

and financial business of all kinds, other than the family concern, goes almost the length of the complete exclusion of altruists from the higher ranks of business employees, because the egoistic habit of thought and action is essential even in serving an employer on a fixed salary. The man who gives a judicial verdict on his firm's goods to an intending purchaser usually does not rise far in that firm's employ, and may have no other chance.

The next question is : Who are the candidates for employment in middle-class occupations ? From what class or classes do they come ? Much has been written in recent years about the ' social ladder '. The opportunities open to sons of working men to gain scholarships for secondary schools, and thence to Oxford and Cambridge, are quoted as the beginning of a great social change whereby all clever boys of working-class families will compete on equal terms with middle-class boys for entry into the well-paid professions. Some authors are of opinion that there is even now a considerable penetration upwards from the working classes to the middle classes. McDougall, for instance, writes : [1] ' The upper and middle classes and also the superior part of the artisan classes . . . have been formed and are maintained by the operation of social and economic competition ; they have long been, and still are, perpetually recruited in each generation from the lower strata, by the rise into them of the abler members of the lower strata.' Later on he writes of ' the draining process by which . . . the best elements and strains have been drained off from the lower strata, brought to the top, and strained off '. But Carr-Saunders in his *Population Problem* (p. 457) does not agree with this view. ' Here we may observe,' he writes, ' that it is altogether misleading to speak, as Mr. McDougall does, of the lower classes as being " drained " by the operation of the social ladder, even in England at the present day where the chance of rising is as great, if not greater, than it has ever been before. A very limited number can and do rise.' My own opinion accords with this latter view. I find it hard to believe that more than about 1 per cent of the boys annually entering middle-class occupations have come from working-class homes, which would mean that little more than one in a thousand of the

[1] *Group Mind*, p. 258.

boys annually growing to manhood in working class homes gain entrance to a remunerative occupation which translates them to the middle class. I refer to England, of course, and not to Scotland or America or Australia, where the chances of rising are much greater.

If the above statement is approximately correct as regards England, it means that the middle class is very largely self-perpetuating; and it is easy to understand why this is so. The birth-rate of the rich and middle class is less than the average for the nation; but so is the death-rate also. The natural increase of the middle class proves quite sufficient, therefore, to fill such expansion of the class as the economic conditions of the country permit. Sons of working men do not seriously compete, partly perhaps because the necessary innate qualities are somewhat scarcer amongst them, but mainly because they have not the same advantages of upbringing in the home, or of school education, as the middle-class boy, who in home and school unconsciously acquires, not only a strong character, but the manners and mental outlook of his parents and friends. Most important, however, is the fact that the middle class can afford to send their boys to boarding or day schools charging high fees, and giving an education far more efficient, or at any rate more effective, than that given by municipal and county schools. The effectiveness, from the preparatory school right through the middle-class public school lies even more in character formation than in superior intellectual training, though this also is largely achieved. But character and manners are very important factors in gaining admission to middle-class employments.

The growing class consciousness of the workers of this country referred to in the first chapter, can be explained, therefore, partly by the fact that the middle class as a whole is largely self-perpetuating. Every thoughtful manual worker knows this well enough : knows that he has no chance of rising into the middle class. Much as we should like to deny it, we have in fact in the English social structure a system of caste. The bitterness and intensity of modern labour unrest in England and some other European countries arise from the fact that the economic struggle between capital and labour in respect of their immediate interests produces an economic cleavage following

5

exactly the line of greatest social cleavage. Education, be it noted, is rapidly increasing the class consciousness of the workers, and hence the economic and social cleavage. It is useless to suppose that the economic opposition and discontent can be allayed whilst social caste remains a fact. The middle class is the great bulwark of our present economic system based on private property, coupled with unlimited competition, or with combination, as self-interest dictates. If we would abolish labour unrest, poverty and destitution, we must be willing completely to alter the social system and all the institutions and customs belonging to class distinctions. We may observe that here, as always in ultimate analysis, we are driven back to the psychological basis of economic reform.

CHAPTER V

DEFECTS OF THE CAPITALIST SYSTEM

THE SCIENCE OF ECONOMICS

IT is most important to realize that the economic aspects of social organization are not fundamental. There is no fixity about economic laws, as the nineteenth century supposed, excepting such of them as are determined by the physical character of the earth's surface, the nature of animate life and the properties of things. For the rest, economic laws relate only to a given condition of society. They depend, to the one hand, on *individual human nature*, and to the other hand, on the existing *structure of society*. It is said that human nature is unalterable ; but this is false. Christianity and liberal thought have changed it. More important still is the assurance we now have that with vigorous teaching and with improved environment, both physical and social, the moral nature of man can be further and permanently changed, so as to replace the selfish by disinterested motives to a degree fully sufficient to create general happiness on earth. That the existing social structure can be altered in concurrence with the will of a majority of the people—a majority strong enough to overcome the resistance of vested interests—needs no demonstration. Hence economic laws not only have no fixity, but are to be discovered for any projected state of society.

It is only within the past forty years that the science of economics has progressed to a point of general agreement among its professors on the broad outlines of theory ; and it is only within the present century that economists have betaken themselves to a detailed examination of the facts of trades and industries as carried on in this country at the present day, and have attempted with success to bring theory to the test of the actual phenomena they observe in progress. This has been done to a sufficient extent to enable us to say that the economics of the present-day capitalist-competitive system as existing in

Europe and America are correctly understood—although, it may be, not completely. But it is only in the most recent books, and in papers published in the scientific economic journals, that the modern theory of the existing economic fabric of society is to be found. All earlier books, even those by famous writers, are erroneous or incomplete.

The economics of the existing capitalistic system to which I have been referring is, of course, a pure science, in the sense that it simply studies existing facts as they are observed, and seeks to explain them by generalizations which are called scientific laws. These are verified by the test of repeated observations by those economists who keep themselves closely in touch with the affairs of practical business. The pure science of economics, when economists confine themselves to it, has no bias in favour of any one social system or any class. It is simply a description and analysis of the existing state of society. It is true that very few economic writers maintain this strictly scientific attitude. Most authors show a certain amount of bias towards the opinion of one school of reform or another.

ECONOMICS OF THE COMPETITIVE SYSTEM

Communism in its permanent form must take account of the economic properties of land and of the machinery and plant necessary for production. These are well known, but it will be advisable to recapitulate those points which have a special bearing upon our subject. After dealing with those economic features which must be determined by the natural properties of things, I shall go on to consider the economic results of the present organization of commerce and industry. I shall show that prodigious waste occurs under the competitive system leading to a quite unnecessary enlargement of the lower-paid sections of the middle classes—among them thousands whose principal energies are used in aiding their employers in the struggle to get the better of one another, and in vast and valueless systems of account-keeping.

RENT OF LAND

The theory of the rent of land is substantially the same

whether the land be rural and put to agricultural uses, or urban and employed for residence or any purpose of business. In both cases we assume the land to be put to the most remunerative use for the time being : and that is what its user always endeavours to secure. In the case of agricultural land this depends upon the prices of the various produce as well as upon the actual fertility of the land, which latter is dependent upon the character of the soil, its improvement or deterioration by cropping, the aspect of the land, and the climatic conditions of the locality. The price realized for the produce *on the land itself* is the price realized in the nearest market less the cost of transport. For urban land the only difference is that when the land is utilized for any particular purpose buildings are erected on it, and much capital is thus permanently fixed upon it. In most cases it is usually unprofitable thereafter to alter the use to which the land is put and erect new buildings until a long period of years has passed. The land and buildings must be taken together, and the latter adapted to a new purpose in the best manner possible. Now, in any one locality different lands differ in their fertility, and thus also in their productivity in terms of money. Owing to competition amongst farmers, landlords can obtain rentals equal to the excess yield of each lot of land above the cost of production in the most remunerative use of the land according to current practice in cultivation, including in the cost of production what the farmers consider necessary to maintain their standard of life. Similarly, in urban land the different sites in a shopping street vary in the degree in which they attract the attention of customers, and thus command different situation rents. In like manner, if we compare the agricultural land in one locality with that in another which is nearer to a railway or a market, there is a difference of rent due to the situation, especially the lower cost of transportation in the latter case.

DIFFERENCES OF CAPITAL GOODS

These differences of different plots of land are characteristic of the differences of all natural objects and of artificially constructed things—termed capital goods—including buildings, machinery and plant of all kinds ; and are even paralleled by the differences between different men. The unique attribute of land is that the supply of it *in any one locality* is absolutely limited. In fact, civilized man can only get more land either by reclamation of marshes and so forth at great capital cost, or by spreading over unpopulated territories—that is, by colonization. Minerals are part of the earth's crust and are still more limited than the fertility of the earth's surface, for they are capable of exhaustion. All other objects, animate and inanimate, are capable of indefinite multiplication according to the will of man.

ADJUSTMENT OF SUPPLY TO DEMAND

Under the prevailing economic system horses, sheep and cattle no less than houses, factories, machinery, railways and ships, are multiplied so long as it will pay to create more of them. The rate of gross profit to be obtained by the use of more of any particular breed of live stock or kind of building or plant is called the marginal rate of return on capital in this industry. The tendency is for capital to be applied in every industry until the marginal return in that industry has been reduced to equality with the marginal return in the majority of industries. Making allowance for the difference of anticipated risks in different industries and differences in the supply of entrepreneurs having technical knowledge sufficient for organizing the industry, an approximate equation of marginal return on capital does actually take place.

By the ceaseless quest for profits entrepreneurs are constantly creating new forms of capital goods, mainly for production of standard articles of commerce, but partly for making totally new commodities—new inventions to serve new wants. Let us take a single instance, viz. the building of new cotton-mills in Lancashire. When the demand in foreign markets—India, China, South America and so forth—as well as in the home market increased, the price of most kinds of cotton cloth increased, giving larger profits to existing mills. Persons ready to start cotton-mills were ever alert for a suitable opportunity. When they saw that, after paying all expenses, the return on the total capital invested would exceed, say 7 per cent, they considered it worth while to erect a cotton-mill. At times the price of cotton goods rose so much that the return to new mills equipped with the latest machinery involving large capital outlay would be (as in 1918–20) anything up to 25 per cent per annum. New mills were erected until, as they one after another came into operation and put their goods on the market, the price of the goods became reduced.

The capital invested in such new cotton-mills is said to be ' on the margin ' with regard to the capital already sunk in the industry as a whole, and the profits which the new mills give on the investment of capital are called the marginal return to capital in that industry. If the new mills already erected still return over 10 per cent per annum, the marginal return of capital in the cotton-spinning industry may still be greater than the prevailing marginal rate of return to capital in all the other great industries of the country, and it will be profitable to put yet more money into building new cotton-mills. Further building does in fact continue until the marginal return to capital has been reduced to the prevailing rate. Usually a slump of trade lowers the marginal return suddenly, and stops further building, which is not resumed until the revival of trade has again increased the marginal return.

This is not the whole story, however. Looking over the whole cotton-weaving and spinning industry of the North of England, we find that many of the older mills are built according to inefficient plans, the machinery is old and its production poor, so that operating costs are high. Again, some of the mills are better situated as regards natural facilities than others—for water-supply, access to railways, or canal, for obtaining the raw cotton or for delivery of the finished cotton goods to the market. Up to a certain limit the increase of size of a mill is itself a factor of economy, and in the present century new mills have been built on a much larger scale than was customary fifty or sixty years ago. The factors leading to lower working costs—such as well-chosen site, large size of mill and latest machinery—may reduce working costs so far that, in competition with one another, the large well-equipped new mills reduce the price of the finished goods to such a level that the old or badly situated mills become altogether unprofitable. Such mills come to be beyond the margin of profitable working ; they are soon obliged to shut down, and the capital which was invested in them years ago is lost. They have run for many years, however, and should have accumulated a reserve or sinking fund out of the profits sufficient to restore the capital, which could then be re-invested as part of the cost of a new mill.

The form in which capital is invested in an industry as a whole is constantly changing, more and more efficient plant constantly replacing that which is old and worn out ; but the fund of capital invested in the industry as a whole normally remains practically the same, or gradually increases. In the actual progress of economic events there is the cycle of trade— alternate booms of trade and subsequent depressions following one another, at intervals usually of seven or ten years, or sometimes longer. A boom of trade is followed by a slump, which passes into a state of depression usually lasting some years. There is a gradual revival of trade, which is followed by expansion, which terminates in another boom ; and so on. The new mills are mostly started during the periods of boom, when profits are abnormally great ; and the old mills become more profitable and their shares rise in price during a period of high prices of cotton goods.[1] But the old mills become unprofitable and are the first to be permanently closed during the periods of depression when a number of new mills put their goods on the market and the demand is also falling off.

LABOUR SUPPLY

One of the advantages of situation which has been of considerable importance in the past is that of the cost of labour ; for in most industries there have been differences in the supply of labour in different places, depending partly on the cost of living, and partly on other circumstances, such as the number of competing industries, great competition for labour having established a higher standard of living. The application of the trade union common rule is tending to obliterate these differences ; or at least to abolish minor local differences, so that it is only in widely separated localities, or large as against small towns, that a different wage-rate is found for precisely the same occupation.

The supply of labour under the competitive system always

[1] As, for example, during the extraordinary boom of 1919–20, when mills (and their shares) changed hands at many times their original cost.

tends to adjust itself to the demand. In other words, if the demand for a particular kind of labour, as, for example, coal-miners, arises in any district through the opening of collieries to meet a demand for coal, men are drawn to the new collieries from other coalfields and also to some extent from other occupations. The accessibility of the new coal-mines from great centres of population, the housing facilities and general amenities for living near the new collieries, and again the price of labour, i.e. the wages offered, are all factors which determine the number of labourers who will offer themselves and settle down as permanent workers in the new mines. In any such newly settled mining area the labour-supply is always short, for the mines tend to develop space for a larger number of men faster than the male population naturally increases. During the first twenty years increase of output is a more important factor to the mine-owner than the rate of wages he pays, and he is ready to pay highly. As time goes on the labour-supply increases through the multiplication of the population settled on the spot. The sons naturally tend to follow their fathers' occupation, and there becomes after a time a surplus of labour offering, unless new collieries are being constantly opened. This latter was the case in South Wales until about ten years ago, and is one of the reasons why wages are so much higher than in the old but small coalfields of the Forest of Dean and Bristol, which have been developing very slowly for many generations past, so that there has always been an ample labour-supply. The coalfields of Durham and Northumberland have been worked on a continuously increasing scale during the past two hundred and fifty years, and the labour conditions are, therefore, quite different from those of the new coalfields like South Wales and South Yorkshire. In Durham and Northumberland the labour-supply increased more rapidly than the demand, and to such an extent that the working of two and even three shifts at hewing the coal became the rule many years ago, thus making it possible to pay good wages for what was before the War a comparatively short day ($6\frac{1}{2}$ to 7 hours). In South Wales, on the other hand, it would be impossible to adopt double-shift working in all the collieries, if desirable on other grounds, simply because there is not sufficient labour. It would be thirty years or more before the natural increase of population, together with immigration to the coalfield, could so far surpass the extension of the collieries as to make the gradual adoption of double-shift working possible throughout the coalfield.

This example well illustrates what happens in all industries, namely, that the labour-supply tends to multiply both by migration and by natural increases of the population until the supply equals the demand. When I say ' until the supply equals the demand ', it must be borne in mind that such equation is relative to the price offered for labour. If the supply of labour is short, and the demand for the commodity is good, the price offered will tend to rise. On the other hand, if the supply increases so as to become excessive the wage-rate offered will be lowered ; but at the same time the number of workmen engaged will be increased. Labour will be employed to a lower marginal productivity, as economists say.

THE STANDARD OF LIVING

It may be asked whether there are any forces tending to limit the growth of the supply of labour offering in any occupations ; and the reply to this question has been one of the great advances in the science of economics during the last fifty years. We saw in Chapter IV that primitive peoples have always been faced with the inevitable tendency for population to multiply faster than the means of subsistence which they can make available. In all countries where the people live under primitive conditions their standard of living is extremely low, and the principal object of life and work is merely to maintain existence. Such a population, therefore, either adopts practices like infanticide to restrict the growth of population, or it multiplies up to the limit of the available means of subsistence. The latter category includes the huge populations of large parts of Russia, India and China. There the cost of keeping body and soul together, with the minimum of clothing and shelter, is what determines the family earnings of the majority of the population. Malthus found this condition to prevail over most of Europe in the later part of the eighteenth century. It is certainly true of more than two hundred millions of the population of India at the present day.

With the growth of demand for labour consequent on the industrial revolution, there came into operation in Great Britain about a hundred years ago a new factor. Owing to many occupations being skilled, so that demand exceeded supply, wages came to stand above the subsistence level for a number of years. Skilled workers in such trades were able to adopt a higher standard of living ; and to this they became habituated. There is nothing to which the persons of any class will cling more tenaciously than the standard of living to which they have become accustomed ; and there are two ways in which they make strenuous efforts to maintain it. If wages become reduced in their own trade below the level to which they have been accustomed, many seek employment in other localities, even overseas, or in other occupations, wherever they find work which will enable them to maintain their accustomed rate of earnings. This migration to other places and to other occupations is one way in which the standard of living tends to be maintained amongst the work-people of any given occupation. The second method is by trade union combination. Indeed maintenance of the standard of living has been the principal motive for combination, the workers in any occupation trying to protect themselves from a reduction of wages. There is great economic pressure to reduce wages when, after a period of growth of the industry, a depression of trade sets in, and the price of the commodity produced continually falls. In periods of depression there may be also an excessive influx of labour from other trades or districts. The more complete and effective the combination of workmen in any trade, the more successful can they be in maintaining, and even in raising, their standard of living. Unemployment insurance is an additional factor operating towards the same result as trade union combination, to prevent transference from other trades and maintain wage-rates.

There are two other important factors, fortunately, which come into play and tend respectively to maintain and to advance the standard of living. In the first place, it is a universal phenomenon that the higher the standard of living of any class of persons the less is the rate of natural increase of that class. This is due largely to the postponement of marriage, because people desire to have their accustomed standard of life assured before they set up a home and undertake the responsibilities of a family. Birth-control is practised for the same object of maintaining the standard of comfort of the family as a whole. Thus the higher the standard of living the smaller is the growth of the supply of labour, as a result of the natural increase of the classes of persons concerned. But we have to notice that this restriction of the size of families leads to a better upbringing of the children of such classes, and therefore increases the supply of well-educated persons. On the other hand, there always remains the submerged tenth of the population which, like the proletariat of primitive countries, has a standard of living no higher than the level of mere subsistence ; and amongst this class large families are common, owing to their improvidence. Consequently we have a continual growth of a supply of almost uneducated, untrained labour.

The only factor which tends to raise the standard of living in advance of wages is education, which teaches people new wants. Intercourse with other people through travel, local and distant, is an informal means of education, and has the same effect. Since the adoption of general compulsory attendance at school, education has become a more and more important factor in raising the standard of living, until now it is spurring on the skilled workers to demand the opportunity of living in decent homes with comfortable surroundings and with some money to spend on neat clothes and luxuries. They are no longer content to maintain by combination merely the standard of life reached during a former period of trade prosperity. They are embarking definitely and rightly on a policy of steadily raising the standard of living of their class.

EFFECT OF TRADE UNION RULE ON SUPPLY

We see therefore that during the past hundred years entirely new factors have come into operation in determining wage-rates. The trade union common rule is peculiarly effective in the so-called ' sheltered ' industries—those which are naturally protected, such as the building trade, railways and all kinds of municipal and constructional work and, to some extent, coal-mining. Where the trade union wage is effectively maintained by combination, or the wage-rate is fixed legally by a wages board, the price of labour is obviously no longer the result of an equation of demand and supply. In this case the price of supply is fixed, and a change of demand expresses itself as a variation in the *number* of workers required at that wage-rate. The demand for labour is affected on the one hand by the demand of consumers for the finished commodity, and on the other hand by any changes in the process of production. For example, if new mechanical contrivances are introduced, these may greatly reduce the demand for a given kind of manual labour; and if the trade union maintains its standard rate for hand-labour, as was the case for many years in the boot trade, there results simply a rapid decrease of the number of hand-workers employed. There would be in most cases, of course, a growing demand for labour to work the machines which were replacing hand-labour ; but the workers attending the machines may be either unskilled, or may require a different kind of skill from the hand-workers displaced.

EARNINGS OF INTELLECTUAL LABOUR

The interest on capital, the remuneration of risk-taking, and the salaries of foremen, managers, and technical and professional men, are all similarly determined by demand and supply, though of course with varying circumstances in each case affecting both the demand and the supply. The remuneration of intellectual labour, which is employed so extensively in this country in every sphere of foreign commerce, banking and finance, and internal trade, in the management of industries, and in various professional occupations, is governed by economic forces similar to those determining the wage-rate of a skilled manual occupation. There is, however, no extensive combination for the support of the price of such labour, excepting amongst certain professions, e.g. law, medicine, architecture, stockbroking and two or three others.

INTEREST ON CAPITAL

Capital is the most fluid of all the factors of production, because in its representative form as money it can be invested in any form of trade or industry which offers the most remunerative return. It is for this reason that the market for capital is not only nation-wide, but international. On the demand side the principal factors are the marginal rate of return which the capital will give in extensions of industry or trade, and the intensity of desire for capital by other would-be borrowers, whether for public purposes, e.g. Government loans, or private borrowers wanting houses, motor-cars, etc.

PROFITS

The remuneration of risk-taking is very elusive, and yet it forms a considerable burden upon the consumer, who has to pay somebody for taking the risk of loss in setting up the production of any commodity. As a rule, in the modern phase of the capitalistic system, viz. joint-stock company enterprise, it is the capitalist who mainly takes the risk, and he gets his remuneration for risk in the shape of the extra dividends which he expects, and does on the average receive. In municipal undertakings the ratepayers assume the risk, and in co-operative distributive societies, which fix prices with a view to paying a dividend on purchases, the risk falls mainly on the purchasing members. The greater the risk in any particular industry the higher the average rate of dividend which the joint-stock companies in that industry must be earning before people will invest in the shares. This is one reason for the high rate of dividends prevailing in metalliferous mining companies, and for the comparatively high dividends amongst those colliery companies which are successful in their mining operations.

So far I have not mentioned profits. This term is used in many different senses, and the economist is obliged carefully to distinguish profits according to their sources. In common speech, the profit of any private business firm includes interest on capital, remuneration to the partners for their work in managing the business, and remuneration for bearing all the risks of their business. It includes also profits arising from special advantages, which in certain cases become extremely important. In a wave of prosperity when prices rise the gross profits greatly exceed what may be called the normal charges against them, that is to say, the remuneration of capital, management and risk-taking. Such a surplus of profits, which may be realized sometimes in three or four successive years, is soon annihilated by new firms coming in and increasing the supply of the commodity ; but while it lasts the surplus is substantial. Such profits due to a temporary rise of prices I shall call *occasional profits*. Then, as another form of special profit, we have that which results from any kind of particularly good bargain, whereby the proprietor of a business has the advantage over his competitors. He may have obtained a better site for building his factory than anybody else, or he may have fixed up some advantageous contract for haulage of raw materials, or have sold his output for many years ahead at a more favourable price than his rivals. Specially good bargains are often made in obtaining capital at a cheap rate by making an issue of debentures or preference shares when the money market is in a favourable condition, or by specially attracting the public to a subscription by clever publicity. Again, some employers are lucky enough to obtain the services of a young manager or technical expert for a term of years at a salary which is far less than his real market value ; and for many years they reap the advantage of his intelligence, industry and initiative whilst paying him the salary of quite an ordinary man.

Another and most important basis of special profits is monopoly. There is nothing that the business man likes better than to secure some kind of monopoly, whether it be by contract with the State or a local authority, by purchase of the whole of some mineral deposit, or by legal power, such as patent and trade-mark protection. So important are the profits, even of incomplete monopoly, in many industries that there are numbers of huge combinations of capitalists formed for the express purpose of limiting the supply of the commodity put into the market, thus creating huge monopoly profits. The movement for the formation of trusts, which has become so powerful in this country as well as in America, is due mainly to the advantage of creating monopolistic conditions, and secondarily to the desire to reap the great economies which are possible by reorganization of plant and management for working on a large scale. These economies are principally of two kinds—the economy which results from using plant each unit of which is constructed upon a larger scale, and the concentration in one big plant of production formerly done in several different places, e.g. the big blast furnaces of the United States Steel Corporation at Gary ; and secondly, the economy in selling and the control and direction of the industrial processes which is obtained by the specialization of managers and technical experts in a very large producing concern.

WASTES OF THE COMPETITIVE SYSTEM

So far I have done no more than summarize the pertinent parts of the economic theory of the competitive system of industry. I shall next point out those inherent weaknesses of the system which are certain to bring it to an end so soon as the people of this country have equipped themselves to establish and operate a better system. From the strictly commercial or monetary point of view, the chief evil of any organization of industry is waste, and the question now before us is most easily solved by finding the principal sources of communal waste in the competitive system. It is true that the capitalist competitive system can be condemned also from the moral point of view, as indicated in another chapter ; but it is important here to demonstrate its weakness from the purely economic aspect, so that we may show that a reorganization on the basis of communism would be superior not only morally, but also in its material results.

The wastes of the competitive system fall under three main headings : (1) waste of productive power (capital, labour, etc.) in the delivery of commodities from producers to consumers ; (2) waste of having an unnecessary number of producing concerns, each a separate complete business entity with separate plant, and of duplicating work in designing, management and book-keeping ; (3) competition in making sales or securing business. Examples of (1) are the overlapping of deliveries of milk, newspapers, etc., in almost every town, and intercrossing of deliveries of coal from the different coalfields, and many heavy goods from various works. During the War, this waste was reduced partly by voluntary agreements amongst retail distributors, often with subsequent sanction and enforcement by the local authority ; and partly, as in the case of coal, by Government orders requiring the consumer to be supplied from the nearest source for obtaining the necessary quality of coal.

The wastes under the second heading, from having an unnecessary number of producing concerns, are to be seen in every industry. Trusts thrive partly by getting rid of such wastes. They close the least efficient plants, group others under combined supervision, introduce standardized systems of accounting and of management in all plants, and have a single highly efficient staff for advertising and sales, instead of many small inefficient staffs. In coal-mining and railways, the waste is prodigious, and well known. There are about 2,500 coal pits in the United Kingdom owned by 1,400 companies and individuals ;[1] but the present output could be raised from 800 mines worked by at most fifteen separate administrations under a national co-ordinating authority. There were some forty separate railway companies actually working traffic in the United Kingdom before the amalgamation of 1922.[2] All the large companies had their own locomotive and carriage- and wagon-building works, each completely equipped to design and build engines and coaches in entire independence of each other, to different patterns. Thus many of the economies of large-scale production were lost. Even now there is too much overlapping of the areas served by the four great companies, and the expense of the boards of directors and higher adminis- trative control could be further reduced by amalgamating all the companies under State control or by nationalization.[3] The most colossal waste is in the private ownership of wagons, of which there are about 520,000 in use for coal alone, and their return empty ; which waste would not be wholly avoided even if all wagons belonged to railway companies so long as the usual rule of returning empty to reload within the owning company's system were maintained. Another tremendous waste is the Railway Clearing House, needed to settle the highly intricate claims of every company on every other company for through goods and passenger traffic. If all railways were State owned all this would be unnecessary, and the tiresome labour of

[1] Report of Royal Commission on the Coal Industry (1925). (Cmd. 2600). 1926, pp. 45 and 240. Many small pits have since been closed.
[2] Not counting city and suburban lines, light and narrow-gauge railways, and companies working short branch lines, which would make the total to about 120.
[3] Since the above was written the pooling agreement between the London, Midland and Scottish, and London and North Eastern Railways made in 1932 has enabled considerable economies to be made by closing redundant goods yards, locomotive sheds, works, etc. ; but much remains to be done.

6

hundreds of clerks would be saved. There are similar wastes on a smaller scale in every manufacturing industry in the country through work being duplicated a hundred times simply because both sales and manufacture are carried on in small lots of goods as orders can be obtained. Instead of this, there ought to be an equalized distribution of work so as to keep all the efficient factories busy by the pooling of all orders through a central office, the inefficient factories being closed.

The wastes of competition under the third head, in making sales and securing business, reach a colossal total for the whole country. Think of the multitude of manufacturers of toilet soaps ! There is no reason why we should not have a hundred and one different kinds of toilet soaps to use with many differences of quality, colour, size and scent, if we wish ; but we do not require fifty different concerns to produce them, every one with its own staff of salesmen, and many of them spending fortunes yearly in advertising—all of which makes our soap dearer.[1] Then think of retail trade—some two or three hundred shops in a medium-sized town doing all, taken together, a much smaller aggregate business than any one of the great emporia of London, but employing about twice as many people. This waste is, indeed, already being lessened, on the one hand by the growth of capitalist retailing companies, and on the other hand by co-operative effort. In some small towns in Scotland and the north of England, where co-operation has taken a firm hold, practically the whole retail business of the town is now done through the store of a single co-operative society, and a score of little shops have closed.

Then we have the insurance companies with their 40,000 agents and canvassers, whose work, so far as it is useful in educating the public to insure, could be better done by one-tenth of that number intelligently directed. Next the banks, with their hundreds of branches—three or four little branches competing in every town—all managed alike, the personal element of the old private banks having been already destroyed. The multiplication of restaurants, cinemas, photographers and

---

[1] Since the above was written the Lever amalgamations culminating in the union with the United Margarine Co. to form Unilever, Ltd., have brought the greater part of the toilet soap manufacture under one control, though brand names are retained. Inefficient factories have been closed and advertising reduced.

every kind of service goes on until the profitable prices at which the first ones started are eaten up in the costs of competition.

These are only a few examples of the wastes of the competitive system—they might be multiplied indefinitely. The total loss to the nation, compared with the practicable results of a scientifically ordered system of central control in every industry, must run into hundreds of millions of pounds per annum.

This waste has also its human aspect, with many deplorable features. It creates classes of persons who live on what is really social waste ; and these persons are undoubtedly to some extent affected in their moral outlook by the unproductive character of their work. Let us take these two points separately.

A wasteful system of trade or industry creates a class of people living on this waste, because supply responds to demand. In most trades and industries there is no conscious organization of the entire business of providing the community with the commodity in question. The only way the public can get the supplies they require is by purchasing from such persons as choose to set up in this line of business and offer their wares. Take retail shopkeeping, for example. If *A* has set up a grocer's shop in a small town, *B* and *C* can also set up shops and get custom for three reasons : (1) *A* has not the initiative, or the power of organization, to arrange his business so as to supply all the various wants of the town in his line of trade : (2) his prices may be high because he has not learned how to buy cheaply from London wholesalers. (3) *B* and *C* can choose sites for their shops where they can intercept some of *A*'s customers, and give them a shorter distance to walk. If the town grows, *D*, *E* and others will open grocers' shops in other parts, one of them perhaps quite close to *A*, but in a position slightly better chosen. Thus there are five or six shops called into existence to do work which with a little organization might equally well be done from one, or at most two centres. But all these shopkeepers and their assistants are men of very limited intelligence and business ability ; for their method of doing business does not demand of them any skill in organization. They are largely engaged in making their windows as attractive as possible, with the object of diverting custom from their competitors ; but much of their time is necessarily spent in idleness, waiting for customers. Thus the effect of the community's demand for groceries is to call into existence a class of persons who, because of their limited business capacity, and owing to competition, carry on the work of distributing commodities at far greater cost than would be incurred by a single organized source of supply. As there has usually been no person, society or constituted authority ready to set up a complete organized distribution in response to the demand for the commodity, the demand has been met everywhere by just such persons as happened to present themselves ; and the cost of their inefficiency has been, and still is, added to the retail price which the consumer has to pay. An interesting experiment in keeping under control and planning in advance the retail supply of goods for a whole town is afforded by the new garden city at Welwyn. The town is planned for 50,000 inhabitants ; but, excepting a few special shops, it has only one shop, the Central Stores, with thirty different departments, from which come all the main supplies, and which is under control of the Garden City Company.

Whole classes of socially unproductive workers are called into existence in a similar manner for want of an efficiently planned economic organization. The host of insurance agents, thousands of bank clerks, and a great number of railway clerks, could be dispensed with, and their services put to productive occupations, if a non-competitive organization of business with centralized control were set up. Some thousands of agents, artists, printers, etc., engaged in advertising the goods of competing producers would no longer be needed. The artists could give us their work in other forms ; though of course a certain amount of artistic advertising of newly-invented or improved goods would always be undertaken. In the management of industries now run upon the competitive plan by a large number of firms with totally separate undertakings, numerous economies could be effected. Thousands of salesmen, commercial travellers, assistant managers and clerks could be dispensed with, whilst maintaining the same output of the commodities ; and these men would be available for other and more fruitful occupations. Clerical labour undertaken for a large number of separate businesses is an extremely badly equipped occupation. The methods of book-keeping have been greatly improved ; but the efficiency of output cannot be much improved in small concerns. It is only in very large concerns where the work becomes specialized, and the numerous American contrivances such as cash-registers, adding, registering and posting machines, can be applied, that something like efficiency of clerical labour is realized.

The important economic principle which I wish to bring out is that all this bad organization of commerce and industry is, in a sense, paid for by the manual worker. In other words, with a better organization the man who actually produces the goods with his own hands could have a distinctly larger share of the total output. In the present chaotic conditions of private enterprise, the multiplicity of employers, of managers, salesmen and clerks engaged in our various industries, and the excessive number of persons employed in the direction and clerical labour of transportation, and in the retail distribution of goods, are indispensable if goods are to be produced for public needs, and the manual worker find employment. Looking at the matter from the wage-earner's point of view, we may say that he is obliged to pay all these people in order to obtain employment. The public's demand for the commodity and his demand for work between them call into existence this host of intermediaries whose present work in organizing the production and delivery of goods could be done by a very much smaller number, backed either by voluntary co-operation of all consumers, or by State authority. It is thus obvious that under the competitive system industry is ' top-heavy '. When private persons risk their capital in competing undertakings, they require the expectation of a high return. The small size of the producing unit in most of our industries means that the capital is employed less advantageously than it might be. In all our industries together some hundreds of thousands of persons are unnecessarily employed in supervising and accounting for the complicated monetary transactions involved in the competitive production and delivery of commodities. Hence it is no wonder that in many cases the actual cost of manual labour in producing a manufactured commodity, including labour expended on gaining the raw material and on all intermediate stages of manufacture, does not exceed 15 per cent of the retail price at which it is finally sold to the consumer. The cost of the use of capital might be halved, and likewise the cost of transport, whilst the cost of retail distribution might well be reduced to one-third. Hence the series of manual workers engaged in producing such commodities might well get a fraction of the retail price, something like twice as large as they do now ; and yet all the managers, clerks and others really needed in production be themselves also better paid than at present, and those not wanted be employed in the industries, like building, which ought to be expanded. These considerations give us some idea of the enormous saving of waste which might be achieved by the reorganization of industry and commerce under a system of communism.

It was stated above that the social waste involved in a system which produces whole classes of unproductive workers is not confined to the loss to the nation of the productive work on which they might be occupied in a better social organization. There is an indirect loss due to the fact that the moral outlook of these persons is to some extent prejudicially affected by the fact that they are doing work which they cannot feel to be of a socially useful character. In Chapter III (p. 43) reference was made to the well-known fact that a person's occupation gradually influences his character. A man who is directly serving the public of his own locality with something they obviously and rightly want takes a pride in rendering effective service whether he be a doctor, a carpenter or a garage attendant. The book-keeper may, and often does, take a pride in doing his work neatly and accurately, but he cannot feel that he is serving any one but his employer. One result is that he has less satisfaction in his work than he would have if he could feel that he was, with his own hands, making things or rendering services in themselves obviously useful to people. Another result is probably that he fails to acquire a habit of thinking of the welfare of others in general. I would suggest that men occupied so that they are obviously at work on something which will be of use to some section of the public, whether they actually meet the consumer (as, for instance, a railway guard) or not (e.g. a baker in a biscuit factory), are thereby led to some extent into habits of thinking of the public they are serving. This habit of thought possibly gives them a tendency to a more altruistic outlook, and a greater readiness to undertake work of social utility in their spare time.

THE AVOIDANCE OF WASTE IN INDUSTRIES

The wastes of the competitive system described above are generally admitted ; but it is argued that such losses are counterbalanced by certain considerable advantages of the competitive system, of which the most important is that it avoids waste due to bad management and want of initiative. Such wastes are all too liable to occur in the processes of production ; and it is pointed out that they are specially characteristic of commercial services managed by the State, by municipalities, and by companies not subject to competition. In reply it may be freely admitted that competition has done much to secure efficiency of production by avoiding waste. When numerous firms are competing in the same industry, the struggle for survival necessitates attention to economy and efficiency throughout all departments of a works or factory. It has been noticed, however, that once a firm or company is doing reasonably well, say, paying a regular dividend of 10 per cent upon its capital, the incentive to make more profit by still closer attention to the business very frequently disappears. The proprietors of the business, or directors of the company, and their managers seem to rest content with the fact that they are making a good return on the capital invested. Extensive observation has convinced me that the very large profits made by many industrial firms are not the result of competition, but arise either (1) from some conjunction of circumstances raising the price of the finished commodity, or lowering the price of raw materials, or otherwise giving a sudden opportunity of profit which comes with little or no effort other than astute buying and selling ; or (2) they result from the elaboration of a system of control of production by cost accounts, whereby a new and almost automatic check upon the efficiency of production is established, which is quite independent of the price at which the goods are being sold and thus of the profit which is being made. Where such cost accounts have been in operation for some years, the directors of a company become accustomed to watch the costs of production rather than the percentage of profits on capital which they are making. They exert constant pressure towards the reduction of costs, and achieve it both by the introduction of labour-saving machinery and by better organization of the work of their entire labour force. The more they succeed in this new ideal of reducing costs as an end in itself, the larger do their profits grow ; until at last competition begins again to act on the price of the finished goods, because nearly all firms in the industry gradually adopt the new system of cost accounts and become equally skilful in the reorganization of their works.

Cost accounting is, indeed, a very great invention, and one for which we have to thank the competitive system. It should be of special interest and importance to socialists, because it forms a bridge which will facilitate the transfer of an industry from the competitive profit-making basis to the publicly controlled non-profit-making basis. The incentive to economy in production provided by private profit-making having already become unnecessary and only operative in a few firms in many of the great industries of the country,[1] there can be no danger to society at large if the profit-making incentive be entirely eliminated from all the great staple industries at an early date. Highly skilled direction and management of the bigger industries under public control would, of course, be necessary ; and the men employed for this purpose who possess special talents and skill, and now gain large rewards, should undoubtedly, during the transition to communism, be paid good salaries. Their duty would not be to make profits for trusts or companies, but to provide commodities for the public at the lowest prices compatible with good wages and proper working conditions for all persons employed. Their system for controlling the cost of production and realizing all the possible economies will be a series of detailed cost accounts and comparative statistics. They will have the same incentive to efficient and economical management that a technical specialist—chemist or engineer— has now, who works more for satisfaction in his achievements and the approbation of fellow-scientists than for profit-making. Successful management will be demonstrable by figures of costs ; and if these be rightly understood by high authority

[1] Because large companies, due to amalgamations, employ fixed salaried managers.

or public representatives, the incentive to good management will probably be stronger than under present conditions.

There is yet a newer and greater source of economy which we owe to the competitive system, and which may likewise be transferred to use in industries under public control, viz. scientific management. This may perhaps be regarded as a development of cost accounting from the passive attitude of merely recording the cost at which the goods are actually being produced, to the active investigation, by a scientific method, of all possible means of reducing the costs of manufacture. From the point of view of technical efficiency scientific management is the supreme art of production by human labour and machinery, in which all knowledge of organization and all natural science is called in to aid the industrial organizer. His object is to find the most advantageous adjustment of machines to the capacities of the workers, having in mind the kind of goods required. A most detailed study of the individual differences of different workmen is undertaken, and each is allotted to the kind of work in which he can naturally excel. Every tool, every instrument of measurement and every machine he handles is worked out in detail with the utmost care, so as to be perfectly adapted to the special task for which it is intended. Numerous ingenious automatic contrivances are utilized for registering work done and also the fatigue experienced by the operating workmen. The planning and supervision of the routine work are divided amongst a number of men on a functional basis, and they become specialists in design, in adjustments of tools, in routine of work, and so on.

Scientific management in its broadest meaning may be regarded from one point of view as the extension to the human actions of production of all those methods of invention and improvement which hitherto have been applied only to machines. The extraordinary advances which have been made in the production of wealth during the past hundred years by the scientific development of machinery lead us to hope that a similar enormous advance will be possible by the further development and extended application of scientific investigation to the labour processes of all industries. When the transitional socialist organization of industry approaches more nearly to placing the whole of the increase of profit caused by the adoption of improvements in methods and technique in the possession of the workers in the industry, they will soon come to realize that cost accounting, scientific management, motion study and labour-saving machines are their best friends, and will increasingly demand their introduction in their own industries. When introduced at the request of the workmen, and with their co-operation, the objectionable incidental results sometimes experienced from such improvements under present conditions will be carefully avoided.

CHAPTER VI

ECONOMIC REASONS FOR EQUALITY

SOCIAL TENDENCIES

IN recent years the social conscience has been aroused rapidly, with the result that the State has already made itself responsible, through contributory schemes or otherwise, for pensions for old age and widowhood, for medical treatment and sick benefit and for unemployment relief on a liberal basis. It has made great endeavours to solve the housing problem at heavy cost financially. The serious growth of unemployment is due partly to the adoption of labour-saving machines and mass-production methods, but very largely in my opinion, to the growth of monopolistic combinations amongst employers as well as workpeople, the *immediate* interest of both being to maintain prices by limitation of output, rather than to adopt the long-sighted view of reorganizing industrial plant at great capital cost and with risks of objections by labour. So long as the State supports the unemployed, trade unionism will be strong, and industrial combinations of employers will be strong, resting on the basis of the common wage-rate, which in most industries effectively prevents serious competitive price-cutting. Extensive unemployment seems likely, therefore, to lay a permanent financial burden on industries and the State. The demoralizing effects of unemployment will also have deplorable results. An economic system in which men are kept idle simply because the organization of industry is such that no work is offering at wages the idle men can accept must lead gradually to national decay.

The public has become very uneasy about unemployment and the relations of capital and labour. Controversies about economic justice are becoming of overwhelming importance, comparable in national life with the religious disputes of the sixteenth and seventeenth centuries. Hence the widespread interest in the study of economics amongst the middle classes of England and America corresponding with the growth of socialist convictions amongst labour.

In spite of the heaviness of the burdens of unemployment and pensions there is no serious thought of shirking an obligation that has been assumed. The country has been prepared (with some grumbling) to shoulder heavier and heavier burdens in favour of the unfit and the unfortunate. A comparison with forty years ago indicates a startling change of public feeling. To some extent this may be due to the propaganda and writings of middle-class philanthropists ; but chiefly it would seem to have been caused by the steady advance of organized labour and its clearly expressed determination to win its rights. One of the most valuable political faculties of the English governing class is their subconscious recognition of a coming storm and willingness to bow to what they cannot avert. Clearly, philanthropy and fear are working in the same direction. Eventually it will be realized how greatly the public burdens are increased by the respect paid to private enterprise. The unemployed, and even prisoners, cannot be put to useful work because every avenue of employment is tenanted by some form of private, i.e. profit-making, undertaking, with which there must be no competition, even though trade union wages could be paid by large-scale organization and State-borrowed capital. The present economic organization has become unstable ; and as it gets worse public enterprise will be advocated more and more as the only solution.

THE DEMAND FOR EQUALITY

A more fundamental view of the changes now proceeding shows that all social, political and economic change is dominated by the growing demand for equality. At all stages of history there have been sporadic outbreaks of ' levelling ' ; but the modern movement has a continuous history only from the French Revolution. ' Liberty, Equality, Fraternity ' has in every decade won some new victory. Political equality—' one man, one vote '—has been won in our own time in most Western countries. Women have demanded, and recently obtained, political equality with men. These, surely, are two events of outstanding importance in the world's history. To this has been added the attempt to give equality of education to all classes of the people ; and this too is slowly being realized. Not one person in a thousand stops to think of the enormous consequences which must follow these innovations, far more significant, as they are, for the world's future than wireless telephony or aviation, or even the motor-car.

Equality of political condition and equality of education are being followed by equality of social status so far as equality of education in the widest sense, including manners, is realized. Religious differences having sunk into the background ; the only form of serious inequality is economic. The demand for economic equality, already voiced, will certainly become stronger and stronger ; at last, irresistible.

THE ORIGIN OF INEQUALITY OF INCOMES

Communism is a very ancient idea. Well-known examples of its practice are Sparta, Heliopolis, and the early Christians. Plutarch has left us an account of the communism of Sparta, established by the laws of Lycurgus probably about the sixth century B.C., and re-established by Cleomenes about 230 B.C.[1] Communism and an austere life was the basis of the former military efficiency of Sparta ; and the victories of Cleomenes filled neighbouring States with alarm and led to a combination which defeated him. Though subject to Macedonia, Sparta retained virtual autonomy in her internal affairs ; but the abolition of communism appears to have been a condition of peace.

It is notable that throughout classical times and the Middle Ages people always looked back to a mythical happy state of existence in which all were equal and had plenty, and happiness prevailed. Possibly amongst the Greeks and Romans this was a tradition handed down through centuries from the time when they were settled as primitive agricultural communities and there was more than enough fertile land for all. When there is no money and no distant trade, and when population has not outgrown the available area of fertile land, a primitive communal life prevails, with practical equality of earnings.

---

[1] *Social Struggles in Antiquity*, by M. Beer ; translated by H. J. Stenning. London : Leonard Parsons, 1922, pp. 61–77. A special Workers' Educational Association cheap edition is priced at 3s 6d.

The first great economic revolution that any country goes through results from the occupation of all the land capable of readily yielding sustenance for a family when worked according to the prevailing method of agriculture. The more egoistic, more adaptable and thrifty begin to accumulate cattle and seed grain ; and when others are in difficulties claim the right to cultivate more land, against a strong public feeling of the villagers. The rapidity of this change has been enormously enhanced wherever British rule has introduced money, security and means of communication. In many parts of India the change is old ; in some recent. In Burma the filling up of practically all of the accessible fertile land could, I think, be dated with fair accuracy at from twenty to twenty-five years ago. In that country, formerly noted for the equality of condition of its people, we see now inequality of incomes arising before our eyes. A non-European landlord and capitalist class has already emerged and is growing rapidly.

The great change from communal village life to individual competition permits the emergence of specialization of labour, which becomes ever more special the more complex become commerce and industry. Our competitive-capitalist system has justified itself up to the present because of the intense specialization permitted by exchange, and of the division of labour facilitated by large aggregations of capital applied to industry. This specialization has given full scope to the different natural aptitudes, and acquired knowledge and skill, possessed by different persons.

The degree in which individuals differ from one another in their inborn qualities cannot be kept too clearly in mind ; and it will be an advantage, therefore, to summarize here the conclusions set out in preceding chapters. Geddes has pointed out how Comte's fourfold classification of men into : chiefs, intellectuals, emotionals and common people has seemingly applied to all races in all ages. With us the chiefs are captains of industry, commanders in the navy and army, masters of merchant ships. The intellectuals are professors, authors, scientific workers, priests of the established Church, and so forth. The emotionals are newspaper writers, revivalist preachers and certain political leaders.

Some men are born altruists and others egoists, with all

stages between. A person's temperamental qualities are considered to be traceable to occupational selection in remote and primitive times. Amongst lonely hunters in the woods or mountains a joy in the chase and a lust for killing was a factor of survival. The shepherd could not succeed unless he had a parental affection for animals ; his factor of survival was a pleasure in preserving life. So the cultivator must be endowed with the constructive instinct to build his home and plan his crops, and must have foresight and thrift. To a large extent he is the prototype of the modern builder and civil engineer. A type that commands men was selected in sea-fishing and coastal navigation. In short, we are all different mixtures of various inherited qualities ; and doubtless the Mendelian law is at work bringing out certain qualities strongly in certain individuals. I may add here, what has not been stated in any earlier chapter, that in my own opinion a type of sexual selection due to free choice in marriage is also having a most important effect in differentiating certain mental qualities more strongly from the average, but without bias to one sex or the other. Especially is this true, perhaps, of intellectual ability, because thoughtful men are attracted by intelligence and mental ability in women. Their children therefore are likely to be well above the average in intellectual ability. Progressive selection in this manner might produce an increased number of ' intellectual giants ', but without affecting much the average intellectual capacity of the race.

Apart from inherited characters we are also very largely the creatures of the environment in which we were brought up. We are born into a certain social organization ; and the people of our country have a certain tradition of knowledge and skill (intellectual tradition), and a certain moral tradition. These traditions vary from class to class, especially the moral tradition, the term being used, in its widest sense, to include social outlook. The acquired knowledge and skill we obtain is largely the chance result of opportunities which come in our way in youth. The character of the education we receive as children is not our own choice, nor, even in the later school years, is it usually selected to suit our inborn capacities.

ECONOMIC CAUSES OF INEQUALITY OF INCOMES

We come next to the economic aspects of unequal earnings, and here we must have in mind the principles briefly set forth in Chapter V. It is highly important to understand that the relative earnings of different persons are not *determined by* the value of the net product (marginal productivity) of their services. That is a misconception too widely prevalent, to which a number of modern elementary and popular books on economics have given currency. That false doctrine is having a serious political result, because it encourages a false ethical dogma ; the assertion that it is just that people should be rewarded according to the marginal net product of their labour, because the marginal net product is proportional to the benefit conferred on the community by an increment of labour.

The truth is that a wage-rate, like the price of a commodity, is determined by the equilibrium of demand and supply. The curve of the marginal productivity [1] of a given kind of labour employed in a given plant, or with a given equipment of tools, etc., is a curve showing what the employer can afford to pay for another unit of labour of that kind when various numbers are alternatively considered as being already employed. Hence the curve of marginal productivity of labour constitutes, in effect, the demand curve for that kind of labour. The supply of that kind of labour in the locality at any given time is independent of the demand *at that time*. It can be indicated by a supply curve ; and the rate of wages actually prevailing is shown by the intersection of the demand and supply curves. Hence the marginal productivity of that kind of labour actually existing at any moment (assuming the employer to engage labour until he can see no further profit in employing more, as he usually does) has become reduced or increased to equal the prevailing rate of wages. Hence the actually prevailing

---

[1] An accurate use of the term *marginal productivity* is somewhat difficult without occupying undue space. It would be more accurate to write ' *value of the marginal productivity* ', as the productivity is usually regarded as measured in terms of the goods produced. According to the terminology of Pigou (*Economics of Welfare*, Part II, Chapter II) the correct term for the quantity which an employer equates to wages is *value of the marginal private net product*. However, it will be sufficient here to understand *marginal productivity* as signifying *value of the marginal productivity* wherever used.

marginal productivity of any kind of labour is an effect of the equilibrium of demand and supply, just as much as is the wage-rate, and is not the cause of the wage-rate.

Apart from combination, therefore, all earnings are determined by the equilibrium of demand and supply for the service in question. Trade union combination may raise wages by 50, even by 100, per cent in cases where the service in question constitutes but a small part of the total of the expenses of production. Combination amongst workers cannot, however, be responsible for so great a disparity of earnings as exists in this country between manual labour generally on the one hand and organizing ability and certain kinds of intellectual skill on the other hand.

The great inequality of earnings can be assigned to no other reason than accidents affecting the demand for, and the supply of, each kind of service. The word *accident* is here used to mean a cause in no way dependent on the will of persons causing the demand or constituting the supply. This may seem at first sight a sweeping statement ; but I beg the reader to think it out carefully. We are so accustomed to conditions of supply and demand not varying greatly within an adult lifetime that we seem to regard them as more or less natural to our race and civilization. In a newly settled country, however, in which there is plenty of fertile land still to be brought under the plough, men will not work for daily wages except at exorbitant rates, and men with organizing capacity find they cannot earn much more as employers than they pay to each intelligent workman. The extra they do earn is to be regarded as interest on capital, compensation for risk and earnings of working overtime. Give the same men with their organizing ability, on the other hand, a cheap and abundant supply of Oriental labour, and the earnings of their organizing ability become hundreds of times as great as the daily wage. As we saw in the last chapter, if the State were to establish many new medical colleges and give liberal stipends to students, the earnings of doctors (men and women) would soon be reduced to those of boiler-makers. Looking next from the side of demand, let us imagine another example, and assume that the drama goes out of fashion and that every one ardently desires to read modern poetry, and chooses with discrimination. Then the

7

fortunes that now go to successful playwrights would go to certain poets.

The progress of invention is constantly disturbing relative earnings. It provides men with special aptitudes and knowledge, and sufficient egoism and prudence, with opportunities of making fortunes, but grinds other men down to the poor-law. Thousands of men who were technical masters of their crafts have died paupers, they and their families, in order that capitalist organizers, and we the consumers, might benefit by labour-saving inventions. If, a hundred years ago, this had not been considered a net advantage to the community at large, legislation would have prevented it before the end of the nineteenth century.

EQUALITY OF EARNINGS POSSIBLE IN THE COMPETITIVE SYSTEM

The prevailing idea that incomes must be unequal because there is supposed to be a natural and inherent difference in the earning-power of different kinds of ability is so deeply rooted that it is important that I should emphasize here the fact that it rests upon a fallacious assumption. People commonly presume that the existing economic system wherein incomes are determined mainly by unregulated competition is the only possible system ; and for this reason it is thought to be ' natural '. The fact that there existed a different economic system, largely non-competitive, in Europe during the Middle Ages, and much later in India, is overlooked. If this superstition were the result of the exercise of their reasoning faculty by those who hold it, there would be little difficulty in giving it its death-blow, for it can be disproved by the logical device of the *reductio ad absurdum*. I fear, however, that the intensity with which it grips the middle classes, including the intelligentsia, is to be ascribed in no small degree to pride and self-satisfaction resting on the belief that it is their ability and industry which enable them to earn so much more than common people. Yet the fact that their particular ability enables them with application and integrity to earn a handsome income is entirely dependent upon their human environment—upon the particular type of civilization into which they happen to have been born. Transport them to the Himalayan hill States (e.g. Nepal or Sikkim), where peasants prefer scraping a bare living from rocky soil by toiling from sunrise to sunset to working for a farmer for wages, or to the fertile wilds of the Northern Territory of Australia, and where would be the earning-power of their special ability ? We must never overlook the fact that in our present economic system earning-power is dependent upon customs and laws, freedoms and restraints, actions and non-actions by government and constituted authorities.

We shall see how true this is if we consider that the government of a country might undertake as a definite and persistent policy the approximate equalization of earnings in all occupations, even though retaining the present monetary economy and free competition. If it should so decide its first step would be to ascertain by psychological tests the inborn capacities of all persons with reference to the various occupations. It would then proceed deliberately to train for each occupation the persons best fitted therefor in the numbers necessary to fill the demand at the uniform rate of earnings. Of course this would take time. The requisite technical colleges or trade schools would have to be established ; and in professions like medicine or electrical engineering, for which a long training, extending over many years, is indispensable, stipends covering the full cost of living and other expenses might have to be given to all students. By completely eliminating the cost of training an almost unlimited number of candidates could be obtained for every occupation which was not peculiarly arduous or disagreeable. These exceptions would be few ; for the unpleasant features of most of the undesirable employments could be completely removed at the expense of the State, which could grant a subsidy for the purpose.

Should it prove impossible, however, as it probably would, to meet the demand for workers in certain exceptional services at the uniform rate of remuneration, a process of modifying the demand could be resorted to. This could be achieved by education directed to altering habits of consumption, by exhortation, or by a number of legal devices, such as rationing or heavy excise duties. Hence, in the course of a long series of years, by the manipulation of the supply and the demand, based on sufficient research and the appropriate government interference, the wages of labour could be equalized in every occupation, manual and mental.

This must not be taken to apply to incomes from monopoly profits, interest or rents. No equalization of these is possible. In a socialist State equal distribution would not be vitiated by such sources of income as these latter, because they would be secured to the State by nationalization. Under communism these kinds of income now arising from monopoly or from property would be, in a sense, merged in the earnings of labour, because the total consumable wealth annually produced would be equally divided amongst all.

The conclusion to be drawn from the foregoing discussion is that there is no foundation for the usual assumption that men are necessarily unequal in their powers of serving the community, and therefore justly receive unequal remuneration. It is all a question of demand relatively to supply. There is nothing inherently more useful to the community in designing public buildings or lecturing on economics than in driving a railway locomotive or baking bread. It is worth remembering that a state of war completely alters relative intensities of demand, and consequently, in the absence of control, relative rates of remuneration. *In fine*, we may say that usually it is not the individual's fault whether he is one of a dozen, one of a thousand, or one of a million, who can do a particular job.

It is evident, therefore, that if an economic system is to be planned so as to achieve social justice, it would not be logical for it to assign different rates of remuneration by time, that is, unequal incomes, to persons working at different occupations, merely on the ground that such inequalities exist under the competitive system. Whether there may be other valid reasons for discriminating between occupations so that labour shall be remunerated by larger incomes in some kinds of work than in others I shall now consider.

PRINCIPLE OF MINIMUM FOR EFFICIENCY

A favourite doctrine of economists, adopted by many socialists, is that in any country at any particular time there exists for each kind of occupation a minimum income for efficiency. Should a worker earn less than this minimum income he would be unable to buy an adequate quantity of food of good quality, or must live under unhealthy conditions of overcrowding, or suffer in other ways which would render him physically, mentally and perhaps morally incapable of performing his duties so well as he could do if he were adequately nourished, clothed and housed, with facilities of recreation in pleasant surroundings. Men whose work entails heavy physical exertion require more food than those whose work is sedentary ; but if the work involves the strain of close attention for long hours, recuperation from nervous fatigue demands a quiet home and garden and opportunities for games or other pleasant exercise.

The contrast is greatest between persons who are engaged in manual labour or routine clerical work, on the one hand, and those whose occupations require either extensive knowledge and skill of a high order, like the surgeon and the sculptor, or exhausting cerebration. It is well-recognized that the dock labourer and the railway clerk can perform their work efficiently on a lower average of earnings than the doctor, the architect or the manager of a large factory. It cannot be disputed that a labourer or a routine clerk can continue to work and give reasonable satisfaction to his employer at a wage that would put a professional man in such discomfort that the quality and, perhaps, the quantity of his work would be seriously impaired. I am assuming equal conditions, of course, in regard to the size of family to be supported. If, therefore, we were to assume that under a socialist régime the national dividend would only be large enough to provide for the whole population, on a basis of equal remuneration, an income no more than a little above the level of subsistence, and that it could not provide for all the means of obtaining the amenities of life, comforts and recreations on a scale decidedly more liberal than the skilled working classes now enjoy in England, then I would agree that higher remuneration for work of an intellectual or nervously exhausting character would be essential.

The present need for higher earnings on the part of mental workers is accounted for largely by the necessity for better housing accommodation than falls to the lot of the working classes. If not fully accomplished before communism arrives, it is certain that one of the earliest tasks to be undertaken by reorganized society would be the demolition of the remaining sordid streets of closely-built workmen's cottages and the housing of the whole population in garden cities and garden villages. Hence quiet, some garden space and proximity to tennis courts, etc., would be available for all who needed them.

When universal' co-operation shall have been realized it is probable, as I shall show in a later chapter, that the national dividend will be substantially increased after a few years from the elimination of wastes, the reorganization of industries and from new capital outlays. The equalized income is likely to permit, therefore, of a standard of living for all equivalent at least to that which a man now earning, say £12 a week (or £600 a year) can enjoy, if he and his family spend wisely. This level of income would almost certainly be exceeded after fifteen or twenty years of industrial reorganization ; but such a figure suffices for my present argument, for I do not think there is any kind of mental work which would be less efficiently performed because the worker had to live at a standard corresponding with £12 rather than £20 a week, or any higher figure, assuming that the education of his children would be entirely free from first to last. In making a comparison with present conditions, in the case of professional men who commonly have working rooms in their homes, the income referred to may be regarded as net, after deducting from present actual income the cost of such accommodation.

PRINCIPLE OF UNEQUAL SACRIFICE

Some occupations are arduous on account of the physical or nervous strain and fatigue incurred, and others are disagreeable on account of unpleasant or disgusting materials or conditions of work. As people tend to avoid such employments, higher wages are paid in them than would be necessary if the unpleasant conditions were removed ; and at first sight it might seem that such compensation would always be necessary. Such an opinion would, I think, be based upon a misconception : upon an underestimation of the great importance which is likely to be attached to equality of remuneration. Indeed, it will probably be argued in the future, I think, that it is more important to maintain the principle of economic equality than to have tasks which employ many persons under conditions unavoidably disagreeable or laborious performed at all, the work, if really needed, being completely changed in method.

Bellamy, in *Looking Backward* (Chapter VII), sought to equalize the supply of labour for the disagreeable and the pleasant occupations by reducing the hours of labour in the former to the necessary extent ; but he believed that compulsory labour, applicable to all young people for three years, would also prove necessary. The difficulty of the inequality of sacrifice demanded in different kinds of work is a real one; but further discussion of it must be deferred until I have dealt with the incentives to labour. I shall only indicate here that the solution seems to lie in the equalization of effort and sacrifice, rather than in varying the material reward in proportion to sacrifice, which is against a fundamental principle of communism.

I believe that it is not beyond human ingenuity to find ways, and to provide the necessary capital, for abolishing all disgusting and degrading labour. One of the earliest directions in which the investment of capital and the control of consumption would proceed would be in the abolition or mitigation of the strain or disagreeableness of arduous or disgusting work. Almost every form of physically exhausting labour can be substituted by some mechanical device ; and whatever the cost it will be supplied. The consumption of meat can be greatly reduced if not abolished ; a tannery can be made clean and sweet ; the coal-miner, we already know, can be provided safely with electric light and abundant fresh air, and be protected from almost all the dangers still experienced. In the last fifteen years methods of street cleaning have been revolutionized by the use of power driven appliances—a good example of initiative by public authorities. If disgusting tasks like cleaning the sewers remain, they will be done by volunteers, who will receive due honour for their readiness to sacrifice themselves in the public service.

The principle of equality of incomes is so important ethically, and for the stability of society, that inequality of remuneration is the last means rather than the first that should be tried in order that necessary but repulsive work shall be done. At the same time it must be realized that precise equality of sacrifice amongst all workers would be an unattainable ideal, owing to personal differences. It certainly does not subsist at present amongst those who are paid equal wages. Probably men will change occupations more frequently than they do now ; and in the long run a rough equality of sacrifice will be the upshot. In so far as some have to suffer when others do not, they must accept philosophically that disadvantage of the system under which they live (whose net advantages they are not likely to question) ; even as the soldier (often cheerfully, sometimes with grumbling) faces the hardest labour, the extremest danger, on a pay that has no relation whatever to his sacrifice.

THE INEVITABLE TENDENCY TO EQUALITY OF REMUNERATION

Too many socialists are guilty of failing to face unpleasant facts, and of sustaining their hopes of a reconstituted society by a confident optimism that means will be found to make it work. In certain respects they fail to take full account of human nature as it is, and so fail to see that the goal at which they should aim is a far more radical alteration of society than they now envisage. I propose to show that an economic system arrived at merely by substituting public ownership of banking, capital and the means of production, and national and local operation of industries and services, for capitalistic ownership and operation for profit, whilst maintaining unequal rates of earnings, will be unstable. I must ask the reader to try to imagine all that the actual working of the type of economic system just indicated would involve. Let me first describe it a little more fully.

All the great industries of the country would be in public ownership and operation, whether under a State department, a national council or board, or under local authorities acting singly or in groups. A large proportion of the distributing business, and some manufacturing industries, would most likely have come into the hands of the existing co-operative societies, extensively developed. Probably some of the manufacturing industries, however, would be worked by large profit-making companies or combines, pursuing a more or less monopolistic policy, to some extent under State supervision.

The smaller industries, and particularly new enterprises, would still be operated much as at present by private capital. Weaving the finance of the whole together would be either the great State bank, formed by the amalgamation of all existing banks, or a banking system under close control by a government central bank.

I have tried to sketch a view of a socialized State as the majority of socialists in this country seem accustomed to visualize it. This national economic system is thought of as a form of money economy ; and every worker for a public body would be paid his wages in money as now. It is assumed that the present inequalities of earnings, so far as salaries and wages are concerned, will largely continue—works managers, textile designers, doctors, lawyers and engineers receiving salaries many times the wages of skilled manual workers, and the latter higher wages than unskilled labourers. Every worker, however, would be guaranteed the national minimum wage at a level which would provide for everyone the means of living in health and reasonable comfort. The spending of incomes would proceed very much as now, so far as the individual is concerned.

The great difficulty of this system, if it be brought into existence, will lie in the fixation of prices and wages ; for, except in merely subordinate industries, there will be no free play of supply and demand. The most important questions of economic policy cannot fail, therefore, to be continually circling around the question of price-fixation. It is true that in many industries at the present day the free play of supply and demand has ceased, and price is fixed by some form of monopolistic combination of producers. There is, however, a clear price policy, although the public has no say in it, unless the combine in its attempt to reach a maximum monopoly revenue overstrains the forbearance of the public and government interference results.

In the case of the great industries, however, which will all be subject to some form of public operation, the price policy that is certain to be adopted will be that of rendering service to the public at cost, as it is now for State railways and municipal tramways. At most the charges will yield only a small margin of profit, to be utilized in relief of taxation or rates ; such profit being justified mainly on the ground that a lower price to the public would involve loss in years of reduced demand.

This policy of supplying products and services at cost is not, however, so simple and logical as it may seem at first sight, for in most industries the cost of production is very largely made up of the wages of the labour employed in the successive stages through which the materials pass. In direct services, like transport, the rate charged is even more obviously the source from which the labour employed is remunerated. It becomes evident, therefore, that the rates of wages fixed for the several grades of employees in an industry must be largely responsible for determining the cost of supply, and hence the price, to the public.

It does not require any undue stretch of the imagination to anticipate that a considerable amount of jealousy will arise as between workers in different industries. When it becomes realized that the adjustment of their wages is a matter between themselves and the consuming public, there being no margin of profit, the resentment which is now directed against the directors and shareholders of capitalistic undertakings will be turned partly against the public, but mainly against highly-paid workers in other industries.

Try as we may to find it, there is no absolute criterion as to what the relative rates of wages should be in different employments. At the time when the State takes over industries successively from capitalist management certain rates of wages will be current in the various occupations in those industries, and the tendency will be for those rates simply to continue. Reduction of wages by the State or a public authority as employer would raise a tremendous outcry. Any increase of wages affecting a large number of workers in the industry would be objected to equally by the public ; because, in default of a considerable reorganization of the industry, it must mean an increase of the price of the produce or service to the public.

In attempting in 1919 to write the book on the economics of a socialist State to which I have already referred I was obliged to face this difficulty ; and ultimately I was convinced that it is insuperable. The permanent wage policy of a socialist State which I devised was to be based mainly upon the two principles well known to economists which have been considered in this chapter. The first is the principle of the minimum for efficiency : that in the interests of the community as a whole, no less than of the worker himself, the wages-rate for each employment should not be less than the minimum which will maintain the worker in a state of high efficiency for carrying on his occupation. As stated above, such a minimum for efficiency may be recognized now for each kind of work, varying according to its demands upon the worker for physical or mental exertion, according to the cost of living in the locality, and also according to the number of dependents in the family. The other principle is the arduousness in mental or physical strain of the work, and its disagreeableness, which may be denoted jointly as the *sacrifice* required of the worker. By careful study of every occupation it would be possible, so I supposed, to ascertain a fair rate of wage for each occupation based upon the amount of sacrifice involved, subject to a minimum on the basis of maintaining full efficiency. State allowances for mothers and children would equalize the personal reward for labour as between different individuals in the same grade having different family obligations. An elaborate bureaucratic determination of fair wage-rates would thus seem to be theoretically possible.

In practice, I am certain, wage-rates so decreed would never be willingly accepted by large bodies of well-organized, low-paid workers. They would not fully understand the principles on which the wage determination was made ; and if they did, self-interest would arouse suspicions that, in their case at any rate, the investigators had failed to understand the conditions under which they had to labour. There could not fail to be recriminations between large bodies of workers in different industries. Already we have had the faint beginnings of such inter-occupational jealousy. For instance, the workers in some of the skilled crafts were lukewarm in their support of the miners in 1926 during their prolonged lock-out, because published statistics proved that the average earnings of hewers and other skilled miners had been higher than those of the skilled craftsmen to whom I refer.[1]

[1] See Report of Royal Commission on the Coal Industry (Cmd. 2600, 1926), p. 157.   See also pp. 305–6 of the present work.

Foreseeing, when writing in 1919, the inevitable rise of the jealousy of workers in one industry of those more highly paid in another industry also in public operation, and finding no solution of this difficulty, I was led gradually to the conclusion that the only logical outcome must be equality of remuneration for all workers. The jealousy between different sections of manual workers would probably become acute ; but it would be outstripped completely by the jealousy of all manual workers of the much higher remuneration which it is likely would still be paid to intellectual workers with organizing ability or technical knowledge. This conclusion is borne out by experience in Russia where, despite the low real earnings of Russian skilled manual workers, the intellectual workers of Soviet citizenship are paid no more, and in some occupations less. The fact is that a system of operation of industries on a basis of public service necessarily destroys the automatic fixation of wage-rates by supply and demand ; and large industries, like the railways or coal-mining, for which there is always an ample supply of labour offering, can only utilize in place of the action of demand and supply a more or less arbitrary system of external determination which can work only with friction.

The more this question is studied the more obvious will it become that an attempt to establish a socialist State on the basis of a money economy with unequal earnings must inevitably break down within three or four decades on account of sectional jealousies ; and the general conclusion will be that, since no agreement is possible as to what are relatively fair rates of remuneration, all must be equally rewarded. It will become obvious, too, that self-interest must be eliminated from a system of industry organized for public service, and that the incentives to labour must be wholly different, as we shall see in the next chapter.

CHAPTER VII

INCENTIVES TO LABOUR

DECLINING EFFECTIVENESS OF INDIVIDUAL SELF-INTEREST

IF the people of a country are to be prosperous and progressive, the whole fabric of society must be so planned and built in its legal and social sanctions as to give full scope to the most effective incentives to labour. This has been true in all ages, and of all peoples, and without doubt will be true of every form which the organization of society may assume in the future. There is no absolute criterion, however, of what are the most effective incentives. The number of different incentives now in operation is larger than most people would suppose without consideration ; and we should understand that every instinct and innate tendency, or its corresponding emotion, may be utilized as an incentive to effort. Which one or more of the various possible and desirable incentives will be the most effective in a given social system depends upon the social organization and positive morality of the people at the time ; also on the state of their material civilization.[1] We have put behind us the fear of corporal punishment and the horror of imminent starvation as incentives to labour. Indeed, for every stage of civilization we find that the prominent incentives are different.

When slavery was the economic basis of society the main incentives to labour were the whip and starvation, with the addition under the Roman Empire of the hope of freedom. Wherever and whenever there has been a development of wants amongst the proletariat and money has come into general circulation, free labour seems generally to have become more profitable to capitalists than slave labour. The incentives in a régime of free labour subject to free competition, such as has prevailed more or less completely in Europe since the break

---

[1] Lest this be misunderstood, see the qualification at the end of this chapter.

up of feudalism and the gild system, then became : (1) starvation, (2) self-interest in the hope of advancement to a higher standard of living, and (3) provision for the family.

It would be absurd to deny the immense benefits in the material sense which civilized peoples have reaped by giving free scope to individual effort based upon the satisfaction of individual desires. In a certain stage of civilized society self-interest, not merely to ward off starvation, but with free play given for a struggle for a higher standard of life, is unquestionably the most powerful stimulant of progress. It has its well-known disadvantages requiring State interference in factory laws and numerous safeguards to labour ; also it is non-moral, when not actively immoral. Self-interest, as the general motive of economic activities, with perfectly free competition of labour seems, however, to be an unstable condition, characteristic of periods of rapid economic change. The industrial revolution at first quickened the struggle of competitive self-interest ; but the separation of labour from capital, and the combination of the former in trade unions, soon made free competition in its fullest sense no longer operative. In short, we have to recognize that at the present time amongst the organized workers class interest has largely superseded self-interest. The results of this change are rapidly becoming socially disastrous, because it leads, whether through false economic reasoning or no, to a certain degree of restriction of output, and to the fixation in the sheltered occupations of a high monopoly price of labour reckoned in terms of goods or services actually produced.

Yet the substitution of class interest for individual self-interest is an advance to a higher moral plane ; and it augurs well for future progress, and especially for the realization of communism. For if men can, as they do, incur immediate, and often heavy, sacrifices for the benefit, real or supposed, of their fellows—not their friends only, but all men of their trade—it will be but a short step further to be able to subordinate their own interests to those of the whole community. In other words, we are not far from being able to make the duty of service to the whole of society a real incentive to labour amongst the organized workers. The present obstacle is the ever-present immediate opposition of interests as against the employing class, with whom the middle class are linked in sympathy, whilst the aristocratic class are considered to be idlers. So long as society includes privileged classes, and a capitalist employing class, with profits going to shareholders having no contact with the workers, a sense of duty in service to the whole community cannot be aroused amongst the thoughtful working classes with reference to the work by which they live. In other fields they widely recognize their duty to their country. I think it is true to say that no other considerable body of men in the world has a greater sense of public service, and is more ready to volunteer for public service in any non-economic emergency, than the organized workmen of Britain.

My purpose will not be served, however, unless I attempt some systematic treatment of the question of the incentives to labour. This I shall begin by considering the present incentives to labour ; and from them we must select and build up, perhaps with others, a system of incentives for a state of communism.

This chapter was written many years ago, and in writing it I could not avail myself of any work by industrial psychologists. There has been published recently, however, an important book entitled *Incentives in Industry*[1] which bears closely on the present subject ; and this has led me to make modifications and amplifications in my list of incentives, but not to consider any change necessary in the analysis or conclusions. Dr. Miles confines himself to discussing the incentives now operating and capable of development in capitalist industry, and does not consider the adequacy of these in non-profit-making undertakings.

INCENTIVES IN THE EXISTING ECONOMIC SYSTEM

The motives now actuating men and women to work and service of all kinds may be divided into two great classes : the egoistic and the altruistic. Taking the former first, we notice that the primary motives of life-preserving activities are (1) avoidance of hunger, ultimately of starvation ; (2) pleasure in the activity itself. For starvation civilized society has

[1] By G. H. Miles, D.Sc., Director of the National Institute of Industrial Psychology. Published by Sir I. Pitman & Sons, London, July 1932.

substituted the social disgrace of the poor-law. Many a work-man goes hungry, however, rather than work for a price below that which, according to the positive morality of his class, he ought to accept—the trade-union rate. Hunger and fear of starvation are only occasionally and sporadically the actual incentives to labour in England now.

Pleasure in the activity itself is in certain occupations a great incentive to labour, the nature of the work which gives pleasure depending on the instinct which is innately pre-dominant in the man. Thus, if the instinct of construction is strong, a man finds genuine satisfaction in his work as a cabinet-maker or carpenter, a mechanical engineer or inventor, or, again, as an organizer of industry in the sense of planning. If the acquisitive instinct is strong, a man becomes a merchant, taking pleasure first in collecting the goods, then in collecting money by selling them. All this combines with his desire for money to satisfy his wants. The school-teacher and the doctor must have the parental instinct well developed, and so forth. The instinct of construction, the creative instinct, is very widespread ; and the successful handicraftsmen of former days doubtless enjoyed their work for the greater part of their long hours. One of the most serious criticisms of the capitalist system, with its mechanical multiplication of goods, is that the artisan no longer has the chance of that pleasure in his work which the architect, the civil engineer and others continually enjoy. The system has in fact allowed *the middle classes to appropriate nearly all pleasurable work to themselves.*

The most widespread and powerful incentive to work in nearly all occupations, except in the salaried professions, is the need of money to satisfy wants arising from the conventional standards of living ; and further efforts will be put forth, up to a certain point, to obtain the means of purchasing luxuries, including recreations, annual holidays, etc., though the latter might be called conventional necessaries now amongst certain classes. We may put in our list of incentives now operative, therefore : (3) desire for conventional necessaries ; (4) desire for luxuries. These would seem to be the main incentives to labour amongst the working classes at the present time, though the fear of having to accept poor-relief or pawn possessions or starve is always in the background. Further, we notice that the desire to make provision out of earnings for old age or support of the family in case of the breadwinner's death, that is to say, (5) thrift, is a powerful incentive amongst the middle classes. It is less powerful, but not by any means negligible, amongst the English working classes.

Another two important incentives to labour are (6) loyalty to one's employer or head of department, and (7) approbation of a superior. Some men by their justice, high character and aims, and their sympathy with their employees, or the men placed under their control, more or less unconsciously win the loyalty of those in their works or department. Loyalty, if verbally demanded, will be given in but small measure : it arises spontaneously where the director or manager acts with high principles which all can recognize, and exhibits no favouritism ; and it is best developed if he becomes a leader and works with his employees in the realization of some common purpose, which has been explained or made evident to them, and of which they heartily approve. The approbation of a superior, which used to be one of the most widespread incentives utilized in industries, is not the same thing. Its effect may be added to that of loyalty, or it may be effective even although the employee has little or no feeling of personal loyalty to his foreman or manager. The latter should, however, at least be regarded with respect for his approval to have much effect. Every good employer knows that sincere and judicious praise of his employees when they do well is more effective in results than blame when they do wrong. The worker's self-esteem is gratified, and he works better in the hope (more or less unconscious) of securing more praise, which, if merited, should be forthcoming again from time to time as a result of the direct observation of the manager or foreman, or the effect soon fades.

Whether a person has (8) interest in his work or not makes a striking difference to its quality and quantity in a given time ; for, if interested, his attention is easily concentrated on it ; there is less effort of will and consequently less nervous fatigue. It is impossible to generalize as to why a man should be interested in a particular 'job' or kind of work. It depends no doubt on the whole of his education, experiences, reading and personal contacts. Employers could, however, do a great

8

deal more than they do to interest their employees in their work by explaining, perhaps in brief lectures, the purposes for which the goods will be used, the ' points ' of the design, and reasons for special or novel parts which are being manufactured. Dr. G. H. Miles describes an ' incentive of knowledge ' and has written a page on ' interest in the firm ' as an incentive,[1] advocating that the employees should be shown over a large works not less fully than the public, whom many firms welcome as visitors. It seems to me that knowledge about the industrial processes in which the worker takes part and about the history of the firm should be regarded as aids to the incentive of interest.

Pride in work (9) is a powerful incentive to a craftsman doing work of which he sees the completed whole and knows its purpose. The opportunities of the stonemason and the cabinet-maker have almost disappeared; and the plasterer and plumber, who were still doing work of real artistic value a century ago, nowadays receive no encouragement. Work becomes more and more repetitive; and trade-union sentiment has tended to deprecate any idea of pride in dexterity and swiftness in doing such work, whether it be laying bricks or turning on the potter's wheel. Nevertheless, public opinion might easily re-establish pride in such aspects of work, if in a changed economic system it would be clear, as it would be under communism, that the gain would be general, going to the consumers, and not, as now, to any individual or set of shareholders. Dr. G. H. Miles has written : ' Pride in the quality of millions of stampings, all exactly alike, that come from a semi-automatic press, is impossible ; but in its place there may be a very marked pride in the deftness with which the machine is operated and in the quantity produced. At such a machine a worker whose gratification is aroused only by the quality of the article would be an obvious misfit, but one who took a pride in manufacturing activity would find much more scope.' [2]

Satisfaction at accomplishment (10) is another frequent incentive to work and to every kind of constructive and organizing activity. The pleasure of getting a task finished and finally out of the way is surely known to everybody. An individual often sets himself a piece of work to be completed

---

[1] Op. cit., pp. 24 and 30.   [2] Op. cit. pp. 20–21.

by a certain time or date, like packing for a long absence, or writing a book ; or a farmer resolves to have a particular field ploughed and sown by a given date. An alert building contractor makes use of this incentive by drawing up, in consultation with his foremen, a program of work to be done, giving the date for the completion of each stage. As each new section of the work is taken up the co-operation of the foremen concerned and the workmen under them is secured to have it completed by the date set. One of the advantages of the ' time and progress schedule ' adopted of recent years in the building industry is that it sets the manager and his men a series of tasks carefully planned so that they can be reasonably expected to be finished by the dates fixed. In any large constructional work or reorganization it is a stimulus to all concerned to divide the work that has to be done into clearly-defined stages, which may be recognized and serve as milestones on the road to completion. The incentive is then almost continuously in operation, satisfaction being felt, or striven for, in keeping the work up to time. It fails only if the time planning has been bad and the workers get too far behind to have any hope of catching up, or too far ahead. The out-standing example, used to energize hundreds of thousands of technical men and workers is the Russian five-year plan.

The extent to which the desire for accomplishment calls forth efforts varies, of course, with different individuals. It is not, I think, another manifestation of the instinct of construction, for the latter makes constructive or planning work itself pleasurable. Satisfaction at accomplishment is just as great, and is perhaps enhanced, when the work itself is arduous and uninteresting. Perhaps in that case it is partly the emotional rebound from a state of constrained attention ; but the fact that a person anticipates the pleasure of having the task completed seems to suggest that it is one of the instinctive satisfactions, the survival value of such pleasurable feeling being obvious. It may be noted that satisfaction at accomplishment is not the result of the utility of the thing made (or done) *to the worker* ; for a man working on time wages, by the week or month, feels satisfaction at the completion of a particular job, and will sometimes work overtime to finish it, if it be nearly done, even though he expects no payment for overtime—will derive indeed no advantage whatever himself therefrom, except the pleasure of completion.

Most of the labour of the great majority of persons is called forth by the foregoing incentives ; but there are others which sometimes become predominant, as with business men, and some professional men, who have accumulated large fortunes. These other incentives are (11) lust of power, sought for through wealth in money and land ; and (12) love of ostentation and notoriety, the former inevitably requiring much money ; the latter also, when making money is a man's habitual business. Love of notoriety is, of course, the motive of many men's gifts to charities and public institutions, and the purchase of titles.

There is another way in which the lust of power evinces itself. We have seen that with a few men it is a powerful motive for continuing efforts to earn more and more money. With others, who have neither instinct nor opportunity for amassing money, it operates differently, resulting in strenuous and prolonged efforts to be promoted or elected to a position of power over others. In the public services, in large commercial and industrial companies, there are men determined to rise, and working twice as hard as others, or in some cases using guile. It is certainly not only the thought of a higher salary which causes these efforts. Hence we may add (13) lust of official power to our list.

Other egoistic incentives I must treat briefly. (14) Desire for distinction, for a label which will command attention and respect, from the good-conduct badge of the policeman to university degrees, knighthood, and aldermanic robes, is widespread amongst all classes, and a very old incentive. (15) Desire for honour amongst men, a subtler and finer feeling than the love of distinction, is responsible for a good deal of the best work done by good men in the public interest—the worker desires nothing more than that he shall have due credit for his work amongst persons interested. (16) The dictates of conscience may lead a man to work hard for his employer, or in the public interest, without desire for special reward of any kind or even that others should know of his work. How far the work such a man does is really beneficial is not a matter which he reopens with himself from time to time. He has a definite moral sentiment in regard to his work, which provides a fixed motive for pursuing it without approbation of others or any relation of earnings to effort. (17) Emulation is the great incentive for serious training for games and sports of all kinds ; but it seems to have little effect on work, except for occasional competitions which some firms organize, and perhaps in the case of friendly rivalry between competitors in the same trade. (18) The team spirit, which would seem to be due to a primitive social instinct of co-operation, has gained attention in recent years. Where all of a group are animated by like purpose, without intrusion of individual conflicting aims, there is a joy in effort which would be tedious to an individual performing his part of the task alone. A boat's crew, soldiers on the march, a party of sappers digging a trench, a gang of men who, as equal co-sharers, have taken a contract, are cases in point. An example showing the efficiency of this incentive in military work was described in the *Economic Journal* a few years ago.[1] (19) Pugnacity may be regarded as an incentive to work in some cases of competition between traders or manufacturers in attracting business. A man of pugnacious temperament may make up his mind to 'down the other fellow', and will work unceasingly till he succeeds, enjoying the fight if the other puts up a good resistance.[2]

ALTRUISTIC INCENTIVES

Turning now to the altruistic incentives to labour, we may note that these seem to be comparatively few. There is (20) compassion or pity, which actuates many women who under-take nursing of the sick or wounded, and workers amongst the

---

[1] Lindsay ; The Organisation of Labour in the Army in France. *Economic Journal*, Vol. XXXIV (1924), p. 69.

[2] The incentives recognized by Dr. G. H. Miles in his recent book are : *Financial incentives*—fear (chiefly of dismissal), love of gain (piece-rates and bonus systems), and hope of promotion ; *Non-financial incentives*—interest and pride in work, appreciation (i.e. approbation) of employer or his repre-sentative, emulation, setting a task or standard to be attained, knowledge, loyalty (*a*) to his firm, (*b*) to fellow-members of a group, interest in the firm, encouragement of workers by seeking their co-operation in certain phases of management, and general efficiency of management, e.g. prompt supplies and efficient tools.

refugees of war or great calamities. Quite distinct from the foregoing is (21) generosity, an impulse to give pleasure to specific persons, with whom usually the subject is personally acquainted. Many little tasks, occasionally serious ones, are undertaken for friends in this spirit. The most important of the altruistic incentives is (22) a sense of duty to another person, or to a particular group or class of people, or to the whole population of a town or a country. With generosity there is a tie of affection ; but not so in this case. A man believes that he owes a duty of service to a certain person, his employer, perhaps, or to many persons whom he serves directly (e.g. a doctor), or to the people whom he thinks of as needing his services, as does the manager of a municipal tramway system ; and this sense of duty is his principal spur to action and effort. The finest soldiers in war-time are pre-eminently imbued with the idea of duty in serving their country at all costs. Ruskin wanted all work to be done in a spirit of service to the community, a thing impossible whilst the capitalist competitive system endures. Sense of duty I would distinguish from incentive No. (16), dictates of conscience, because the latter seems to me to be impersonal, in the sense that the worker does not have in mind a person or persons for whom he is working, and whose interests he is thinking of. The person actuated by (16) seems to me to go on blindly doing what he is satisfied is right, according to his fixed belief.

INCENTIVES TO LABOUR UNDER COMMUNISM

The economic success of communism will depend very largely upon giving full scope to those incentives to labour which are appropriate to that social system. There seem to be three important ways by which the selected incentives can be marshalled in action so as to secure efficiency. In the first place, industry must be organized with this end in view ; secondly, the laws of the country must give their support— positively, by requiring of every person in a position of responsibility that he shall exercise his functions with due regard to the motives which ought to actuate persons he directs, and negatively, by prohibiting profit-making ; and lastly public opinion must emphatically support the right incentives.

Communism must be democratic ; and the importance of public opinion is obvious, therefore. It must be an educated public opinion, however, which will give social censure with due discrimination. Herein lies the difficulty of introducing communism, and the necessity of delay until such time as the public shall have been educated in the fundamental conceptions of the economics of communism, and shall be prepared to condemn the slacker, the ' sponger ' on society, as an enemy of the people. Such education must take many years ; but that is all the more reason for beginning it without delay.

No single incentive to labour will suffice under communism. Under the competitive system numerous incentives are in operation, two or three being predominant : so must it be under communism. William Morris was continually advocating the pleasure of the work as the natural and most effective incentive to labour. Also he insisted that the work should be useful—should be ' worth doing '.[1] In other words, he recognized that the workman should have a consciousness of being of service by his work. Making frippery for rich ladies, or the thousand and one meretricious articles with which the vulgar rich and too many others, fill their homes, was no true service. The workman could not feel an interest in making such things, which he knew were to be thrown aside, or regarded with indifference, as soon as the first novelty, or pleasure of acquisition, had worn off. Morris's views I accept.

It would seem most probable, therefore, that, when the industrial system of communism is fully developed, the two principal incentives to effort will be the pleasure of the work and a sense of duty in service to the consumer and to the community at large. There is no doubt that a man will work with greater interest, and hence with less effort of will, if he has in mind a particular person who is going to use the thing he is making. He will also be ashamed of scamping the work, or running up the cost unduly. This sense of responsibility is always strong where there is a personal relation with purchaser or employer. It could be made equally strong in relation to

[1] See lecture on ' Art and Socialism ', fourth paragraph. It is worth recalling that Fourier, more than a century ago, proposed to reorganize society on the basis of ' attractive industry ', the object of the organization being to make all socially useful occupations pleasurable.

the users of factory-made goods, and to the community at large as regards diligence in keeping down costs, by the simple means of an educational propaganda within the industry directed to this end. The principle on which William Morris laid emphasis—the right of the workman to feel that he is doing useful work—would necessarily be conceded under communism, where, as a matter of general policy, production would be limited to meeting the needs of reasonable consumption. To make practically all work pleasurable would require, of course, skilful organization of industry to this end. The creation of a sense of duty in work as service to the community depends on public opinion more than on anything else ; and opinion will doubtless be rightly led and quickly formed when the time comes, though preparation for this formation of opinion before the actual period of transition is reached is essential. In a limited number of workers the sense of duty in service may be powerfully extended to a kind of missionary zeal to invent and discover new ways of doing things and to teach these new ways, for the general benefit, to the organizers and workers in the industry wherever the industry is carried on.

The conditions which make work pleasurable would appear to be : (1) That it is of a kind suited to the person's predominant instinct and other inherited qualities ; (2) that it is of a kind in which for any reason the worker is interested ; (3) that the worker believes the product of his labour to be of exceptionally good quality, or in some other way to bear the mark of his individuality, so that he can feel pride in it ; (4) that the time and place where the work must be done meet the worker's convenience, the workshop or factory being light and airy, and kept at the right temperature, and without a noisy racket, glaring lights, etc. ; (5) that the worker is in good health, which condition will be realized largely by diffusing information as to suitable diet, and the care of health generally.

As I have said, skilful organization will be necessary to make work pleasurable ; and the most difficult part of it will be the fitting of everybody to the kind of work for which he has the right instinct and other qualities, so that he may be occupied with what is for him the pleasantest task. Morris, of course, wanted everybody to have the pleasure of creative work, by hand or brain. It would seem, however, that capacity to experience pleasure from such work is closely associated with the instinct of construction. Hence it is doubtful whether everybody does derive pleasure from creative work, though no doubt in most countries the majority do. The greatest difficulty would be to provide for those persons having pre-eminently the acquisitive instinct, who are now traders and financiers. Perhaps there would be openings for them in foreign trade ; but in the main the younger persons of that type, if they are to be fitted into the new scheme of society, must have such of their abilities as are related to some secondary instinct developed by education.

The problem of fitting people to the most suitable occupations is too complicated to be followed further here. On the one hand, it involves a great development of applied psychology, with elaboration of experimental tests,[1] and records of children's work and play at school, and the establishment of a classification of persons according to temperament, instincts, mental abilities, and so forth. Organized research on a scale comparable with that now being devoted to aeronautics would probably solve the psychological difficulties in ten or fifteen years. On the other hand there is the difficulty of the adjustment of the supply of persons with particular aptitudes to the demand for corresponding services ; for it cannot be expected that the numbers offering and demanded will be anything like equal as regards certain types of people. Any kind of ordered adjustment would be infinitely better than the present haphazard system by which so many individuals have the unhappiness of getting into wrong occupations, and discover too late that family obligations close all avenues of escape. Possibly the processes of industry will be modified to meet the need of making work pleasant to people of all aptitudes, so far as practicable without serious inroad on the national dividend. Morris not only desired, but certainly anticipated, a reversion to handicraft for the production of certain kinds of goods.

Any labour unduly prolonged becomes unpleasant, and

---

[1] This important work is being carried on in England by the National Institute of Industrial Psychology, and in U.S.A. by Harvard University, the Personnel Research Federation, N.Y., and the Bureau of Personnel Administration, Chicago.

finally a painful effort. Work of some kinds may be so interesting and engrossing that a man will find it pleasurable for the whole of a long day. Probably this must always be the exception ; and many kinds of work, though interesting and not unpleasant for the first two or three hours, become thereafter arduous from monotony or nervous fatigue. It has been suggested as a practical present-day measure that all men who so desired should have one kind of work for the morning and another for the second half of the working day. For a few men this would be advantageous ; but it seems doubtful whether many would care to divide their day in this way. Henry Ford points out that there are men of an indolent disposition who prefer monotonous repetitive work.[1]

The two main incentives—pleasantness of the work and a sense of duty to the community—can be fortified by the adoption of others, all of which were mentioned in the preceding section as being in operation to some extent at the present time. Taking them in the order of the importance which they would probably have in communist industry, I should put first the approbation of superiors. Next in importance would seem to come interest in work, and perhaps pride in work. Then there is the team-spirit. Socialists have already widely recognized its potentialities ; and the Committee of the Industrial Council for the Building Industry, which reported on Organized Public Service in the Building Industry, regarded the introduction of the team-spirit as the key to the whole problem of production. An organization of industry would surely be practicable which would give a task in production to a group of workers who voluntarily associated themselves for the purpose. They would undertake to finish it in a certain time, but would be autonomous in the matter of dividing the work between them, and in many cases might have their say as to the character of the product and the methods of manufacture to be followed. On this supposition in some industries the staff of a big factory might consist of many such groups ; and co-ordination might be obtained by a managing and technical staff not belonging to the groups, assisted by a representative committee.

Satisfaction at accomplishment is a simple incentive which,

[1] *My Life and Work*, by Henry Ford, pp. 105–6.

even nowadays, could be utilized far more widely than it is. In job-work, like printing, and in constructive work other tha n mass production, the worker can readily estimate what he has done ; so, also, in all kinds of piece-work. Automatic counting devices are attached to many kinds of machines. In works and factories under communism various ways might be found to divide up work into lots or parts, for which each man (or sub-groups of two or three men) would be responsible to his group (team), or to the management ; and there would be ways of affording each worker a continuous measurement of the amount of work he had done.

Love of distinction (14) might be used to a certain extent. Bellamy thought so ; [1] and Wells, by postulating a class of *samurai* wearing distinctive clothes,[2] is using this incentive in a general way. I am inclined to think, however, that a society so far advanced as to accept economic equality will regard distinguishing marks, whether in clothing, titles or university degrees as a crude appeal to a low instinct ; and that public opinion will ban all distinctions. The desire for honour amongst men (15) will remain, however, as strong as it is to-day, in all probability. It is a socially constructive desire, and will probably be encouraged by giving credit to whomsoever it is due, in the humblest as well as the highest tasks. Suitable means of appraising work and of publishing specially good results could be found without difficulty.[3]

In so far as people in the future will have a fixed moral array guiding their actions, as many have now, the dictates of conscience (16) will be a valuable incentive to labour. It will only be necessary to see that conscience is rightly formed ; and this will be a question of education. The lust of power over subordinates (13) is a powerful incentive ; but it is also danger-ous, in that a man may seek promotion not by really honest work which genuinely satisfies him, but by pleasing the authorities, and even by intrigue. This incentive will have to be used with discretion ; and too great ardour for promotion might well count against a man, for presumably appointments

[1] *Looking Backward*, Chapter XII.　　[2] *A Modern Utopia*, Chapter IX.
[3] Cf. the London Street Architecture Medal now annually awarded by the Royal Institute of British Architects for the best design of a building erected within four miles of Charing Cross.

would not be made without consultation with representatives of a man's fellow-workers.

All others of the egoistic incentives would either be useless under communism, or against its spirit. A sense of duty in service, and its extension as a missionary zeal to invent and diffuse benefits, having been mentioned above, there remains the altruistic incentive generosity (21). As this involves direct service to a person for whom affection is felt, it can only be of limited application, as in household service. In so far as the manager of an industrial establishment inspired genuine personal affection in the workers under his direction, generosity would dispose the latter to work hard so as to give him the credit of a good output from the works.

Although it is very true, as was stated at the beginning of this chapter, that the character of the social organization and positive morality at the time determines which particular incentives will be most effective out of all that are possible, this should not be interpreted to mean that it is merely a question of deciding which are the best incentives to fit the existing state of society. The social organization itself will require modification in the three ways previously mentioned—in its laws, in the technique of industrial management, and in social customs reflecting public opinion—before the absolutely best results can be obtained even from the group of incentives which does fit the prevailing state of society better than any other group. For instance, a general recognition by public opinion that manual labour, as the basis of wealth production, is more honourable than office or professional work would go far to make a sense of duty in service to the community an effective incentive to quality and output. So also in methods of management, such as the attitude of foremen to the workmen, or ways of consulting the wishes and utilizing the ideas of skilled workers, or again of measuring work, changes must be made from time to time to keep pace with the progress of society. Without such changes new incentives suitable to the new stage of social organization and morality cannot become effective. There is much room for experimental investigation on these questions even at the present time.

It is impossible to foretell, of course, how the practice of utilizing the various incentives I have mentioned in this chapter would develop ; but perhaps the subject has been followed here sufficiently to show that proper organization, and the development of public opinion, could find an adequate basis in human nature for securing the performance in the communist society of all labour considered necessary.

CHAPTER VIII

THE OBJECTIVE

MORAL GAINS

EVERY person who believes that a society of equality is a desirable end, and is convinced that incentives to labour of a morally higher order can be substituted for lust of gain and power, or fear of the poor-law, will want to know how such a society would organize itself to provide amply for the wants of all, and what kind of life its citizens would lead. This perhaps is the most convenient stage of our inquiry at which to consider the bearing of the proposed new economic relationships upon some non-economic aspects of the daily life of the people of the future. It is to be hoped that ideals and culture will evolve differently when society is placed on a new and stable economic basis ; that activities and relationships not directly of an economic character will change so as to make for greater happiness. Economic ideas ought to occupy a subsidiary place in public attention. They have done so in many periods of history ; and the new social order, once it is established, must admit of adequate public attention being given to progress in the higher spheres of life. It is not going too far to say of all ages and peoples that the success of the economic system may be judged by the freedom which it gives the *whole population* to attain a life on a higher moral and spiritual plane, to love the beauties of nature, to practise and appreciate all the arts, and to follow intellectual recreations.

The moral gain arising from the adoption of communism is likely to be much greater than might be assumed at first thought. Our present economic system is to blame, I think, for the hypocrisy with which we English are charged by foreigners, and from which no impartial observer could altogether acquit us. Thousands of earnest appeals from the pulpit have not succeeded in inducing business men to apply on weekdays the moral code they hear laid down, and sincerely accept and believe in, on Sundays. The English may be regarded, I would suggest, as a singularly well-intentioned people. They are sincere in professing belief in a high standard of conduct. They are usually upright in social relations, and honest in the routine of commerce. But in the fundamentals of business—its policy, its negotiations, its finance—the standard of moral judgment is elastic. The high principles proclaimed by preachers and politicians, bankers and authors, are conscientiously believed in by business men, and even practised ' so far as practicable '. This saving phrase means that there are occasions when necessity gives its dispensation. It must be within the experience of every man that there comes a point at which the high moral code of Christian teaching seems to have no relation to the actualities of business. He is forced to do as others do, or do nothing.

The truth of this, and the reasons for it, become clear when we consider the conditions which make for honesty in business. Competition is a hard master, and the weakest must go to the wall. If a man cannot succeed when he runs his business with strict honesty, he may be able to make a good profit by practising some form of dishonesty—adulteration, or inaccurate description of his goods. It is probably safe to say that in almost every kind of business, from selling real estate or horses to manufacturing carpets, only the man supreme in knowledge and in judgment can afford to be strictly honest. The able man loses by his honesty some part of the profits he can make by his superior skill in management. The common saying that ' Honesty is the best policy ' is by no means necessarily true, especially under modern conditions.

We may consider this point a little further, and notice first that different kinds of business differ markedly in the extent to which honest dealing is financially profitable, even in the long run. There are many trades in which a reputation for honest dealing becomes easily known ; and in these it is the best policy because it pays best in the long run. But there are transactions of a kind which people make so rarely, or things they buy with qualities so recondite, that no man could earn a reputation for right dealing unless he himself were to educate the people at large as to the risks they run—probably at an

expense which would ruin him. Thirty years ago people knew
less about houses and health than they do now, and no speculative builder could afford to ask the price necessary for good
work. I doubt whether, even to-day, the speculative builder
can afford to go beyond conforming with the by-laws, and
giving such good work, or appearance thereof, as will satisfy
sharp eyes.

So we English, whilst sincerely trying to be honest and
straightforward, being generally well-intentioned, have to
gloss over the motives which lead us at times to bow to ' necessity '. A man *must* provide for his family : he works for their
future needs, according to the customs of the trade, with a
consciousness that he is doing right. If the public be deluded,
well—that is due to the ignorance and folly of the public.
There are so many grounds on which rather unscrupulous
business can be justified that a trader or financier whom the
strict moralist may condemn, yet can himself feel conscious
of the utmost rectitude. It is worth noting here that this habit
of mind—the easy justification of transactions which are in
accordance with custom—we carry into international affairs.
Hence, after our publicists and statesmen have professed our
high ideals and utter disinterestedness, the business man's
mentality asserts itself at the stage of negotiating an actual
settlement.

This tortuous morality (for it is no less) I can only ascribe
to our economic system. Where livelihood depends upon
competition, and the public does not enforce strict honesty by
its discrimination, or by legal process, dishonesty of various
grades, variously camouflaged, must be the result. For comfort of mind it is necessary to justify this ; hence the hypocritical habit of thought and speech.

Communism offers the opportunity of sweeping away completely this moral miasma. Indeed, the moral atmosphere
would be cleared automatically by the abolition of private
profit and the establishment of equal incomes for all. There
would be no inducement to subterfuge, no object in the elusive
kind of dishonesty by which trade customs (using the term in
the widest sense) prevent the consumer from getting beneficial
service. People naturally prefer to tell the truth and have the
truth told to them ; but now we accept lying advertisements

and the glosses of salesmen as a well-understood part of the ' game '. But it is no game ; buying and selling is a deadly serious part of daily life ; and we sap our moral vitality by such constant contact with distortion of the truth. In a social system which would permit no advantage by the practice of lying and concealment, they would quickly go out of fashion ; for people would see at once that there was no longer any reason to tolerate them.

Furthermore, it may be expected that secondary reactions of a most welcome character would follow automatically the abolition of the immorality of commerce ; for the habit of tolerating distortion of the truth vitiates all our relations, social and political, no less than economic. When no possible ill consequences could follow from open frankness and free speaking of the truth, everybody would naturally speak thus, and would expect this to be the rule. Misstatements and concealments, in politics and every phase of life, would be censured by public opinion in a manner so drastic we can hardly imagine it. This, then, I think, will be one of the greatest of all gains from communism—a universal straight-forwardness and honest truthfulness of purpose, speech and writing, which will create for all a sense of freedom and mutual confidence to us unknown.

Men will enjoy not only the happiness of this new freedom and confidence : the changed moral atmosphere is likely to prove a favourable environment for an expansion of human nature difficult for anyone now even to conceive. The way would be open to the growth of generosity and love as motives of conduct. Try as we may, we cannot altogether forget that the teaching of Jesus demands that all our actions, and thus the fabric of society, be based on love—brotherly love for all about us, for all mankind. No man can preach so now with the genuine belief that his hearers will take him seriously. Not until communism is established can love for all men become the dominating motive of our lives. It will not be a matter of preaching. When there is no economic conflict, no business chicanery, mutual confidence cannot but expand into mutual love.[1]

[1] This does not mean that morality will not have to be taught during the preparation and transition (see Chapter XII) ; nor does it mean that children will not always have to be taught the supreme importance of the virtues of love and truth, of industry and thrift, meaning by the last control of consumption.

9

THE SPIRITUAL GAIN

Many great thinkers, William Morris amongst them, have held that happiness is a proper object to pursue. Some would go so far as to say that happiness, pursued, not selfishly, but in the interest of all mankind, is the only ultimate aim of civilized society which can be rationally conceived. To me it seems that in a broad search for the happiness of all are harmonized the teachings of philosophers of nearly every school. What is ultimate good but the happiness of others, now and hereafter ? What is self-realization in its highest sense, but, on the one hand, the finding of satisfaction in actions undertaken for the happiness of others, near and far ; and, on the other hand, the ability to find pleasure in those activities of art and intellect which develop the capacity for aesthetic enjoyment still further ? What is spiritual life but the acceptance of images and ideals to give us a fixed guide in the interpretation of the mysteries of life, and in regulating our conduct, such fixity of ideas contributing to happiness by the removal of worry and indecision ?

Whether it be for happiness or no, man in every age has wanted spiritual conviction and an imagery of ideas and ideals. Furthermore, he has degenerated and ultimately suffered, in proportion as he has outgrown the spiritual tradition of his ancestors and failed to replace it with another. Individuals who become engulfed in materialism always ultimately suffer from mental torment. Woeful is the fate of the nation which sinks into materialism, and spurns its old idealism, its spiritual cult, without effort to replace it by a new conviction. The ultimate test of communism, therefore, will be the spiritual life of the people.

In all times religion has been the organized expression and source of spiritual life ; but it would be a mistake to suppose that spiritual life has been limited to religious experiences. Particularly untrue would that be of the last hundred years or so, unless an unwarranted extension of meaning be given to the word religion, as, for instance, when people speak loosely of socialism as a religion. What they mean, and this is important for us to realize, is that socialism occupies for many of those converted to it the place of a religion. Socialism is an ideal—

or, perhaps more correctly, a body of principles and ideals—which stirs the emotions of generous-minded persons, and incites to efforts and sacrifices. More and more the idea of economic equality calls men out of grim materialism, and fills them with aspirations for the welfare of their fellow-men. Thus whole-hearted belief in communism as an ideal state of society, which every one must make personal sacrifices to attain, does, and will more largely, form a part of religion.

When the state of communism is actually realized, however, what will then be the expression of spiritual life ? Man is an emotional creature and must have lofty ideals, whether personified or not, before which to abase himself : ' must have ' both for his own good and for the needs of society, which otherwise perishes in materialism. It would seem probable that, when communism is established, there will be two lines of development of spiritual experience. The great body of the people, having set themselves free from theologies and the traditional doctrines of the Churches, will embrace with eagerness a new and simple Christianity, without dogma, and resting only on belief in communion with God and on admiration of, and devotion to, the teachings of Jesus. On the other hand, perhaps the more intellectual part of the population may largely satisfy their spiritual needs by an idealization of the life of mankind. With their eyes always on the future and the possible, they will seek to increase the happiness of all men by extending a knowledge of the philosophy and art of life, including all social relations, by teaching and encouraging the practice and appreciation of all the arts, by striving for a feeling of union and amity between all the races of the earth, and by trying to benefit the peoples of every country.

Whatever the exact character of the religious or spiritual life of the people may be, one thing seems to stand out clearly : the high standard of morality in all affairs of daily life to which communism seems likely to lead automatically, will give scope for a wider, more sincere, and, therefore, more effective and satisfying spiritual life. Thus religion, or its spiritual analogue, will come into close contact and harmony with daily life. Religion was in close and daily relation with all phases of life in the Europe of the Middle Ages ; and is so to this day amongst non-Westernized Hindus. It may well be hoped that under communism, when the practical affairs of life will be regulated on principles in no way conflicting with the highest morality, spiritual life and thought will revive as a preventive of mental distress, and expand as a great source of energy stirring men to actions for individual and social good.

THE REVIVAL OF ART

William Morris rightly insisted that the exercise of the creative faculty in craftsmanship ought to be one of the great sources of pleasure in life. Not only should the appreciation of beautiful things be widespread amongst the people, but also the desire and the ability to produce needed things with grace of form, true proportion and beauty of ornament or pattern. He saw that the capitalist system, especially the cheap multiplication of copies by machinery, was antipathetic to art. He admitted the great benefits of machinery to man in relieving him of arduous physical labour, and of monotonous or disgusting tasks, but deplored the destruction of the skilled handicrafts by the competition of mechanically-produced goods.

There is no reason to suppose that the use of machinery is necessarily inimical to art. It is rather the state into which society is thrown by the growth of capitalism, the competition of profit-seekers, and the uncertainty of employment caused by changes of production, which is responsible for the decay of art amongst the people. My own view is that art arises naturally amongst a people in a stable civilization ; that is to say, when no considerable economic change is taking place, neither progressive nor retrogressive. Such was the condition of affairs in Europe during the Middle Ages, and in India, China and Japan until the invasion of Western trade and capitalism in the nineteenth century. In those countries at those times, and particularly in Japan, art seems to have entered into the very life of the people, finding its expression not only in architecture, but in all the objects of daily use— clothing, household utensils, and even tools. When visiting Japan some twenty-five years ago I was deeply impressed with the beauty of all household appointments : even kettles and cooking-pans had graceful shapes, and often bore some simple design or ornament.

Amongst the primitive agricultural people of Europe and Asia the handicrafts have always, from the earliest times, developed form or ornament of artistic merit, sometimes of marked individuality, and of the beauty which comes from a graceful adaptation to purpose. I would venture to put forward the theory that some kind of artistic expression, in the construction of his house, or in the design of things which he makes for use or sale, is natural to every man, if he has leisure to produce things to his satisfaction. In olden times the people at large had few wants, and the pressure of population on the soil was comparatively slight. Society was in a state of equilibrium ; and, apart from war or famine, occurring usually at long intervals, every one was practically certain of his livelihood from youth to old age. He worked long hours in leisurely fashion, but the work itself was interesting, and every new idea in design was discussed with his friends. There are backward parts of Asia where such conditions still survive. The people live with an economy still practically self-sufficing ; and their handicrafts exhibit a natural inclination to artistic expression of a high aesthetic value.

If we look for the causes which destroy the habit of artistic expression amongst any people, I think we may find them in wars and economic and social upheavals of all kinds, which disturb the relations of classes. They produce uncertainty of employment, and thus of income ; they cause migrations of labour and the mixing of classes. Perhaps it is an undue extension of the meaning of the word ' upheaval ' ; but, for my present purpose, I must extend it to cover a slow, but fundamental, economic change. In this sense the greatest of upheavals has been the rise of a ' European ' world-wide commerce from the sixteenth century on, and the growth of capitalist production, with the application of power. These changes introduced the mass of the workers to a struggle to live somehow—anyhow. Certainly the standard of living of the working classes has been gradually improving so far as necessaries and material comforts are concerned—yet in the oft-recurring periods of depression of trade the struggle has been renewed again and again. The industrial revolution provided for a few the opportunity for a scramble to get rich. Success has usually required much hard work it is true ; but that in itself is an evil from the point of view of art : all energy has been directed to the increase of output and every means of making money. The successful manufacturer has had no time to acquire artistic taste himself ; and, if he had taste, would find no time to exercise it in his own factory. Designing has become a specialized function ; and the best ' artist ' is the man who can produce the greatest number of the most saleable designs in a given time. This deleterious specialization, Morris has called ' disintegration of labour ' ; and he pleaded for a re-integration of labour wherein the workman should have a part, if not the whole, of the responsibility for the design of the goods he was producing.

The conviction to which I have been driven, and which I wish to emphasize, is that the tendency to artistic expression in the fashioning of all kinds of objects is inherent in most men of all races. The condition that it may develop is that a man has no doubt as to the adequacy of his income for all reasonable needs from birth to death, and that he is not pressed by an employer, or by a low price for his product, to a rate of production which gives him no time to think of varying the form or pattern of each article according to his ideas of improvement, or mere passing fancy. The limitation of membership by the medieval craft gilds provided the security of income and the opportunity of leisurely work here regarded as an essential condition for the vitality of art in craftsmanship. The social system of the Middle Ages, with its threefold organization around Church, feudal tenure and free city, adapted its means to well-understood ends, as we perceive more clearly now that the mists of nineteenth-century *laissez-faire* thought are rolling away.

I repeat that when society is in a static condition economically, and the people are prosperous and happy, they seem naturally to become artistic in production. There seems to be no evidence that the *primary* cause of artistic craftsmanship flourishing in any age is a demand from consumers for artistically produced goods. Rather the initiative would seem to come from the work-people themselves, who, if they have time, produce things artistically. The public gradually becomes educated in good taste to prefer things having real merit in design, and an artistic style becomes prevalent. But taste may easily be degraded again by the offer of new kinds of things of tempting novelty, convenience or cheapness, but executed in bad taste. The machine-made goods and toys with which shops became filled during the middle of last century completed the destruction of public taste in England, which had already suffered seriously from luxury demand met by production in organized workshops with division of labour. The degradation of public taste by goods of cheap European style is not quite accomplished in India, China and Japan. The tragedy may be seen in progress.

This discussion of the relation of popular art to the economic system has seemed desirable in view of Morris's oft-repeated hope that the realization of communism would mean a revival and glorious expansion of popular art, from which a large part of the people would derive much of their pleasure of life. When society has settled down in a communistic organization it will be once again in a condition of equilibrium. There will be a gradual progress in economic wealth and welfare, but with no fundamentally disturbing internal processes at work, as in the era of four hundred years or so now approaching its end. In a society which will become wealthy, in comparison with our present condition, by the proper organization of production as a social service, there will be leisure to produce artistically, mostly by handiwork, all durable things with which man surrounds himself, e.g. the furniture of houses, and the china and metal-ware in daily use. The making of things by hand might be a form of recreation for many, and of half-time work for many others ; but doubtless there would be craftsmen also devoting their whole time to production to their own designs, by hand mainly, but not necessarily wholely without the aid of power-driven tools. I think, however, that machinery will recede in importance only in making certain articles for personal and household use, and a few materials used in building. In most of the other branches of production it will be applied ever more extensively and efficiently.

There would seem every reason to believe, with Morris, not only that the capitalist-competitive system has destroyed popular art, but that communism will restore it, with untold possibilities of development. Above all we may hope for *co-operation* in artistic achievement, where the designers are inspired by a common emotion for some public end. Only so can we hope ever to equal the glories of the medieval cathedrals. The present individualistic system impels architects to rely on their own ideas, with suggestions from partners and salaried assistants occasionally. More appropriate and beautiful architecture would probably arise if every public building were evolved from the original conception by consultation between sympathetic men of equal experience, and if, in its execution, some liberty in detail were given to men of proved ability as workers in stone or wood, in cement or plaster. Undoubtedly the spirit of communism will encourage and stimulate co-operation in art, as in work of every kind.

INTELLECTUAL LIFE

All aspects of social life are knit closely together. Every great economic change has its origin partly in moral and intellectual changes which precede it ; and the economic change then reacts to produce further changes in the moral and intellectual life, and ultimately in the spiritual life, of the people. Actions and reactions occur, intellectual and moral changes assisting or impeding further economic change. We have seen that communism is likely to provide an environment favourable to straightforward and sincere morals, to the expansion of true art, and the growth of spiritual life. What, we may ask, will be its influence on intellectual activities and enjoyment ?

The result unquestionably will be a great stimulation of intellectual energy. As I shall show in later chapters [1] the attainment of communism without risk of social disaster will entail extensive researches in psychology and sociology, and a remodelling and extension of secondary and adult education. Studies in applied economics and public administration must be carried farther than has yet been thought of. The realization of communism can only be the result of a great intellectual effort, as well as of a spiritual and moral renewal. By that time there will be a general appreciation of the value to the whole community of the human sciences as well as of the natural sciences.

We are familiar at the present day with the important role

[1] Chapters XIV, Preparation, pp. 258-61, and XVI, The Transition, pp. 308-9.

which the natural sciences play in modern industry. So far the most notable advances have been made by the application of chemistry and physics to industrial processes, to the making of new substances, to the production and distribution of power and to the standardization of materials. Other natural sciences have a more limited application : geology in mining, botany in medicine, agriculture and forestry, zoology in medicine and fisheries. Year by year the applications of physical science to the service of man become more numerous and important.

Possibly because they form a compact and ordered body of concrete knowledge, the natural sciences seem to attract the men of keenest intellect, and keep them ; which in many respects is a social disaster. A vast field for knowledge concerning man himself, internally, mentally and socially, remains unexplored ; and such little systematic and reliable information as has been gathered by a few able inquirers remains uncoordinated. The scientific method is applicable in every field of human inquiry ; and further research of a high order carried out by a number of trained workers is badly needed in sociology and psychology.

Scientific research may be undertaken either to gain knowledge for its own sake, which was the genesis of all the natural sciences, or for some utilitarian end—that is to say, some future definite object of benefit to man. A well-known example of the latter is the recent development of the theory of aerodynamics with a view to assisting the construction of safe aeroplanes. The grandest example is afforded, however, by the medical sciences, the development of which has been constantly stimulated and directed by the aim of saving life and alleviating suffering. The growth of the medical sciences gives us the keynote for all future human progress. In every kind of communal activity, and in every branch of industry, safe rules of action towards a predetermined end may be established in similar manner by precise observation and ordered thought.

Competitive industry is the result of leaving things to chance. Probably it was the failure to understand, or even to believe in the possibility of understanding, the complexities of industry and trade sufficiently to determine what, if any, interference or initiative by the State would be beneficial, which lent support to *laissez-faire* until near the end of last century. It may be said generally that there was no serious application of intellectual energy to industries during the most part of the nineteenth century, except in the technical aspects of industry, i.e. the development of machinery and processes. The introduction of cost accounting, of scientific management, of motion study, of methods of administration based on exact knowledge of working results and on suitable divisions of functions amongst members of the managing staff, has enabled the formation of business units on a gigantic scale which fifty years ago was regarded as impossible. Yet the science of industrial control is still in its infancy, the human, mostly psychological, factors having received too little attention. Studies of industrial efficiency in relation to the individual's psychological reactions, and in relation to climate and other factors of the environment, as also studies of industrial fatigue, constitute a beginning in the direction required. Much needs to be done in the study of the economic problems of the administration of individual industries, somewhat in the manner in which the subjects of railway economics and railway administration have been developed in recent years. Before communism is established detailed studies of all the great industries, and the successive stages of their reorganization under communism, must be published. When communism has come into being the continuation of economic research in the administration of whole industries is sure to be necessary.

Regional planning and town planning will gain greatly in importance ; and, as will appear in the next chapter, industry planning as regards the whole country, and occupation planning as regards each locality, will be important subjects of professional study. The economics of consumption and production as a whole, and in connection with foreign trade, will be a central and continual subject for research, with the increasing experience and organized knowledge in all the cognate and subsidiary subjects. Certain it is that reforms will be based more upon exact knowledge than has ever been the practice hitherto, except perhaps in public health.

These anticipations will, I think, lead any reflective person to the conclusion that competitive industry is the way mankind has adopted of getting things done without science applied to the organization of industry ; and that communism demands the reverse—a system of industry planned and controlled throughout in accordance with scientific principles, many of which have yet to be discovered and formulated. The success of the new society will depend largely upon the availability and accessibility to the public of a body of scientific knowledge with regard to the organization of industry and all social institutions. Communism cannot succeed until the nation first learns to know itself in all its existing complexity, and then learns how it is to improve itself.

Perhaps I have devoted too much space to the intellectual activities connected with production. Essential as these will be, they will not divert attention from the search for knowledge for its own sake. Public interest in science is likely to grow ; and every branch of learning is likely to benefit by the new outlook, by the casting off of prejudices and presumptions, and by the spirit of co-operation in research. There is likely to be a general appreciation of the importance of extending knowledge in all directions, the ultimate utility of pure science to mankind becoming generally recognized. It would seem likely, therefore, that investigators in all subjects will have at their disposal a personal freedom and an amount of resources of which present-day scientific workers can only dream with envy.

The universities will, of course, be, as now, the centres of research in the social and natural sciences ; and I think it will be found advisable to have a great deal of the technical research needed by industries also carried on at the universities—or at least in association with them, even when the work must be conducted at an industrial centre. All difficulties of financing the extension of university activities, in the present sense of finance, will have disappeared in a régime of communism. Every member of the staff, and every recognized research-worker, will be entitled to the same general allowance (i.e. income) as everybody else in the country, whatever his occupation. The universities will continue to be self-governing bodies ; and their freedom will increase, if they rise to the occasion and take their due part in national and local life, because they will not be dependent on Government for finance.

The university of the future, as I see it, will simply have to obtain sanction to the total number of members of its teaching staff and of research-workers ; and it may then appoint whatever persons it likes up to the sanctioned number. Every person, it must be remembered, draws his general allowance, whatever his occupation, or whether employed or unemployed. His only obligation is to offer himself for some sanctioned employment. His income is always available wherever he goes and whatever he does, short of contravening the law. A university will have to indent for its apparatus and materials for teaching and research, except those which it produces in its own workshops ; but there is no reason to fear that the public will grudge large staffs and liberal supplies, if the universities fulfil their important functions efficiently and adequately. Two things in particular the university authorities must watch : (1) to keep in touch with the life and thought of the people, (2) to appoint only efficient men to their staffs. A university divorced from the active life of its time tends to a barren scholasticism, and in economic and social affairs to a particularly obnoxious dogmatism. The university staff and research students should become acquainted with the problems confronting administrators and technical men in industries and public business, and aid in finding solutions. Probably the ideal urged by the late Professor Sir Patrick Geddes—' The University Militant ', which shall study and initiate reforms, especially in the affairs of its own locality—will be realized under communism, if not in the nearer future.

Outside university circles intellectual activities will surely be far more widespread, useful and satisfying than at the present day. Although the universities may train men for executive and administrative positions in industries, it seems certain that every industry will require a number of technical colleges of its own situated in convenient centres. Quite possibly every manual worker in industry, after some years in the factory or workshop, will be encouraged to take a one-year course in college before he is twenty-five years of age, with the object of qualifying for more responsible work, or, if he has the ability and industry, of fitting himself for promotion to the managing staff, which might require a second year of study, taken immediately, or later. Very likely also there will be in every town local colleges not of university standard at which lectures and classes will be held in early morning and evening, so that adults may improve and extend their knowledge in any subjects in which they may be interested without being candidates for a degree or diploma. They might develop in connexion with the now existing technical colleges, polytechnics and commercial institutes, and from what we now call university extension centres and educational settlements, but would have a definite building and organization of their own, and the nucleus of a permanent staff. Perhaps the public library of the town would be in the same building, and a college of music and the arts. These adult educational facilities will not be provided by any department of the central government. They will usually be organized and managed by the people of the locality ; and evening lectures will be given by people in their spare time. The provision of a full-time staff would require the official sanction of the Ministry of Occupations, acting perhaps on a petition of the Municipal Council, but the selection of the teachers would probably be left to the local committees.

As regards general public education, I think it will be developed so as to provide much greater variety in objects and methods of teaching than we have now. Perhaps by that time English spelling will have been reformed by the efforts of a revived Simplified Spelling Society, thus saving much time in the child's school years, and aiding that development of the power of logical thought which must become more and more the goal of education. Practically every boy and girl will go through a secondary school, no child's school education being complete till the age of seventeen. The secondary schools will be of very various character, some probably having an occupational bias, as towards agriculture or the principal industry of the locality, others specializing on art and others on preparation for the university. At all the schools an important aim would be the inculcation of studious habits and the teaching to every one how to learn serious subjects by the reading of books and without other assistance. Athletics and games will have their due place, without the over-emphasis sometimes given to them now. Dancing on the village green as a recreation, and eurythmics, or Greek dancing, as a fine art of the highest type, are sure to be popular at schools, as well as among adults.

POLITICS

A profound economic change in the life of the nation can hardly come to pass without considerable modification of the British Constitution and a realinement of political parties. It is widely recognized that constitutional development in the direction of relieving our overworked Parliament is already overdue. The following are at present the principal kinds of business for which Parliament is responsible :

(1) General (non-economic) legislation for Great Britain.
(2) Economic legislation for Great Britain.
(3) Financial business of Great Britain.
(4) Relations with the Dominions and India.
(5) Government of the Crown Colonies.
(6) Foreign affairs.

At various dates before, and soon after, the establishment of communism Parliament is likely to delegate or surrender some of these functions. It is possible that the Imperial Conference may become a permanent Imperial Council, which will take over the discussion of foreign affairs and the ratification of treaties, also the regulation of the mutual relations of the self-governing units of the Empire. For economic legislation a subordinate legislature will need to be established, which may be compared with the Social Parliament proposed by Mr. and Mrs. Webb,[1] to which in the next chapter, where it is briefly described, I give the name ' Legislative Assembly for Economic Affairs '. Financial business will disappear entirely with the realization of communism, the sole business of Parliament in place of the budget being to determine the number of men in the navy and army, and in the administrative civil service, as indeed it does now, and the quantities of munitions and materials with which they shall be supplied. There would remain, as the principal business of Parliament, numbers (1) and (5) of the above list, with occasional debates on the other subjects, in exercise of its power of revision (or referring back) decisions of the Imperial Council and Economic Assembly on certain grounds.

[1] *Constitution of a Socialist Commonwealth*, 1920, pp. 110 et seq.

I imagine there would be ministers for each of these subordinate legislatures, having amongst them certain members of the Cabinet ; and also representative ministers of the subordinate legislatures in the Cabinet. This would be a system of ' interlocking ministries ', for the purpose of closely co-ordinating the three legislatures, analogous to the interlocking directorates by which combined action of industrial undertakings is secured.

The supreme legislature will probably consist of two houses and the King, as now. It seems likely that the British genius for political compromise and recognizing the inevitable will avoid a violent revolution, and that the House of Commons will continue in existence (despite William Morris), all the more efficient for having a smaller number of members and a reduced scope. The House of Lords will perhaps have been altered almost out of recognition into a Senate or House of Elders, one-fourth of the members being officials, nominated by the Government, one-fourth elected, shall we say, from amongst aldermen by the city councils, and the rest elected from amongst men or women over forty years of age. I see no reason why the Constitution should not continue to be monarchical so long as the ruling House maintains its present democratic sympathies and consequent remarkable popularity. In theory communism should result in social equality, following on political and economic equality ; and after a time doubtless it would do so, the only exception being the King himself.

One of the greatest changes is likely to be in foreign politics, especially after other European countries have also reorganized themselves on the basis of communism. I anticipate that the League of Nations will slowly approximate towards a federal government of the world ; and that the League Assembly will be directly elected on the basis of one representative for each ten million or less of the population.

What will be the political parties in England under communism ? This is a question, of course, which it is impossible to answer. That cleavages of opinion will exist on many vital problems of the time would seem certain. Probably the most acute and enduring opposition will be between those favouring the rule of authority and those believing in the maximum of independence for the individual and the group within the larger group or State. The former, whilst ready to confer extensive powers of interference on the League of Nations, would advocate the maintenance of the British Empire, and ultimate supremacy of the British Parliament therein. They would also favour a bureaucratic policy in the administration and management of industry. The latter party—those who believe in the maximum of individual independence—would be more concerned to safeguard countries from encroachments by the League on their independence and sovereignty, except for prevention of war, and would advocate offering independence to constituent parts of the British Empire. In industry they would press for democratic control, election of managers, and so forth. At times the party divisions might run quite differently in the Economic Assembly and in Parliament ; the question of a general reduction of hours of work, for instance, might become, for a time, an acute question in the former. It may be assumed that elections will be as hotly contested as now, and more numerous in kind. There will be no political funds and no professional election agents, though perhaps a man or woman might get two or three months' leave to act as a candidate's agent. Printing would probably be done by the press which issued the local newspaper of the party, there being a rule to limit the amount of work permissible according to the number of voters. The registration of electors would be done officially, the only qualifications being age and six months' residence in the country. Persons convicted of a penal offence, or on a charge of refusal to work, or of malingering, would be disfranchised.

THE CONTENT OF LIFE

If I had not an intense conviction that life under communism will be fuller, richer and happier than now, I should not have undertaken the writing of this book. Yet, for the convincing of others, I must try to state briefly in what manner the then prevailing conditions will, as I conceive, yield a fullness of life and happiness. Let us consider what will be the social values of that day, and what will be the human and the physical environment ; for it is by reaction with their environment, in its widest sense, that men rise to higher things. I am not, of course, denying the individual his power of willing to be good,

or the satisfaction he may get from conceiving himself successful ; neither do I deny that occasionally there are born or bred
persons capable of rising superior to their environment ; or,
more likely, who have the force of character to find, perhaps
even to a large extent to create, the environment necessary to
their higher life. On the whole, however, human beings respond
to their environment just in the same way that plants flourish
or fade according to soil or climate.

There is no difficulty in understanding that communism,
once fully established, would provide all the conditions for the
growth of men in the higher virtues and in culture. As was
indicated earlier in this chapter, the maintenance of a high
moral standard will be largely automatic ; because the very
existence of the State demands honesty in service, truth of
statement, and the prevalence of altruistic motives. Every
cohesive and healthy society, or class of society, always
demands of its component members, by the force of public
opinion and the sanction of social ostracism, conformity with
such rules of conduct as are essential for its safety and well-
being. Hence there will be a general atmosphere of truthfulness, frankness and straightforwardness, a mutual confidence
very pleasant to experience. I have no doubt that a much
higher standard will prevail in all true virtues, as distinct from
those which are merely relics of chivalry and class exclusiveness,
of ecclesiastical dominance or of a money economy.

To-day we live amidst struggle, self-assertion, misery and
self-indulgence. This is very largely because we have no fixed
ideal, no guiding star to direct our efforts. The scepticism of
science, spreading to the people at large, has destroyed all the
old standards. Communism is an ideal which, once it is understood, will fire people's imaginations. Once it is realized it will
have cleared the field for a practical and literal application of
the teachings of Jesus.

The mass of the people, as my mind's eye sees them after
a generation of communism, will be of a type which now claims
our honour and affection, but is all too rare. I mean the
serious-minded person with settled convictions—broad-minded
and tolerant, sincere and straightforward in affairs, good-
tempered and with a sense of humour. He or she is capable of
throwing off the serious mood and enjoying life intensely ; is

10

fond of fun, but does not make a business, so to speak, of pleasure. Such a person has ' poise ' in life, has a soothing influence on all around, and draws out the best that is in others. Under communism all the conditions will be such as to allow these good qualities to develop ; indeed, the idealism that lies at the root of communism, especially its foundation on the love of one's fellow-men, and its stimulus to intellectual activities, will foster this type. Happiness is contagious, and it will be multiplied manifold when many of the persons with whom each is surrounded are such as have poise and a joy in life.

Perhaps the most fundamental gain from communism will be the mental satisfaction—one might almost say spiritual comfort—it offers in presenting a comprehensible, just and ordered scheme of life. Much doubt and positive unhappiness arise now amongst all classes from the apparent aimlessness of life, as well as from the hard economic conditions with which the workers, whilst nominally free, are normally confronted. On all hands one finds the bitterness of disappointment— almost as much amongst the salaried middle classes as amongst the manual workers. Is not the cramped and often futile life of suburbia possibly due largely to the fact that its inhabitants unconsciously feel that they are doing little or nothing of social value—the men mainly adding up figures or seeking to down their competitors, and most of the women who employ servants not working at all ? Dwellers in communist England will all have the satisfaction of feeling that they are working daily for the real good of their country ; for every able-bodied man or woman will have to offer, and will be accepted, for a suitable occupation ; and all permitted occupations will be socially useful.

The settlement of economic life on a rational basis cannot but lead with little delay to every other phase of life becoming regarded and treated in a similarly logical and straightforward manner. The problem of happiness in married life, complicated as it is now by the growing independence and self-assertiveness of women, will surely adjust itself as soon as people lose all their preconceived ideas. English marriage laws, and customs in regard to sex, have probably had a mixed origin, partly in the instinct of primitive man claiming a woman as his property, partly in the economic necessity of limiting the growth of population, and also to safeguard the mother and child from suffering—in early times from actual starvation. It requires little imagination to see that an economic system which will provide support throughout its life on an equality with everybody else to every child born, within the marriage contract or without, in a society which has generally accepted birth-control, will radically alter the sex position, and the customs and laws relating to marriage. The immorality of the present English divorce law, which requires actual adultery or the fraudulent representation of it, could never be tolerated when communism is established. The custom will prevail, I think, of warning young people and requiring them to consider very carefully about getting married ; but no obstacle will be put in the way of divorce for proved incompatibility, which interferes with happiness and makes genuine home life impossible. Married or divorced, the upbringing of the children will always be equally a public charge, as will be explained later in Chapter XI (see p. 215).

Social life will be informal and pleasant, people following their inclinations. There could be no snobbishness on the basis of wealth, because all will have equal incomes. Ostentation by living in a large house with much furniture, even if possible, would be a poor and burdensome undertaking. Lavish expenditure on dress or housekeeping would perforce disappear with the absence of wholetime servants, even if a non-expansible income permitted it by economy in other directions. It would soon be recognized as the right thing to live in modest style in artistic simplicity of dress and house. People will lead a free and easy, unconventional life, with no display ; but I think there will be plenty of simple hospitality. Affectation of superiority on the ground of learning or of travel, or the holding of a highly responsible position, will be regarded as intolerable ; and the culprit will be told so with a directness which is not the custom now.

The sincerity of all social life will contribute to happiness ; so also will the freedom from care and daily worries. There will be no money to handle, no rent, rates, taxes, water, gas or electric light bills to pay ; and the monthly credit of the general allowance at the store will be automatic and inevitable under all circumstances.[1] The worries of housekeeping will amount only to common prudence in spending and to keeping things clean—a simple process with vacuum-cleaning apparatus, and gas or electric cooking, in every house, and fires of smokeless coal, if open fires be used.

Critics of socialism and communism are never tired of reiterating that public operation or control of the country's industries must necessarily abolish all opportunities for individual initiative and enterprise. They imply that the taking of risk in some commercial venture and the battle for success are themselves sources of enjoyment, no less than of strength and character and of powerful leadership. That there is benefit as well as heavy loss in the present scope for individual initiative, I would be the last to deny. The answer to such criticisms is that the advantage of giving scope to individual initiative is not likely to be overlooked in the organization of communist society. There is no reason to suppose that the country will be at the mercy of a huge industrial bureaucracy; for the dangers of stagnation and inefficiency in a bureaucracy not subjected to external criticism and control are too well known. A system of checks and counter-checks will be established, both expert and popular criticism being so organized as to be useful and effective.

Much freedom will be allowed, I have not the least doubt, to local and individual initiative. Probably any man who could get the moral backing of a local council and persuade any recognized expert that there was something in his scheme, would be given leave to try it and be provided with all necessary resources in plant, materials and labour. His venture must cost him much hard work in plans and organization, but it would be ardently given for the sake of putting his idea to the test of practice. Ultimately, of course, he must exert himself for the sake of his reputation as a man who has been trusted. If he should fail through laziness, negligence or ignorance, this would be duly recorded by some public authority; and he would not have a second chance of wasting public resources anywhere in the country.

My own view on this important question is that the wisdom

---

[1] Unless a person offends against the law to such an extent as to require his detention in a penal colony.

of allowing clever men to make special studies, to travel abroad and to make experiments, would be amply recognized ; and that a man of ability and energy would only have to apply in the proper quarter for leave to devote his whole time to any activity in which he thought he could be useful and successful, and it would be readily given, if the result seemed likely to be of social utility or scientific interest. For persons having an instinctive love of adventure and danger, as many in Britain have, there will be aviation and many other difficult and dangerous occupations. In the annual holiday of a month's duration which every one will have, they can go mountaineering ; or, by saving up leave, explore the recesses of the Himalayas or the wilds of northern Siberia. Only a few people require freedom of initiative ; but those who do will be sufficiently numerous to demand and obtain the opportunities for exercising it. Such initiative must be sensible and disciplined ; and then, by giving it scope in positions of responsibility, the vitality and progress of society as a whole will be ensured. There will be a net advantage in giving scope to initiative and enterprise, even at the cost here and there for a time of a slight loss of routine efficiency. Even an originator of a new style in art or literature, though it be contrary to then existing taste —regarded even as ugly—will, I think, be given whole time for his work after he has first proved, perhaps in his spare time, that he has energy, and will produce something that at least arrests attention. One of the great principles on which the whole of the communist society must be built up is a complete tolerance and impartiality on the part of the committees and councils dealing with the allocation of persons to occupations.

Turning now to consider the physical environment, we may ask : How will it be made to contribute its quota to the fullness and happiness of life ? The obvious course will be to leave the beauties of nature unspoiled in places where man's works can be avoided ; to assist nature to restore as much as possible places of beauty already spoiled ; and, wherever there must be houses, factories or bridges, to make them beautiful, in harmony with their purpose and in keeping with their surroundings. We may be sure that all advertisement hoardings and vulgar street-signs will instantly go, serving a more useful purpose as firewood ; and that an immense building and rebuilding of towns, finely planned on garden city lines, will commence from the early years of communism. The sordid slums of our great cities and hideous rows of workmen's ' cottages ' will then soon be gone for ever. Probably a score or more of satellite towns will be laid out around London at various distances, thus reducing the population of what is now the built-up part ; and almost the whole of that will, no doubt, be rebuilt with ample garden space, fine avenues and open squares of grass and trees. The smoke-pall will no longer be tolerated, not even in any industrial town ; and the beauties of flowers and trees will be found everywhere in the towns in full view of the streets. So, in return to nature and art, will all the conditions of life tend to pleasantness and refinement. Ugliness and vulgarity will be banished for ever.

PART II
ECONOMIC ORGANIZATION

CHAPTER IX

NATIONAL ECONOMY

GENERAL PLAN OF ORGANIZATION

NO belief in the theoretical advantages of communism would induce a practically minded person to advocate its adoption, unless he were convinced that a national economic organization could be devised which would function efficiently. It is only because I have become so convinced that I have written this book. The scheme here put forward should be regarded, however, more as an embodiment of an analysis of the conditions which must be fulfilled than as a final opinion of mine as to what the precise organization should be.

One school of writers has believed that communism would involve the breaking up of the present politically organized States into practically self-governing communes, each covering but a small territory on a regional basis. State socialists, on the other hand, start out with the existing political government as the central organization from which the whole economic organism will develop, being national in its extent. My own view inclines to a compromise, giving local initiative the utmost possible scope, consistent with the exercise by national authority of those ultimate powers of compulsion which are necessary to ensure co-ordination. Moreover, the advice, and in certain respects the control, of the central authority will always be necessary ; and no one can deny that transport—both the internal transport of goods and foreign trade—must be nationally organized, because in these respects each nation is already a closely knit economic unit, and control is already exercised nationally.

There is another principle of great importance : the need of the authority of the State. Guild socialists appear to have believed that a national guild, consisting entirely of workers in the industry, would be entirely self-governing ; also that in most industries they could arise by the metamorphosis of the

existing trade unions. I am unable to accept either view as
the normal condition. No body of workers, if money economy
and markets be done away with, can adjust its work to the
needs of the community at large, in most cases the whole
nation, without external channels of information ; nor is it
likely to function smoothly without external advice and the
exercise, from time to time, of external authority. How, for
example, is the plant of an industry to be renewed or enlarged
by the work of other industries without either a money economy
or a state organization ? As to trade unions changing into
national guilds, it would, I feel sure, be the exception rather
than the rule. In complex industries technical management
is all-important. Managers, engineers and other specialists will
be ready enough to serve their country when the time comes,
on a basis of economic equality ; but it is likely that only in
small numbers would they be ready to work as members of a
body having the traditions of a workman's organization of the
old system.

In the final building of the new order the authority of the
State will be needed at every point, and so the new organization
must be introduced by comprehensive legislation. I agree with
Mr. and Mrs. Sidney Webb that a dyarchy, which would separate economic from social and political legislation, is perfectly
feasible. The spectacle of Parliament trying to settle the coal
strike of 1926 was one proof of its futility in the industrial
sphere. I should propose, therefore, that a Legislative Assembly
for Economic Affairs should be established by Parliament on
the basis that Bills passed by the Assembly must be reported
to the House of Commons, which could return a Bill for
reconsideration, but not amend it. A membership of three
hundred would be amply large enough for the Assembly, about
half the members being directly elected, the rest to be partly
officials, some of whom might be ministers, and partly nominated
by various organizations.

The general business of directing all the economic activities
of the country would fall to three bodies : a Council of Occupations, a Council of National Economy and a Council of Industrial Welfare. The business of the first would be to see that
every adult in the country was engaged in some immediately
or remotely useful occupation. The employment exchanges

throughout the country would be under it ; and in close touch with each exchange would be a ' registrar of occupations ', who would maintain a register of every person in his circle, showing changes of employment, leave taken, etc. No one could escape being on the register, because the stores supplying goods would automatically report to the registrar every new person supplied and every discontinuance. All direct services of every kind would be treated as professions—even household service ; [1] and all professions would be represented by a Council of Professions, which would be subordinate to the Council of Occupations. The latter would deal with industrial labour also in its social aspects, i.e. hours of labour, conditions of leave, etc.

The Council of National Economy would be in charge of all industry and the distribution of goods. It would be an ' apex ' council, as it may be called, having under it three councils corresponding with the three main lines of economic activity : production, foreign trade and internal distribution. These would be : (1) the General Council of Industries, which would have subordinate to it a Council at the head of each industry ; (2) the General Council of Foreign Trade ; and (3) the General Council of Supply, the last being the agency for distributing goods to consumers through local ' commissions of supply '— in other words, the organization for satisfying demand by supply.

The Council of Industrial Welfare may seem to be magnified illogically by placing it on a basis co-ordinate with the Council of National Economy ; but I am not prepared to believe that under communism all need for checks and balances will disappear. Ordinary industrial safety would doubtless be provided anyhow ; but under communism society is setting out to relieve the worker of the oppression of daily toil, to abolish obnoxious employments, to make all work pleasant and educative to the utmost extent possible. The business of the Council of National Economy would be to find goods to meet the demand. Outside pressure of an authority concerned with the other aspect of work might often be needed. Getting

[1] Probably there will be no servants in the sense of a woman employed as such for a single family. With labour-saving appliances in every house a woman would do the work of her own house and two or three others if she chose housework as her profession.

rid of undesirable occupations, and reducing the monotony of ordinary employments, are highly technical questions, which might require large investments of capital, and in other ways interfere with the development of output. Thus an independent body of specially interested persons conducting research, giving advice and, when necessary, exercising pressure, in all matters of the welfare of workers, seems to me essential.

For the purpose of co-ordinating the work of the three great councils named, those of Occupations, National Economy and Industrial Welfare, I would suggest that there should be a Supreme Economic Council, the membership of which should consist of half the members of each of the three great councils just named, elected by each Council on a constituency basis, with the addition of a few members to be nominated by other important bodies, say, about sixty members in all. I think all members of the Supreme Economic Council should be *ex officio* members of the Legislative Assembly for Economic Affairs. The Supreme Council would have an Executive Committee, each member having a portfolio. There might be twelve such ministers in charge of the following subjects : transport, mines, metallurgical industries, agriculture, textile industries, minor industries, foreign trade, supply, professions, industrial welfare, occupations and vocational education. These ministers would be members each of several appropriate councils, thus securing interlocking.

THE ORGANIZATION OF PRODUCTION

It is probable that specialization of occupations will be carried further under communism than at the present day, except in certain directions where disadvantages become clearly recognizable. At the same time narrowness of outlook would be avoided by specialists being expected to devote spare time to study of related branches of learning, of professions and of industry. Since division of labour in industries must exist to a great extent even to maintain the present national dividend, monotony of labour arising from that cause is unavoidable. The probable tendency would seem to be to push the division of labour much further, wherever economy of workers' time could be achieved, thus enabling a shortening of working hours. Those taking pleasure in constructive or artistic handiwork would spend a short working day, perhaps on the half-time basis, in the factory at a mechanical task, and the balance in a workshop, such handwork being done as public work—that is, the work required of everybody in return for the guaranteed livelihood. The manufacture of pottery and metal goods for household purposes is likely to revert very largely to handwork, for artistic reasons ; but probably the tendency will be not to restrict it to a comparatively few whole-time workers, but, as far as possible, to give the opportunity to all wishing to do handwork to do it during part of their working hours.

At present industry is organized and reorganized with a view to cheaper production. Under communism the object will be to get pleasure not merely out of the consumption of goods as now, but first out of the production of the goods, and then out of their consumption, the pleasure on both occasions being enhanced by the individuality, more or less artistic, of the workmanship of many kinds of durable goods. The necessity for lowering the production cost in workers' time of machine-made goods will never be lost sight of. As now, the consumer who wants hand-made articles will have to pay the cost of them, though the price may be arbitrarily reduced to some extent ; [1] but we may be sure they will be in great demand.

The economies of large-scale production would lead in certain industries to the concentration of producing units : in extreme cases the whole country's supply of a commodity might come from a single factory. In several industries, however, there would be tendencies militating against concentration. For example, industries particularly suited for the employment of women might not be sufficiently numerous to provide for every town the one great factory of some one industry ; and, even if that were possible, the inhabitants of towns would probably demand some variety of occupations. At present there are industrial towns and areas (e.g. the South Wales coalfield) where there are many idle women, because there is no industry organized to employ them. With better

[1] See Chapter XI, p. 199, and Chapter XII, p. 225.

household equipment, and perhaps joint housekeeping, many women could spare half- or whole-time from household and maternal duties. There might result, for instance, a wider distribution of the textile industries. At present the initial commercial risk of going outside an area where experienced labour and markets already exist is too great. Some industries, like machine knitting and some classes of weaving, could be distributed in homes, or in small workshops, by using electric power.

These, and other considerations, show that it is impossible to predict which industries will be more highly concentrated and which more diffused. Each industry will doubtless be investigated from time to time with a view to adapting its organization to the convenience of workers, and to maximizing output. It will be realized that one of the chief objects of industrial organization should be to provide work economically for everybody : to have no able-bodied man or woman idle— and this without too much shifting or aggregation of the population. Town planning, occupation planning (from the point of view of the town) and industry planning (from the point of view of the country as a whole) will all be closely linked.

THE CONTROL OF INDUSTRY

A subject so vast as the control of industry under communism merits a series of treatises for itself ; and it is obvious I can only offer here a few leading ideas. The conception I have formed of what will probably be the most efficient management is *single-man control* modified by consultative committees. Every producing unit, and even every department of a large factory, must have its committee, consisting of representatives of the workers elected by them annually.[1] The appointment of a manager would be made by higher authority, but subject to an appeal by the works committee. It might prove advisable that, when taking action contrary to the advice of his committee, the manager should be obliged to disclose and record his reasons. A three-fourths majority of the committee should

---

[1] On the subject of the workers' sphere in the government of industry the reader may with advantage consult *A Grammar of Politics* by H. J. Laski, 2nd ed., pp. 440–2, and the books by Mr. and Mrs. Sidney Webb mentioned in Appendix III of the present book.

be entitled to petition for his removal. Departmental committees might be granted similar rights as regards sub-managers.
Although departmental committees would consist entirely of
workers, one-fourth of their membership might with advantage
consist of workers of other departments ; and the factory,
mine, or works committee might have two or three members
representing cognate industries and the consumers' ' supply
committees ', to be described later. It seems to me desirable
that outside views should be represented at meetings of the
committees so as to avoid the friction that might arise from
narrow self-interest or uninformed altruism amongst a body of
workers.

At the head of an industry, for purposes of administrative
direction, would be a council of the industry in general control.
It would be composed, on the same principle, mainly of workers
—that is to say, manager, technical specialists and rank and
file—probably partly elected ; and there would be some
outside representatives. Each industry would have its council ;
and each great industry would probably have under its general
council divisional councils, one for each regional division, with
limited but clearly-defined powers. The geographical divisions
suitable for an industry would not necessarily coincide with the
administrative areas for supply and other economic purposes.
The functions of these councils administering each industry
would be : (1) the review of production per worker in each
establishment, and making further necessary inquiry and
taking consequent action ; (2) the giving of orders as to the
increase or diminution of output and the recruitment or
reduction of labour (by transference) ; (3) the consideration of
the state of the plant and its improvement; (4) major
alterations of the designs of goods produced. In the normal
course of business orders as to kinds, qualities and quantities
of goods to be produced in accordance with the program of
production for the year would be received by the factory
manager, or the director of the division, direct from the commissions of supply. If a special or extra order not included in
the program were received, which could not be easily executed, the council of the industry would be entitled to make a
representation to the corresponding commission of supply as to
any difficulty in complying with the order.

For the management of each industry a considerable establishment, or secretariat, would be maintained under control of the council, divided into three branches : secretarial, technical and directive. The last would be under a director, or director-general, who would deal directly with managers of producing units in the smaller industries, and with the divisional directors of the regional divisions in large industries. A divisional director would be responsible for managerial and technical supervision of all producing units in his division, in consultation with the divisional council ; and on routine matters he would deal directly with the regional commission of supply, that is to say, as regards fulfilling orders, small changes of patterns or quality, complaints, etc.

Industries would indent for replacements of plant as a matter of routine ; but large schemes of improvement, or new works, would be subject to the approval of the Council of Equipment, whose business it would be to direct the whole national flow of labour available for fixed investment into the channels socially most beneficial, on the balance of advantages from all points of view. The Equipment Council would be continually taking evidence from consumers' representatives, as well as commissions of supply, from the councils of industries demanding plant, and from those supplying plant. It would be organized in a number of branches or departments corresponding with the major industries and groups of minor industries ; and it would need a considerable staff of experts and a large secretariat.

It is probable that the development of agriculture will receive continuous attention. I think it will be organized mainly for large-scale farming, on account of the greater productivity of labour thereby obtainable ; and that the dairy industry will doubtless receive a great development on the most modern lines. The use of margarine would probably be discouraged. Except in the environs of towns, where land would be reserved for allotments for spare-time work, all agricultural land, including many of the present great private parks, would be divided into farms, with improved housing for the farm-workers. For purposes of control and the sharing of certain kinds of machinery the farms might well be grouped into units averaging about 20,000 acres of cultivated land and pasture, preferably with variety of soil. In charge of each such unit would be a superintendent, having a consultative committee, mainly of its workers, similar to a works committee. Such groups of farms would lie in divisions, each under a divisional director, and each division would have an agricultural college.

The training of its workers would be an important part of the organization of every industry. Every factory and works would have its own training class for probationers, i.e. applicants for employment in skilled work. Every industry would also have a technical college, and great industries many colleges, to which men and women who had already been in skilled employment would go at the age of twenty-four to twenty-eight for a one- or two-years' course leading to higher appointments. Those who were university graduates in science would usually pass through the technical college in one year ; but preliminary experience in the manual operations of the industry would be essential.

THE ORGANIZATION OF SUPPLY

The organization necessary for the supply of goods does not seem to present any serious difficulties. The system which will be outlined here is that which would naturally be adopted, as it seems to me, in early years after the adoption of communism. I do not postulate so radical a change of present-day human nature (if the phrase may be allowed) as Sir Thomas More and William Morris, who believed that people would be entitled to be supplied from the common stock to the full extent of their wants. That the simple life will be cultivated almost goes without saying ; but I cannot believe that, within any period of time which it is worth while now to consider, all individuals will gain sufficient control over their wants for it to be possible to give them freedom to satisfy them fully. If any large number of persons abused such freedom, not only would the principle of equality be violated, but consumption would outrun the national production and exhaust stocks held in reserve.

Private property is sure to be recognized in personal things and the smaller household goods ; but not in houses, and possibly not in furniture, the larger pieces of which might be

11

made for the house, and remain in it. As will be explained in Chapter XI, every person will receive an equal *general allowance* by monthly credit, and all purchases made to satisfy his daily or occasional needs will be debited to this. Goods so acquired would unquestionably be regarded as his private property, in the sense that he could keep them or dispose of them as he wished, otherwise than for profit.

It seems to me probable that unusually costly things, such as houses, motor-cars, fine grand-pianos, and unique works of art, would not be treated as private property—at least during the earlier stages of the introduction of communism, and perhaps permanently. They would be assigned for use by arrangement to those who seemed likely to make the best use of them, or else in turn. Doctors, and all men whose business required much getting about in the neighbourhood, would have cars assigned them as instruments of their work. Other cars would be available from central garages for business or pleasure whenever desired. Everybody would be able to drive, and anyone wanting a car would go to the nearest garage and take his usual car, or any other that happened to be in, and sign for it. If used for pleasure, he would be debited at a rate which would include cost of petrol or electricity, lubricating oil and depreciation only. The use of trams and local omnibuses would simply be free ; and so would be the postal and telephone service, and the supply of water, gas and electricity. To measure the service and do all the clerical work of making debits for such services would cost more than the social saving that would ensue from the prevention of unnecessary consumption. Wilful waste would be regarded as a serious offence. Local railway travelling would no doubt be free by permanent pass ; but not long-distance travelling for pleasure. A free pass for the journey would be given if there were any kind of public or educational purpose in travelling. For expenses when travelling a person would simply carry with him a credit card, or book for a thousand miles, the total amount of which would have been already debited to his home account.[1]

---

[1] Compare the 1,000 mile tickets now issued by the L. & N.E. Ry. Co., which consist of a book of 1,000 small coupons good for one mile each, the requisite number being torn out for each journey, and given in exchange for a ticket.

HOUSING ACCOMMODATION

Housing would be in charge of a committee for each town ; and in large towns there would be sub-committees with co-opted members for each ward. There would be a permanent staff of housing officers working under direction of the committee. The business of some would be to find a suitable house for every applicant, as far as possible in the part of the town or suburbs he might desire. Others would be in charge of repairs. The occupier might often do minor repairs or decorations and alterations with his own hands in his spare time. As a rule, however, the building industry in its repairs division would be called in. Possibly large houses or hostels, with separate suites of rooms, but also common dining and sitting rooms, will become popular. Some existing large houses of sufficient architectural merit are likely to be allowed to survive and be converted for the purpose. So far as practicable houses would doubtless be allotted to suit the size of the family ; and the need for additional space, if any member of the family should carry on his or her work in the home, would be taken into account. Whenever a shortage of accommodation appeared likely to be more than temporary, the housing committee would call on the local building director (in charge of the building industry for the town) to build more houses, after submitting plans for approval. In all towns, and many villages, building would be constantly in progress ; for, if the population were not increasing, the replacement of old houses would proceed till all were housed according to the new and high standard which would be possible.

It is probable that a very much greater advance would take place in the standard of the housing accommodation of industrial workers than in the satisfaction of wants of any other kind. The present pressure of the rates on the satisfaction of this particular want would disappear entirely. It would be widely recognized that the re-housing of about 90 per cent of the people should have the first claim on the surplus labour which would become available by abolishing the wastes of competition. Hence the personnel of the building industry would be expanded to three or four times its present number ; and the efficiency of labour in both output and quality would be greatly increased by improved organization and by the adoption of new methods, as the result of motion studies and experiment with new materials.[1] During the initial period of thirty years or more which this complete re-housing would take, it would seem inadvisable to charge any rent at all for houses, for people would often have to live in houses larger or smaller than they wished. New houses would be allotted partly according to need and partly according to order of application. New houses and flats should, of course, be built with considerable variety as to size and style of equipment, so that eventually the condition contemplated by Bellamy could be reached—that families preferring better house accommodation to other lines of expenditure could do so by paying a correspondingly higher rent. When this stage had become possible the general allowance would be increased so as to include average rent.

STORES AND THE SUPPLY OF GOODS TO THEM

All kinds of commodities which we commonly purchase from shops or co-operative stores in such quantities as our individual needs and tastes dictate would be obtainable from a central general store, or from many branches thereof in the larger towns. The store would be the universal provider for all daily needs other than those of the classes mentioned above. It would be convenient for the store to act also as banker. Every person would be registered at one of the central or branch stores, and must have a running account there. On this he might as well be allowed to draw cheques, and have his general allowance credited monthly in its books. It would be a wasteful duplication to keep ledger accounts at a bank and a store for every person. There being no money in circulation, the only function of the national bank will be the setting off against one another of surpluses and deficits of public authorities and industrial managing committees. Special articles required by any person from London or abroad could be ordered direct from London on the purchaser quoting the town and number of his account, to which the debit would

[1] See Gilbreth, F. B., *Motion Study*, 1911, Chapter III, and *Bricklaying System* (N.Y.).

quickly find its way. The management of a store would be supervised by a 'store committee' elected by the persons having accounts there ; and there might very likely be a small committee for each branch store.

The mechanism of the stores themselves would be simple enough. A more interesting question is how they are to be supplied with goods and linked up with industries and foreign trade. Here would come in what I have named above Commissions and Committees of Supply.[1] A commission of supply would consist of a group of commissioners—whole-time officers, each in charge of the supply of a related group of commodities in his division ; and each important town would have its committee of supply. The commissioners would exercise the functions of wholesale merchants, or of directors of the Co-operative Wholesale Society ; and for each division there would be a headquarters town, in which the commissioners for the various departments would have their offices, as close together as possible. Associated with them there would be a commissioner of transport, who would take up with the local traffic superintendents of rail, road, water and air transport systems questions of deliveries of goods and arrangements for special consignments. The whole body of commissioners for a division would meet from time to time as the Commission of Supply to co-ordinate supplies and deal with certain matters on joint responsibility.

I do not think that the town councils could effectively discharge the complex duties of the committees of supply in addition to all their other duties. The committees of supply should therefore be bodies of citizens elected *ad hoc*, who would serve voluntarily in their spare time for the purpose of focusing public opinion as to the inadequacy or poor quality of supplies, or as to changes desired. Complaints would come before them through the medium of the stores committees, or direct ; and the commissioners would be obliged to follow their orders, so far as these related to interpreting the desires of the public for the

---

[1] The term 'supply' is better than 'distribution', which is in use at the present time to describe the business of getting the goods from factories to the consumers, for the word 'distribution' implies a process starting from the producer. In reality the business is undertaken in order to satisfy the consumers' wants. The psychological result of recognizing this in the terminology may be important.

kinds and qualities of goods to be supplied. In technical matters like prices and sources of supply, and quantities to be ordered, the commission would be the final authority, and the committee would have advisory powers only, subject, however, to appeal to inspectors of supply under the General Council of Supply. I take it the committee of supply for a division would be not unlike the municipal council of a large town in its organization, having its sub-committees for the various classes of goods ; but the area from which members would be elected would be larger than a single town, except in the case of towns of over half a million population, which, with all their suburbs, might be divisions in themselves.

The inspectors of supply mentioned in the preceding paragraph would be officials of one branch of an exceedingly important department under the General Council of Supply—that concerned with research, inspection and complaints regarding the goods and services supplied through the stores. In the absence of competition under communism a definite organization designed to ensure that all legitimate wants and wishes of the people are supplied to their satisfaction will be essential. As in every problem, a solution can be found by the patient application of the scientific method ; and it is interesting and important to realise that the foundation of the technique of supply has been laid already by the adoption in Great Britain since the War of scientifically devised ways of increasing sales and producers' prices, such as market research and National Mark grading.

The existence of committees of supply is proposed partly because of the importance of the economic organization of communism having a democratic basis locally as well as centrally, and partly to ensure the proper functioning of the Central Research and Inspection Department above mentioned. The really important part of the work of giving satisfaction to the consumer would be done by that department.

Market research involves a close study of the qualities of goods of a certain brand, of the suitability of packing, of how far they meet consumers' wishes and compare with competitors' products, and of the opportunities for enlarging sales or offering new products. Goods are compared by physical tests and chemical analyses, by having samples tested by large numbers of persons, by actual tests of wear, and so forth.[1] Elaborate house to house enquiries are made, and numbers of typical consumers are invited to reply to questionnaires. Such research is usually undertaken by large manufacturers selling their products under brand names ; but a few wholesale distributors and chain store companies are beginning to organize such research in qualities and prices of the goods they handle. The Co-operative Wholesale Society has a research Department for testing goods it buys and for improving its productions.

Grading involves both laying down exactly the characteristics of each quality or grade of a product, and the maintenance of a staff of qualified experts to assess the grade of each lot of produce submitted. The method of sampling for this purpose also has to be studied. The work of grading is usually done on a non-profitmaking basis, either by a trade association or by a government department. The statistical theory of testing and grading is likely to prove a fruitful field of research as may be judged from two important recent publications.[2]

Market research, and grading and testing, are now organized by manufacturers, or on behalf of primary producers, to enable them to extend their sales by better pleasing their customers. There is much overlapping through competitors investigating the same problems ; and the results are usually kept secret. The proposed Central Research and Inspection Department would be carrying out such work on behalf of the general body of consumers. Its methods and results would probably be to a large extent published ; and necessary information not published would be made accessible to the committees and commissions of supply concerned or desiring to be informed.

Statistics of stocks would be sent weekly for some commodities, and monthly for others, by all stores in the division to the commissioners, who would quickly note by means of graphs any change of demand from the normal for the time of year, and act accordingly.[3] Transferences from store to store,

---

[1] See *Market Research* by P. Redmayne and H. Weeks, London : 1931 (Butterworth).

[2] *Economic Control of the Quality of a Manufactured Product* by Dr. W. A. Shewhart, New York and London : 1932 ; and *A Survey of the Uses of Statistical Method in the Control and Standardisation of the Quality of Manufactured Products* by Professor Egon S. Pearson : Journ. Roy. Stat. Soc., Vol. XCVI, 1933, part I.

[3] An elaborate system of statistics entirely suitable for this purpose has already been put into operation by the London Co-operative Society, Ltd.,

or even from one division to another, would always be possible. Stocks actually kept in any locality would probably be far smaller than are now usually kept in all the shops and wholesale stores of a town. This fact, and a systematic arrangement of warehouses, would greatly reduce the area of land utilized for supply, as compared with the present chaos of shops and warehouses.

The supply of direct services will require only a simple organization. Presumably there would be a medical council for each division to assign doctors to circles, in which they would work in groups, including specialists. Each division would have one or more hospitals controlled by the medical council. Household service would be transformed by labour-saving appliances, and would occupy but little time compared with the present inefficiency. A woman of the family would do everything necessary for her house in two hours or so a day ; and, if not looking after her own or other children, would then go on to do neighbours' housework, this being her assigned duty. In a hostel, or communal house, three or four of the women living there, aided by the men in their spare time, would probably be able to do the work of ten or twelve families. In each town or each ward there would be a committee of household service, which would authorize women, and perhaps some men, to be engaged in household service for whole or half time. On such authorization being notified to the registrar of occupations the household duty would be treated as public work. Other committees would authorize freedom of women from public work on account of maternal duties. There is no reason to think these committees would be unpleasantly inquisitorial. A full statement of facts would be made before the committee, and the business would go through quickly on the basis of rules or well-understood policy. Doubtful cases would usually be the applicant's own fault.

The professions of art and learning are likely to demand and to enjoy great freedom. There would probably be guilds of painters, sculptors, illustrators, musicians, authors, artist-craftsmen in wood and metal, and so forth ; and so long as a guild were recognized, every member it admitted would be

for controlling the two hundred and twenty branch stores of the Society, and similar systems by other large co-operative societies.

entitled to treat his art as his public work. Persons already in other occupations could acquire proficiency in their chosen art in spare time or leave time, and obtain a transfer when admitted by the guild. The universities, as stated in the preceding chapter, would decide whom they wanted on their teaching staffs and for appointment as research fellows ; and normally the limit to the size of their staffs, and particularly to the number of research fellows, would be elastic. It would probably be an advantage if organized research for social and scientific progress gravitated to the universities, rather than have it all bureaucratically concentrated in London.

It may appear at first sight that the organization of industries and the supply of goods as here foreshadowed involves the functioning of a very large number of councils, commissions and committees, and that the system is too complex. Any such appearance must be ascribed to the fact that I have attempted to describe within a brief compass the economic organization of forty-five million people. When it is considered how many thousands of boards of directors, and committees of co-operative societies and trade-union lodges there are in England now, it will be seen that the number of such bodies here anticipated will not greatly exceed the number of corresponding bodies now existing. At the same time I think it is true that there will be a considerable multiplication of committees under communism, perhaps to an extent much greater than I have indicated. Universal co-operation is the essence of communism ; and committees, official and non-official, will be the means of securing fruitful results from co-operation, and of meeting people's wishes. Perhaps almost everybody will serve on some committee or other for a few years in his or her lifetime ; and so, with widespread experience in committee work, we may expect that people will learn to handle business efficiently and expeditiously.

CHAPTER X

PRODUCTION AND THE NATIONAL DIVIDEND

THE economic problems involved in the distribution of wealth, the fixation of prices, and the equilibrium of demand and supply can be approached in a simple manner from the standpoint of the national dividend. To obtain a clear idea as to what the national dividend is constitutes an essential preliminary, for there is some confusion amongst economic writers as to terminology, if not as to ideas. I shall proceed from the ideas pertaining to the present system of money economy as a convenient stepping-stone to understanding the national dividend in the economy of communism.

All readers will be familiar with the comparisons of average income per head in different countries which have become a common, if sometimes misleading, statistical exercise in recent decades. The income per head is simply the *national income* divided by the population. The national income is not the Government revenues, but the total earnings and other incomes of all the people of the country, expressed in terms of money. Only a rough estimate is possible ; and there are difficulties, such as the effects of a change of the general level of prices, and whether the rental value of a house occupied by its owner is to be included.

The national income from this point of view is the sum total of the *net* incomes of all persons in the country—in fact, their incomes as they would be reckoned for income-tax if everybody were assessed. Another view of the national income is that it consists of the sum total of the money value of all the goods and services annually produced in the country. These two conceptions are inconsistent. In the first view, the interest on capital invested in industrial securities, representing plant and machinery, is counted as income, and so is the rent of house property received by a landlord, or the equivalent rental value if the owner occupies his own house. But the plant and machinery and house property, when built or manufactured, were sold, and the successive receipts from such sales provided the incomes to the persons who took part in making them. The investors who bought the said plant and machinery (or shares representing them in limited companies) and house property, afterwards permitted some one else to use them on paying interest (or dividend) and rent ; and this interest or rent is counted as part of the income of such investor. It is true that money changes hands both when the machinery or house is built and sold and when it is afterwards used by some one else than the owner. From the social point of view, however, that is to say, from the point of view of the well-being of the whole population, it is evident that such durable goods are being counted twice over : firstly, their capital value when originally built, and secondly, the annual value of the use of each, continuing throughout the whole period of its life in use. The second conception—the total money value of all the goods annually produced in the country, whether for immediate consumption or for continued use—is, in fact, the one more nearly appropriate to our purpose.[1]

TOTAL PRODUCTION STREAM

It is unnecessary here to enter into the intricacies of the definition and measurement of the national income (or national dividend). It is simpler for the purpose of the approach to the economics of communism to exclude the idea of money altogether ; for, after all, money is only an intermedium

[1] It will be convenient to explain here the classification and nomenclature of goods of all sorts adopted in this chapter as they differ somewhat from those common to most text-books on economics. Goods of all kinds are firstly broadly divided into *Consumption Goods* and *Capital Goods*, the former being all those which are directly used or consumed, as a house, a pen, clothes, food, or matches, and the latter being the tools and plant by which consumption goods are made and the stocks of raw materials. Each of these two great classes can be further divided into two sub-divisions, according to whether they are perishable or non-perishable. We thus have four groups, as follows :

(1) Durable consumption goods (here called *usable* goods), e.g. a teapot, motor-car, clothes-brush, etc.
(2) Non-durable goods, which are destroyed in the act of consumption, e.g. food, cigarettes, coal (here called *consumable* goods).
(3) Durable capital goods, often called fixed capital (here called *instrumental* goods), e.g. all tools, machinery, plant, and buildings used in production of any kind.
(4) Non-durable capital goods, constituting the so-called 'circulating capital', e.g. raw materials and partly-finished commodities of all kinds and fuel for power.

between producer and consumer, its main function being to help them find and deal with each other. What is of vital importance to the community as a whole is the real annual production of new wealth, that is to say, the stream of goods and services resulting from all the work done in the country. What share of it is diverted to monopolists and owners of land and capital by the present constitution of society we need not now inquire. The monopoly profits and rents of lands in their natural condition (i.e. site values) are pure waste from the social point of view ; and the payment of interest is, from the same point of view, a clumsy way of securing that a certain number of workers shall be maintained in the production of fixed capitals goods—buildings, machinery and plant generally.

This will become obvious if we concentrate attention on the total of goods and services themselves which annually result from all the work done in the country, and ignore their money value, for money is only the medium whereby the competitive system distributes the goods and services amongst the various members of the population. I propose to call the total of goods and services annually flowing from all work done the *total production stream.* It is well to think of it as a stream, or, rather, as a stream which is the aggregate of a very great number of smaller streams, each the output of one kind of commodity or service. It embraces every kind of work. The civil servant, the municipal official, the minister of religion, the nigger minstrel, the tea-taster, even the bookmaker, who provides his clients with the pleasurable anticipation of uncertain gain—all are rendering services, though they may not all be services which a wise, reconstituted society would continue. The total production stream may be said to include all activities carried on with the intention of meeting other people's wants and one's own future wants. It includes, there-fore, much unpaid work of a public, educational, or benevolent character ; but it cannot be said to include such work as that of an advertising agent who spends his time inducing people to buy one brand of cigarettes rather than another.

By concentrating attention on the stream of goods and services produced, rather than upon their money value (the national income), we avoid many pitfalls. For instance, the money value of goods which are only partly manufactured, and form the raw material of another industrial process, must not be added to the full sale value of the goods of which they become a part. When thinking in terms of the actual commodities and services themselves we are not so likely to make the mistake of counting them twice over, for we only need to think of the individual streams of goods and services which actually go into consumption in the country, or go abroad by way of foreign trade in exchange for streams of goods flowing into the country.

The production of many kinds of goods exhibits periodic fluctuations ; as, for example, in agriculture, due to the annual character of the harvests, and in certain other industries on account of the seasonal character of the demand. All industrial work is interrupted from time to time by strikes, by accidental stoppages and by holidays. It is convenient, however, for some purposes, to think of the total production stream as a continuous flow of unvarying volume month by month, and even day by day. Unless a stoppage is lengthy, normal stocks of the finished goods are but little depleted, and the stream of consumption goes on with smooth regularity. For our present purpose it is unnecessary to take account of seasonal, or even cyclical, fluctuations of the production stream. Probably in future industry will be so organized that the fluctuations of production will be much less than those which are now experienced. The effect on consumption of the cyclical fluctuations of seven or ten years might be almost nullified by allowing stocks to vary in size, a result which may be contrasted with the prejudicial effect of the cycle of trade on the workers in certain industries under the capitalist régime.

THE CAPITAL FUND

The capitalist system has brought into being an immense quantity of buildings, machinery and plant of all descriptions devoted to production and transport. Such fixed capital, along with skilled organization and the division of labour, is the indispensable basis of the modern efficiency of production. Much the greater part, but by no means all, of this fixed capital is in the hands of profit-seeking capitalists. There are, however, municipal tramways and electric supply systems ; in many

countries the railways and various industries are State enterprises. Roads and their bridges, and river and harbour
improvements, are important parts of the fixed capital of the
country, mostly in public ownership. Co-operative enterprise
too is everywhere increasing its investment in machinery and
productive property of all kinds. All this fixed capital, in
whatever ownership, and all the immense stocks of raw
materials and finished goods in the hands of merchants and
manufacturers, constitute the capital fund of the country.

The capital fund is subject to forces tending to reduce it,
and to others tending to increase it. Amongst the former
the most important is deterioration, due on the one hand to
wear and tear of the plant and machinery in use, and on the
other hand to the action of the weather and natural agents of
all kinds, including rot and decay. Obsolescence of machines
and buildings due to the progress of invention and reorganization also tends to reduce the capital fund ; but not seriously so,
unless there is also at work an active increase of the capital
fund with more efficient instruments of production, which
throw out of use existing plant long before it is worn out. The
way in which the increase of the capital fund takes place
is by the investment of new capital ; this is provided by
the accumulation of individual savings, through the mechanism of joint-stock companies and loan issues, and by the
reservation of their surplus profits by firms and companies
for reinvestment.

A review of the industries of the country shows that many of
them are engaged entirely in the maintenance and enlargement
of the capital fund in this and other countries. The engineering
industries, for instance, are mostly occupied in manufacturing
machinery and plant and in building ships. The building trade
repairs and constructs factories and works of all kinds. The
glass-making and other industries contribute part of their
output to the manufacture of instruments of production.
These machines, buildings, ships, railway material, and so
forth, are being produced for two reasons: (1) to replace
machines worn out, or otherwise deteriorated or obsolescent,
and (2) on account of the expansion of the industry using the
machines or other instrumental goods. The mere replacement
of machines which have become worn out or otherwise useless

does not, of course, increase the capital fund : it merely prevents its decrease. Such replacement is provided for by a depreciation reserve or sinking fund, which forms part of the normal price of the goods which the machines produce. Any considerable expansion of the output of an industry, on the other hand, usually requires the investment of new capital, and this constitutes an addition to the capital fund.

A large proportion of the workpeople of the country are engaged in the industries devoted to the maintenance and increase of the fixed capital of the country. The larger the capital fund already is the larger must be the output of machines, etc., needed for replacements, unless the durability of machines, buildings, etc., is extended by the use of better materials or workmanship. It is impossible to tell which of the tools or machines a factory turns out are being made for replacements and which for expansion of industry, except by inquiry and computation. The replacements are being constantly provided for out of the income from sales in every well-conducted business, an accurate estimate of the necessary financial provision being made for the cost accounts. As mentioned above, the increase of the capital fund comes from reinvestment of the surplus profits of businesses, and from savings of individual persons through the medium of companies, public borrowings and life-insurance concerns.

The relation of the capital fund to the total production stream is so important that it must be clearly understood. Suppose that the various industries making machines and all other instrumental goods had an output which was only sufficient to effect all necessary replacements. Clearly, then, there would be no growth of the capital fund, assuming the stocks of raw materials and goods, i.e. free capital, to remain unchanged in quantity. If the output of the industries making instrumental goods be insufficient even for replacements, as notably in Russia from 1917 to 1922, there is an actual decline of the capital fund. This is a usual occurrence in any country when it is invaded in a great war. On the other hand, when the output of the industries producing instrumental goods exceeds the requirements for replacement, the capital fund is being increased.

The economic significance of the term national dividend will now be clear. The dividend of a company is that portion of its profits for the year which it divides amongst its shareholders. Any portion of the profits placed to reserve is invested, either in the company's own business or in some other form. In any case, profits placed to reserve or carried forward are not called dividend. In strict analogy with the use of the word dividend in company finance the term national dividend, when correctly used, means that portion of the total production stream which is distributed amongst the people for consumption. Machines, etc., produced for replacements cannot be part of the dividend. They have to be produced in order that the dividend may be maintained. So also the extra output of instruments of production which goes to increase the capital fund obviously is not dividend for consumption. Hence we see that the total production stream consists of three main parts : the national dividend, instrumental goods needed for replacements, instrumental goods added to the capital fund.

The national dividend itself may be subdivided into three main parts : (1) consumable goods, whether non-perishable or perishable, large stocks of the former being kept ; (2) durable goods, which may last in use either a few weeks or a century ; and (3) direct services, which are necessarily consumed at the time they are rendered. The recording of music on a gramophone record must be regarded as the production of a durable commodity.

Foreign trade introduces an apparent complication into the subdivision of the total production stream just outlined ; but it is more apparent than real. Instrumental, usable and consumable goods are sent abroad in exchange for goods belonging to those classes, but in quite different proportions. Thus the country may specialize, as England does, in making instrumental commodities, and so export more machines and ships than she imports. The result is that the number of persons employed in the industries making instrumental goods is larger than it would be if there were no foreign trade, and the national dividend partly accrues in the form of imports received in exchange for exports—the imports being mainly raw

materials and food, but including machines of foreign manufacture. If there were no foreign trade, we should have to
produce all our own raw materials as well as food ; and as
labour would be highly inefficient in producing many of them
in our conditions of soil and climate, the national dividend
would be very much less than it is.

In considering the subdivision of the total production stream
into three parts, and the further subdivision of the national
dividend as above described, the imports are simply to be
considered as substituted for the exports. The relative size of
the industries producing instrumental goods (machinery, ships,
etc.) and the industries producing goods for consumption will
depend, therefore, upon two factors : (1) the extent to which
the total labour power of the country exceeds the labour force
necessary to produce the national dividend, i.e. the goods that
go into consumption, and (2) the ratio of the demand abroad
for English machines, ships, etc., relatively to our demand
for foreign machinery. Neither of these factors can really
be taken alone, and be considered to be acting separately ;
for it is only on account of there being foreign trade that
the labour of the country is in excess of that required to
maintain the national dividend at our present standard of
living.

The magnitude of the national dividend relatively to the
population, which determines average earnings and places
a limit on the standard of living, depends on several factors
almost too obvious to need attention. The more efficiently a
person works, whether in output or in quality, the greater is his
contribution to the total production stream. His efficiency
depends in most cases more or less upon manual skill ; but
since the industrial revolution it has depended much more
upon the employment of suitable machinery, which tends ever
to be more automatic and standardized, and also upon effective
organization upon a larger and larger scale. The authorities
in control of industries under communism will indubitably
make the fullest use of machinery, division of labour, and
large-scale organization both in industries directly producing
consumption goods and in those creating the instruments of
production. We may be sure, however, that the use of
machinery and organization will be guided not solely with a

12

view to maximizing output. Pleasantness and satisfaction in work will always be ought for.

Attention has already been called to the fact that under the capitalist system the growth of the capital fund depends upon the decisions of boards of directors and partners of firms to reserve profits for investment, and on the decisions of individuals as to their savings. These decisions, according to the knowledge, or the delusion, of people as to the safety and profitableness, or otherwise, of investments, determine, in conjunction with foreign demand, on the one hand the magnitude of the industries producing instrumental goods as a whole, and on the other hand the relative magnitude of the different branches of those industries. Under communism the total volume of production of instrumental goods for home use and foreign trade, and in particular the relative rate of production of new equipment for each industry, will be determined after full investigation by the appropriate governing bodies described in the preceding chapter. The Council of Equipment is the body which will decide the relative claims of industries for new instrumental goods (other than for replacements). It would base its decisions on a variety of considerations, such as increase of output, reduction of price, or removing dangerous and disagreeable conditions of work.

The determination of what shall be the total production of instrumental goods for use in the kingdom (i.e. apart from export demand) will be a matter of high policy, which must engage the attention of the Council of National Economy, and probably also of the Supreme Economic Council; for it is evident that the Council of Supply and the Council of Equipment will often be in opposition on this matter. For instance, they might very likely make conflicting demands upon the Council of Occupations for the allocation of labour. In spite of great liberty being allowed to men in the choice of their occupations, there would usually be large numbers who could be employed at similar work in making either usable goods (like motor-cars) which form part of the national dividend, or instrumental goods (e.g. engines and machines of many kinds). Moreover, many men have no very definite choice as to their occupation; and sometimes the interests of demand might be held to overrule the worker's choice. Hence there would be some freedom in the allocation of labour to one industry or another as required.

The Council of Supply will be, so to speak, in charge of the national dividend, and the Council of Equipment in charge of the growth of the capital fund. True, one of the best ways to increase the national dividend is to equip the industries which produce its goods with machinery of greater productive power per worker ; so that in the long run the interests of the two councils would be identical on this point. Their immediate interests are opposed even as regards output ; but still more so when the Council of Equipment wants to increase its manufacture of plant in order merely to improve conditions of work, without increasing output, under pressure from the Council of Industrial Welfare. Men cannot work in two places at once. There is only a given amount of productive power in the country at any one moment ; and public opinion ultimately must decide how far the increase of the national dividend is to be sacrificed to the growth of the capital fund, and with what objects the latter is to grow. This is an instance of questions of economic policy which the public must understand, for the various councils can only be organs for focusing public opinion and carrying out its behests. One great advantage of communism is that the economic organization will be astonishingly simple and easy to understand, in comparison with the economic organization under the capitalist-competitive system. The great issues of economic policy are likely to become commonplaces of the secondary schools, and will become generally understood.

OCCUPATIONS AND THE NATIONAL DIVIDEND

The greatest immediate source of the increase of the national dividend would be the setting to work of all idle persons ; and the next would be the elimination of unproductive occupations —that is to say, those concerned with the advertising and selling of goods, the handling and accounting of money, and so forth—which would become superfluous in a rationally organized society. In this connexion it will be of interest to review all the occupations at present carried on, and to classify them according to the economic character of the service rendered. On this basis nine classes may be distinguished, varying greatly in the relative number of persons belonging to each, as follows :

(1) Persons rendering direct services, either
    (a) General, like Government and municipal officials, police, army and navy, preachers and musicians who play in public free ; or
    (b) Special, as doctors, lawyers, teachers, musicians, etc., whose services are rendered to individuals desiring them, such persons usually having to pay for them.
(2) Persons employed in public utility services, such as the supply of water and electricity and the post office, telegraph and telephones.
(3) Persons employed in mining (mainly coal) and manufactures of all kinds of goods for consumption, including managers, technicians and book-keepers.
(4) Persons engaged in transport services of all kinds.
(5) Persons employed in the manufacture of durable instrumental goods.
(6) Persons engaged in producing durable works of direct utility, either :
    (a) General, like roads, bridges, and town halls, or
    (b) Special, such as houses and residential accommodation of all kinds.
(7) Persons engaged in the distribution of goods, namely, merchants and shopkeepers, and all their employees and agents.
(8) Persons engaged in finance of all kinds, such as banking, insurance, company promotion and secretarial work, tax-collecting and accountancy.
(9) Persons of the professional class rendering indirect services, such as authors and artists.

A classification by crafts, that is, the nature of the work done, would of course be different from the above, which is based upon the economic significance of the ultimate service rendered.

To complete our review of the population in relation to occupation there is needed a classification of persons above school age not employed in any socially useful manner, or grossly under-employed, and the following may serve our purpose :

(1) The idle rich, pursuing amusement and travel.
(2) The partly employed rich—directors of companies, Members of Parliament and county councils, landlords managing their own property, etc.
(3) Unemployed workers—mostly manual workers, but some intellectual workers also.
(4) The unemployable—mostly men who have deteriorated through a long period of idleness, or through casual employment or drink—some are on the rates, some vagrants, others dependent on public or private charity.
(5) Women of all classes not occupied, or but little occupied, with duties of motherhood or housekeeping, be they spinsters, married or widows.
(6) Prisoners, both under trial and sentence, the work done in prison being of little use socially.
(7) The mentally defective in asylums and homes.
(8) Permanent invalids, cripples, war victims, and others physically defective, except some, especially the blind, who do useful work.
(9) The aged, at whatever age they have become too old to serve at the pace of modern industry.

It would be a conservative estimate to put the total number of able-bodied and mentally sound men and women not employed on socially useful work at about 6,800,000 in Great Britain, at a time when not more than 2,500,000 persons are officially on the unemployed register. In the total of about 6,800,000 I have assumed about 3,200,000 to be women who are not now employed, though family duties would permit of their working, either because they are of the middle class, or because no suitable work is offering. As I have explained before, under communism every woman not wholly occupied with motherhood or household duties will be expected to do public work, and if partly occupied therewith, then a half-day's work. In no previous state of society have women been idle to the extent that they are under the capitalist system : many idle, others overworked. Under communism work would be found for the physically defective, and many of the mentally defective, according to their several capacities. Persons under restraint for offences (I will not call them prisoners) would be required to work at socially useful work like free men, and, so far as possible, not under more disagreeable conditions.

There are over 16,000,000 registered workers in this country of whom 13,500,000, and some unregistered workers, are actually at work. This indicates that the national dividend might be increased by something like 50 per cent merely by setting to work everybody who could work. At present, amongst those classes, or in those parts of the country, where women are accustomed to live on their husband's or family incomes, it does not pay any one to risk capital in starting a suitable industry on the chance that a sufficient number may offer themselves ; for at times when the men's earnings are low, trade also is bad. Neither can Government set the women to work, nor even the unemployed, the prisoners or the mentally defective ; for any work these people could do would be an encroachment on the ' right ' of private enterprise to carry on business for profit without competition from so-called ' subsidized ' undertakings, and the ' right ' of skilled journey-men workers to the employment which the existing firms in the trade provide. Government may only employ people on making some of its own requirements, like parliamentary papers and postal bags, or in picking oakum : so we remain poorer than we might be !

OCCUPATIONS UNDER COMMUNISM

It will be instructive now to make a corresponding classification of occupations and non-occupations under communism. The classes are placed in the same order, and given the same numbers, as follows :

(1) Persons rendering direct services, either

        (a) General, like government and municipal officials, police, army and navy, musicians, etc., or

        (b) Special, as doctors, teachers, etc. (lawyers, if any,

being very few in number), rendering services to individuals who usually will not be required to pay for them.

(2) Persons employed in the supply of a commodity, the consumption of which is restricted only by reasonable need, e.g. matches, pencils, daily newspapers.

(3) Persons engaged in mining and in the supply of goods the consumption of which is restricted by the fixation of a price.

(4) Persons engaged in transport services of all kinds.

(5) Persons engaged in producing durable instrumental goods, such as the buildings and plant of industry and transport.

(6) Persons employed in producing durable works of direct utility, either

(a) General, like roads, bridges, town halls, or

(b) Special, such as houses and residential accommodation of all kinds.

(7) Persons engaged in the distribution of goods, i.e. the staffs of commissions of supply and of stores.

(8) Persons rendering indirect services, mainly intellectual, and not auxiliary to industries, such as authors, cinematograph actors and artists, surveyors making maps, town-planners, etc.

It will be observed that there is no class corresponding with Class (8) of occupations under capitalism, namely, persons engaged in finance, for the simple reason that money will be non-existent. Simple accounts of time, materials and stocks will be all that will be required in industry. In the stores only accounts of stocks, and personal credit accounts, will be needed. Persons at work on these accounts are analogous with the book-keepers, which were included in Classes (3) and (7) of the schedule of capitalism ; and the wholly monetary occupations will disappear, freeing many intelligent, upright and honourable men and women (e.g. cashiers) for better work.

All the eight essential classes of occupations under communism above enumerated exist at present ; but the mechanism of the capitalist competitive system is such that the proportions of the number of persons in each class are wrong, and also the proportions of persons following particular types of employment within each class. Take, for instance, Class (7), engaged in the distribution of goods ; surely one-fourth of our present number of wholesale merchants and their clerks would amply suffice for the commissions of supply, and not more than one-tenth of our present number of shopkeepers and their assistants would be needed in the stores, even including the keeping of the credit accounts, as there would be a tendency to a standard organization and a lavish use of labour-saving office-devices. Not one per cent of the persons now engaged in advertising— writers, artists, printers, etc.—would be needed for the mere giving notice of novel goods and of coming events. The salesmanship of proprietary articles is immensely wasteful, commonly absorbing, in retailer's and wholesaler's gross profits and the manufacturer's selling cost, including the expenses of travellers and advertising, from 50 to 80 per cent of the retail price.

The immense savings possible in the distribution of goods, and by the abolition of money, dwarf all others ; but throughout industry and transport further great economies could be effected by the elimination of competition, by more perfect organization on a large scale and by the division of functions. The amalgamation of railway companies and the formation of trusts and combinations in industries has begun this process ; but the complete elimination of private enterprise alone can carry it to its logical conclusion. Competition involves failure, and the loss of the capital invested in the less efficient businesses ; and many enterprises in which much capital has been invested are strangled a year or two after birth. The liberty which people now have to start companies for ill-considered enterprises (even with no fraudulent intent) is itself a source of waste. Under communism freedom to develop inventions and new processes of production will be regarded as highly important, and will be assured ; but labour and capital will not be devoted to such development until the inventor's or projector's plans have been rigorously examined by independent persons attached to the Council of Equipment and to universities, as well as by the industry itself.

A complete consideration of the facts regarding the occupations of the people and of private initiative in the investment of capital would take us too far. We may come at once to the important conclusion that those persons alone are contributing to the national dividend who (1) are actually engaged in doing the manual operations of production, or in planning or controlling them or making absolutely necessary records of them ; (2) are engaged in unavoidable work in the distribution of goods and services to the consumers ; (3) are rendering direct services.

A further important question is the theory of the proper distribution of labour power when communism is established. Examined in detail, this would be a very complicated question ; but the general principle is simple and clear, and in accordance with a well-established principle in current economic theory. Obviously the endeavour would be so to apply the labour power of the community throughout all kinds of work that there would be no great advantage to the community in transferring labour from any one kind of work to any other. The significance of this statement turns on the meaning given to the word 'advantage'. In the capitalist competitive system there comes about a rough distribution of resources—that is, the factors of production, land, capital, organization, and labour—such that the application of a marginal unit [1] of each factor (combined with others in the most favourable proportion) results in approximately equal gain of utility in whatever branch of production the additional unit is assumed to be applied. 'Gain of utility' should be understood to mean merely the satisfaction of wants as they exist at the moment, whether in accordance with long-standing custom of our civilization or newly created by advertisement. It finds its measure in terms of money through market prices.

Under communism other considerations besides securing equal marginal utility in the supply of all goods to the consumer will unquestionably enter, as has been stated in other words in preceding chapters. The community might be deliberately stinted of certain goods by an artificially high price (a method comparable with our present practice of imposing customs and

[1] The marginal unit of any factor of production in an industry is a small quantity considered as an increase of the total amount of that factor employed in the industry by one unit. For example, a marginal unit of capital might provide another machine with appropriate covered space : a marginal unit of labour might be one man more or less employed, or a slight increase or decrease of the daily time worked by all persons employed on a certain process.

excise duties on luxury or harmful articles) in order that more labour might be transferred to work of a pleasant or educative kind, or for the purpose of eliminating certain arduous or disgusting kinds of work.

Hence the marginal significance of a unit of resources will take full account of the effect upon the worker and his family of its mode of employment (in the case of land or capital), or of his mode of employment (when the unit of resources is the man himself), as well as of the community's need of the product or service. The welfare of workers is not susceptible of money measure, and must always be the subject of estimate. The fact that relative estimates will vary from time to time, and from region to region, does not affect the validity of the principle.

SOCIAL RESULTS OF CAPITALIST WASTE

Much the larger part of the waste of the present unorganized society lies in shopkeeping, salesmanship, advertising, and all the professions and callings connected with the handling and accounting of money, from the stockbroker to the rent-collector, and half the varieties of clerks. It will be seen, therefore, that the capitalist-competitive system has caused an undue growth of middle-class or ' black-coat ' occupations. Statistics show that the class of non-producing workers, the majority of whom are employed in distributive or clerical duties, has been growing in recent years at a greater rate than the manual workers, so that it has been forming a larger and larger percentage of the total population.[1] The main cause of this no doubt is the increasing efficiency of mechanical production, combined with the inefficiency in selling caused by increasing competition. To this must be added the immense growth of insurance and banking, in both of which the competition is highly wasteful.

William Morris foresaw the possibility of some such evolutionary excrescence of the capitalist system, which might operate to delay the realization of socialism, because its votes, and even its organized resistance, would help to retain political power with the privileged and capitalist classes. Amongst the millions of the ' respectable ' workers, men and women, it is a pleasant surprise to find a socialist. The essence of lower

[1] Some statistics are given in Appendix II.

middle-class feeling is imitation of the rich and contempt of the ways of the manual workers. Here and there, as amongst the railway and insurance clerks, a change of feeling is becoming evident ; but a vigorous socialist educational propaganda alone will remove this formidable political obstacle.

The propaganda must be of the highest moral and educational value, for reasons which I shall outline in a later chapter. It can hardly be expected that the change to communism would appear attractive at first sight to the many thousands of shopkeepers and clerks, and others of their class, who would have to turn to manual employments, or at least would expect to find their children driven thereto. This very natural feeling can be overcome only by insisting on the dignity and patriotism of all socially productive labour : that which is directed to meeting the true needs of the people, not the whims and fancies of the rich. Manual work which is now disagreeable or disgusting would be either abolished or made tolerable. Work which is now dirty could, in many cases, by proper arrangements be made clean ; and, in any case, workers in dirty industries would have facilities for washing and changing before leaving the premises. Noise can be reduced, and perfect ventilation and comfortable heating can be installed in all workshops.[1] Thus, with no differentiation of pay and with no obvious disadvantages all employments would become equally respectable. Indeed, we may well hope that the fundamental economic principles of national well-being will become so well understood by the public under the simple economic organization of communism, which every one can understand, that productive work will come to be honoured more than clerical work. People will tend to ask about every one : Is he doing socially useful work ? Since all productive work helps to swell the national dividend, and every one has a share of the dividend, all will resent any obvious waste of labour.

THE INCREASE OF THE NATIONAL DIVIDEND

There is no difficulty in pointing out how great is the number of persons in the country rendering no socially productive

---

[1] The subject of disagreeable work has been discussed more fully in an earlier chapter. See p. 103.

labour at the present time, either from idleness or from the competition and complexities of the capitalist system ; but it is not so easy to form a trustworthy estimate of the extent to which the national dividend would be increased by setting them all to productive work. The only estimate I can offer is no more than a thoughtful guess. I think it may be said safely that setting to work the 6,800,000 odd men and women now idle, but capable of working, would be likely to increase the total production stream by about 50 per cent ; and that at least 30 per cent increase could be obtained by transferring to productive work nine-tenths of the people now engaged in advertising and the wholesale and retail distribution of goods, and in all occupations concerned with money and money accounts. Thus we should have from these two sources alone something like 80 per cent increase of total production. We may assume that it would be decided to allot this additional labour in approximately equal amounts to the increase of the national dividend and the rate of addition to the capital fund. Of course, if nearly all the extra labour were allotted to the national dividend the immediate increase might be greater ; but not much, because to employ the additional labour efficiently would require additional plant and machinery.

On the basis of a detailed census of occupations, together with a simultaneous census of production, it ought to be possible to estimate with some degree of accuracy the increase of the total production stream that would be likely to ensue from employing idle persons and transferring the unproductive workers as above described. The census would need a cross classification, showing on the one hand the industry or pro-fessional group in which one person was rendering service, and on the other hand the kind of work he was doing—whether directional, manual or clerical, and so forth. The census of 1921 was the first in which this double classification was effectively attempted. The census of production of 1930 was taken in an abnormal year. The next census of production should give full details of the mechanical equipment and plant of each industry and its productive capacity—plant regarded as probably obsolete on account of high working cost being separately recorded. It would not be wise to contemplate a fundamental change of the industrial system of the country except upon the basis of the acquisition and study of the most complete statistical information. The nation must have the same kind of information about its industrial business which the directors of a big company obtain as the indispensable basis of their policy.

There remains for mention the increase of the national dividend which may be confidently expected to accrue from the introduction of improved kinds of plant and machinery, from a larger ratio of capital invested to labour in certain industries, and from improved methods generally. The public is not sufficiently alive, I think, to the inefficiency of some of our great industries in comparison with the standard of achievement in America, and in some respects in Germany and even in Japan. I mean that the output per head of persons employed is much greater in America, and in certain industries in other countries also. Of all our industries the building trade is the least efficient, and coal-mining and railways are far below what they should be in output and carrying capacity respectively per person employed. Many branches of the engineering industries could double their output per head if labour co-operated heartily with modernized management in enlarged and improved plants. Of course there are industries in which we are reasonably efficient, like textiles, but yet the output per head is much less than it might be if all mills were equipped with the latest machinery and if labour could be induced by satisfactory guaranteed minimum wages to co-operate with the management in working more looms and more spindles, or at higher speeds.[1]

To a large extent the unsatisfactory condition of our basic industries is due to want of enterprise on the part of capitalist employers. They hesitate to scrap plant which is still running as perfectly as when it was installed. The rate of invention and of increase of the size of units of plant has become too rapid for the English tradition. For nearly a century one of the chief aims of English makers of machinery has been durability ; and during the nineteenth century, when the rate of interest was generally low, and the progress of invention was British progress only, it undoubtedly paid the manufacturer to give a

[1] After the settlement at the end of 1932 of the more looms dispute, the above statement is still true.

somewhat higher price for a machine in order to have it last much longer. In America and Germany, with a higher interest rate, and the probability of obsolescence kept more prominently in view, the fashion has been to buy cheaper machinery with a short expectation of life. Moreóver, the mobilization of capital in trusts and cartels in America and Germany has enabled the establishment of plants upon an enormous scale, as in the steel industry; and economies have thus been realized which no British concern has been able to equal.[1] Combinations of producers in England have generally been formed with the object of maintaining prices and restricting output. There has usually been no great reorganization of plants.

It must be admitted that the inefficiency of some British industries is due also to the methods of organized labour. With the dread of unemployment ever present, workers in many industries are accustomed to set a limit to their output with the twofold object of keeping up the price of labour per unit of work done and of spreading out the available work so as to postpone unemployment for themselves or their fellows. There is a tacit, if not overt, opposition to the introduction of more efficient machinery, which exhibits itself in the union rates for working on the new machines being such as to show so little advantage to the employer from installing them that he refrains. In following these practices, which have prevailed in the building of ships as well as of houses, the workers in the trade in question appear to be acting against their own real interests. It is true that, in the long run, to a great extent, they are acting against the interests of the working-class as a whole as well as against the interests of the middle class. But the capitalist system is not organized on a basis of altruism —especially remote altruism. The interests of a particular group of men at a particular time are frequently in direct opposition to the interests of their class and of the whole country in the long run. The more educated working men become, the more do they follow the commercial policy favoured by their employers : seek immediate profits—monopoly profits, if possible—and let the public pay ! That is the inevitable and ingrained weakness of the capitalist system, which is slowly

[1] For information regarding cartels, amalgamations and trusts in Germany and America, see *Cartels, Concerns and Trusts*, by Dr. Robt. Liefmann (English translation revised to date) ; London, 1932. See also Appendix III, Part II.

but surely bringing it to its end. The capitalist system can only flourish with ignorant, apathetic and unorganized labour.

The danger that British workmen will carry over with them into the industries of communism a habit and tradition of bargaining as to the price of labour is one that must be squarely faced. An educational propaganda in national economy will probably be necessary ; and here the simplicity of the economics of communism, to which I have already alluded, will come to the rescue, and make it practically certain that the economic results of restrictive and obstructive tactics will be well understood. Every man will be aware that he and his fellows in the industry would gain nothing except lazy self-indulgence, and the contempt of their fellow-citizens, if they were to limit their rate of work below the normal healthy rate. They will realize that as workers they will lose nothing whatever by facilitating the introduction of improved and labour-saving appliances ; whilst as members of the community they will stand to gain by lower prices along with every one else.

There is no undue optimism in believing that the workers, when they have been freed from wage slavery, and have gained a large measure of control of their own industries, will welcome improved machinery, reorganization of plant, and the introduction of new methods, aiming at increasing the output per worker.[1] Such reorganizations might inconvenience a few, through their being compelled to remove to other towns, perhaps even to learn new work ; but under communism there would be no question of unemployment or reduced earnings for any one. Public opinion would undoubtedly strongly favour improved methods and plant both for bettering the conditions of labour and for increasing output, the latter having the desirable result of enabling the Council of National Economy either to increase the national dividend per head, with a consequent reduction of prices, or to curtail the normal working hours. I look forward confidently, therefore, to great activity in reorganizing and re-equipping industries as one of the earliest results of establishing communism.

[1] The above was written in 1925. It was interesting to find the miners in 1926 loudly demanding the reorganization of the coal-mining industry with improved equipment. In the other great industries the trade union leaders understand the economic advantage of modernized plant ; but they prefer to demand a better sales policy and unified economical administration, because substitution of labour-saving machinery would increase unemployment.

Knowing what we do of the increased output already obtained from modernized works,. mills and factories, I have no hesitation in anticipating from such reorganization and improvement of plant, after, say, twenty years of reconstruction, with the present number of employees, the increase of the national dividend to four times its present amount. We have already seen that the setting to work of the idle, and eliminating the wastes of competition, would be likely to increase the dividend by 80 per cent. Hence it is likely that twenty years of reorganization and improvement in all directions on a national basis would enable the national dividend to be multiplied at least seven times.[1] Whether public opinion would favour utilizing this greater command over wealth partly for reduction of working hours,and lengthening the annual holiday, or wholly for increasing the standard of living, cannot be foretold. In any case, I think millions of existing workmen's cottages will be replaced by small houses in garden cities and garden suburbs, thoroughly well built at a speed which would now astonish us, and completely equipped with labour-saving devices for household work. It is better a woman should work half-time daily for a few years making automatic electric cooking-stoves, electrically driven vacuum-cleaners and wash-ing-up machines, than spend more than half her time for her whole life over the present kinds of household drudgery. The freedom from the sordid cares and worries of life now enjoyed by the rich is attainable by all if we have the will to achieve and the power to organize and labour for a common end. That we have amongst us many men of great organizing capacity, and that all English men and women are capable of hard labour for a cause which stirs them, cannot be doubted. The new ideal, when all men understand it, cannot but rouse in them the will to achieve. Thus will be opened the door to the higher life in which once more, amidst happiness and freedom to most of us unknown, art, both individual and communal, will become the visible expression of man's spiritual thought.

---

[1] This appears to be a conservative estimate in view of the astonishing results of recent American invention in the field of labour-saving machinery revealed by the Energy Survey of North America. Some figures illustrating these results will be found in Appendix II.

CHAPTER XI

THE DISTRIBUTION OF WEALTH

THE Theory of Distribution is the name given by economists to that part of their science which treats of the causes determining the differences of people's incomes. It relates to the distribution of the national income, or national dividend, amongst the inhabitants of a country : not to the distribution of property in the static sense, but to the distribution of the stream of wealth produced. It has seemed appropriate to discuss under the same title the analogous subject of the relative incomes and direct benefits which people will enjoy under communism.

It will be conceded readily that the question of the distribution amongst people of the actual satisfactions they enjoy from economic activities is of greater importance than the question of the distribution of money incomes, or even of the goods and services which may be purchased with money. Money is only a means to an end. To be able to live in beautiful surroundings in the country, where the quality of foodstuffs is good and rent and rates are low, is accounted by many a good compensation for a small income. If prices in general fall, and money wages or incomes remain unchanged, the *real* wages in terms of the goods and services which the money wages will enable the recipient to enjoy are thereby enhanced.

We must go a step farther, however, and observe that we only purchase certain goods, or engage services, such as a doctor's or a hairdresser's, for a psychic reason. In other words, we only make use of goods and services for the immediate, or ultimate, purpose of either increasing our own enjoyment of life or someone else's. Goods or services either afford us pleasure at the time of use or consumption and in anticipation thereof, or they operate to remove discomfort, mitigate suffering or relieve anxiety. Whether the use or consumption of a thing is pleasant, or merely prevents or reduces discomfort or pain, it is said in either case to have a positive action on feeling ; and, conversely, anything which is unpleasant or painful, or reduces the pleasant reaction of something else, is said to have a negative effect on feeling. The great majority of economic actions result from deliberate decisions to adopt that course which, as we believe, will sooner or later influence our feeling in a positive sense. Of course we frequently make mistakes, and do not get the expected beneficial result ; and this indicates that all economic activities have their basis in a psychological reaction. A man believes that if he does a certain thing a net benefit or satisfaction will follow : therefore he does it ; and perhaps with a net result quite different from what he anticipated, owing to his having overlooked an unpleasant indirect effect.

If it be objected that all economic activities are not deliberate, I would reply that, even when economic actions are reflex (resulting from an established habit) or instinctive, there seems usually to be a pleasant reaction of feeling accompanying or following them. For instance, a man who has the constructive instinct strongly will find his fingers itching for work, as did William Morris, and will find pleasure even in the monotonous operations of weaving, if his interest be centred in the growth of his own design. The vast majority of actions connected with work unquestionably are deliberate and the outcome of a conscious preference or balance of feeling.

It will now be evident that there are three kinds of income, whether we consider individuals or the whole population collectively. The first is the income in money ; the second the income in the form of the actual goods and services which the money income will purchase ; and the third is the psychic income, or net income of pleasant feeling, which those goods and services produce in the person who consumes, uses or receives them. When we aim at economic equality, in which of these three kinds of income are inequalities to be measured and equality to be established ?

We may at once rule out the psychic income, for the very good reason that no way has been discovered of comparing the intensity of feeling which one person experiences with that which another is experiencing. In fact, we can only compare the ratios in which people find enjoyment or utility in two different events or things. We can recognize that·one person may consider an apple or twenty nuts to be equally desirable, and be uncertain which to choose ; whilst another person, liking nuts very much, or apples very little, would consider ten nuts the equivalent of one apple. We can only in a very rough way say that one person is happier than another ; and then our estimate is of the happiness caused by *all* the person's experiences, imagination and will-power. The economic causes, positive and negative, cannot be disentangled from other causes.

It being admittedly impossible to equalize psychic incomes, it would seem that any basis giving the nearest approach thereto would be desirable. If it be suggested that equal incomes in terms of goods would give the nearest approach to equality of psychic income we may at once negative the suggestion. Equality of incomes in terms of goods could only mean that each person should have apportioned to him the same share or ration of every kind of food and all other things as every other person. A standard ration for all kinds of goods is on the face of it ridiculous. Theoretically, the fact that it would not maximize enjoyment may be explained by observing that each individual would find that the marginal utility of certain commodities was high and of others very low : i.e. that he had too little of some and much more than he wanted of others. This would certainly not maximize his psychic income.

The only possible common measure of all the various commodities of a market is money ; and this is the only form of income which can in practice be equalized for all persons. We must accept this fact and consider what will be the psychic results of equal money incomes for all adults, men and women alike.

THE ABOLITION OF MONEY

In a planned and regulated economic system like communism the term *money*, if used at all, must have a different signification from that with which we are familiar in a society based on exchange. It will be entirely unnecessary to have any actual money in circulation, whether in the form of coin or paper money. It would, of course, be possible to abolish money even in our present society, and conduct all exchanges by means of book transfers on a universal State bank—an extension of the post office cheque system widely adopted on the Continent of Europe. This, however, would involve so much labour in book-keeping, when the mass of small payments characteristic of our present life is considered, that it would be uneconomical to abolish money.

In a regulated national economy, however, a host of small payments could be completely abolished by rendering the services gratis to an extent sufficient to meet every person's reasonable need. Not only could water, electricity, newspapers and gas be supplied free, but omnibus and tram fares and local journeys by train need not be charged ; neither should the services of the doctor and the barber. Many kinds of goods usually bought in small quantities, such as pins and matches, might very likely be supplied gratis, as is done now, for instance, in a small community like an ocean liner ; eventually, perhaps, also bread, butter, milk, sugar, salt, soap, and so on. With the almost complete abolition of petty payments would come the possibility of effecting all the consumer's purchases of goods and services by means of book debits against a single account kept for each person in some central place.

The system which I suggest as being the simplest is that every person should be allowed a credit income (termed *general allowance* elsewhere in this book) stated in terms of money units in the ledger of the general store at which it is most convenient for him to make most of his purchases. The credit income would be the same in amount for every adult man and woman ; and marriage would not alter either party's income. Every man and woman would have to select the store at which he or she wished usually to deal, and he or she would then be credited monthly in the office of that store with one-twelfth of the total credit income for that year. A numerical system of distinguishing accounts would be economical and would expedite business. Every store would probably be denoted by a group of three letters, and each account kept at that store would be assigned a number. Thus if a person had his account at a branch store in Nottingham the letters NM might signify the town Nottingham, the third letter the particular branch store, and the number following the particular account at that store. Thus, a person's account might be NMd–7815. London would need so many branch stores that the first letter L alone would be used to indicate the town, and it would read somewhat as follows: Lbh–11589. The British Monomark system supplies an existing precedent ; as also the system of letters and numbers adopted a few years ago in London to indicate telephone numbers owing to the introduction of automatic exchanges.

The system here suggested is similar to that described by Bellamy in *Looking Backward* ; but he postulated the existence of ' banks ' for keeping these credit accounts. It seems to me obvious that ledger accounts would have to be kept at the stores in any case, and that the simplest plan is to debit the cost of services of every kind, including railway travelling, foreign telegrams, and so forth, to the one account, namely, that kept at the store. Wherever a person travelled throughout Great Britain he could go to any store and purchase any article. There being no money he would not, of course, pay for it. He would simply quote the number of his account at his home store, and, excepting for small sums, might be required to sign a debit voucher, of which he would be handed a carbon copy. The store at which he made a purchase would then simply forward the voucher to the store indicated by the letters which the purchaser had given, and his account would be debited with the amount.

It may be thought that this system would be widely abused ; that some people would draw very freely on their accounts when travelling without being careful not to overdraw. This, however, is merely a question of custom or habit. I think the usual rule would be that no person might overdraw his account by a greater amount than the equivalent of the monthly instalment of credit. He would be expected normally to have his account in credit ; and a person who was continually overdrawn would receive an official reminder that he must curtail his expenditure. If he ignored the reminder he would be penalized by a fine from succeeding months' credit. Persistent abuse of his privilege would, of course, bring him sooner or later before a court of justice, with the liability of being sentenced to detention in a penal colony. We may well believe that public opinion would so strongly censure any person who deliberately ignored the law in regard to obtaining goods from stores other than his own that a person convicted or sentenced for such an offence would become more or less of a social out-cast on his return from the penal colony. We may be sure that society as a whole would give effect to its desire that such a convenient system should be workable.

In this book I have given the name *general allowance* to the credit income at the stores, because it is quite conceivable that there might be special allowances for certain purposes ; as, for example, for holiday travel, for purchase of books by teachers, perhaps of alcoholic liquors, use of motor-car, etc. This would amount to rationing particular commodities and services.

THE NEED OF VARIETY IN METHODS OF SUPPLY

In the organization of supply the principle to be aimed at should be to build up a system which would embrace every method of dealing with the consumer, and to adopt for each kind of service and every class of goods that method which would accord best with its physical character and the economic nature of the demand, that is to say, its elasticity, the relative magnitude of transactions, and so forth. Various writers have advocated different methods of putting goods into consumption. In *Utopia* and *News from Nowhere* people are allowed to take gratis from the stores whatever quantities of goods of all kinds they require. Bellamy appears to have intended that all goods and services should be paid for through the credit income. Other writers have assumed a rationing system—an elaboration of the manner in which soldiers are housed, fed and clothed.

In reality the utilization of all these three methods at once will serve best to meet the very varied character of goods and services. The first method, free supply without limit, is particularly appropriate for at least four different classes of goods and services, namely : (1) goods and services commonly used in small amount at one time, e.g. rides in tramcars and omnibuses, lead pencils, matches, etc. ; (2) goods which every one wants to consume and the supply of which requires much labour or costly apparatus to measure and account for, e.g. supply of water and electricity ; (3) goods for which the demand curve for nearly all persons is inelastic, e.g. salt, spices, soap, ink, and a host of minor commodities ; (4) the services of doctors, dentists and provision of nurses, hospital treatment, medicines and everything connected with maintenance and restoration of health.

The second method, namely, payment by debit at the stores against the general allowance, is appropriate for all kinds of goods the demand for which is elastic. The third method, the supply of a regular quantity per annum or per mensem, either by means of a ration determined in quantity, or by means of a special allowance, would be advantageous only in a few special cases in a society which had reached a stage of advanced economic well-being, such as America or any of the western European countries. In these countries commodities might be rationed (1) on account of their deleterious character, such as alcoholic drinks, cigarettes and drugs ; (2) on account of temporary shortage of supply ; (3) in cases where it was desirable for some reason to fix the price of supply decidedly below the demand price for the quantity per annum at which it would be practicable to supply to the public all that it would buy. The last class of cases would probably include some particularly beneficial or pleasing kinds of goods or services, as, for example, hand-made table-ware, certain foreign artistic goods, or seats at the opera, theatre, or concerts.

NATURE OF ' MONEY ' UNITS AND ' PRICES '

In the case of those goods and services which are supplied through the general or a special allowance a ' price ' must be used for purposes of accounting. We must be clear exactly what this ' price ' is, and how it will be determined. It differs in two ways from market prices, or even the retail prices of shops, with which we are now familiar. From the point of view of theory the difference is so considerable that the adoption of a new term would seem advisable. To this course, however, there are two objections : in the first place, the word ' price ' is at present in use in special cases with a meaning closely analogous to that with which it is here used ; and in the second place, whatever term might be adopted for theoretical purposes would never be likely to come into common use, because the connotation of the term price can be so easily extended to the meaning which it will have in connexion with the general allowance that people are sure to make this extension and to continue to use the term.

From the abstract point of view the general allowance must be regarded as a measure of the call which every citizen is entitled to make upon the products of the labour of the community. It must be expressed in terms of some unit ; and this might be ' labour-hours ' or anything similar. The number of units which have to be given for a unit of any kind of goods is sure to be spoken of as the ' price ' of that article ; hence it will be more convenient to use the name of a familiar monetary unit like the pound or shilling. The nature of this unit I shall consider presently. It will evidently bear a close analogy with what is called *money of account*. In former centuries it not infrequently happened that accounts were kept in some monetary unit representing a coin which had been in circulation at some previous time. Thus the coins in actual circulation differed in name and value from the money of account which, at the time, had become purely arbitrary, depending for its relation to current coin on a legal ordinance.

Whatever the monetary units may be in which the general allowance will be calculated, units by weight or otherwise of each of the various commodities and services offered will be supplied for different numbers of units of the general allowance. We may, therefore, define ' price ' in the system of communism as the number of units of the general allowance which will be cancelled for one unit of the commodity supplied. This price will be arbitrarily determined by authority, and not by demand and supply ; though considerations relating to the demand and to the supply of the commodity are likely in nearly all cases to enter into the authoritative determination of the price.

We need not search far for analogies in the present state of society. Municipal corporations often supply water for certain purposes by meter, charging perhaps sixpence per thousand gallons. This is a purely arbitrary price which may be greater or less than the actual cost of supply, but is undoubtedly determined with reference to the cost of supply and with reference to the demand for the purposes in question, mainly industrial. Arbitrary prices, too, are fixed for the services of the post, telegraph and telephone, and to some extent in railway transport, as for example, workmen's fares, and perhaps season tickets on State railways. It is not only public authorities, however, who fix arbitrary prices. Public utility companies operating services having the type of a natural monopoly, as, for example, electricity and gas supply, and commercial and industrial combinations which have achieved a practical monopoly throughout a country, or a large part of it, adopt the policy of fixing their prices only with general reference to maximizing monopoly revenue. In the one case they may be subject to legal limitations, both maximum and minimum, or they may think it advisable to set a reasonable limit to their profits ; and in the other case, though legally free to vary the price, trade custom and the habits of the public require the maintenance of fixed prices over periods of a year or more. Well-known articles such as typewriters or proprietary medicines are sold in all parts of the country at a fixed price, which remains unchanged for many years in spite of changes in the cost of production. Thus there are many precedents, both public and commercial, for arbitrary fixation of prices, with only general reference to the conditions of demand and supply.

What should be the nature of the units in which the general allowance is to be computed is not so simple a question as might at first be thought. Writers of the early nineteenth century advocated labour notes being put in circulation, labour time being thus assumed as the basis of the distribution of wealth. According to this suggestion every unit of a finished commodity, having required for its production and transport so many hours' labour of one or more persons, its price should be stated as the total of ' man hours '. The idea of basing prices upon labour time solely is very attractive to the socialist, and it might be thought that the units of the general allowance could be made to represent ' labour-days ' or ' labour-hours ' ; the price being the sum of all the hours and minutes during which every one of the several workers in each of the different stages of production was occupied in contributing to the fashioning of the finished article. There is, however, a difficulty in this, as I shall explain farther on. Certainly the units could not be consistently named ' labour-hours '.

In all probability, when ' the Day ' arrives for the change

over to communism, the name of the then existing principal
money unit—in England presumably still the pound sterling—
will continue to be used to denote the arbitrary units of the
general allowance. Habit is so strong in the average person
that this emphasis on the analogy to credit transactions in
money would facilitate the transition. Whether the total of
the general allowance credited to each person were to be £200
per annum or £10,000 per annum would, however, be entirely
arbitrary, the level at which prices were to be fixed depending
upon the total assigned for the general allowance.

INCOMES AND SATISFACTION

We have now to enter upon a somewhat difficult part of our
subject, with a view to inquiring more closely what is meant
by economic equality, and how far we may expect this ideal,
whatever it·is exactly, to be realized by any practicable
arrangement of the distribution of wealth. We are forced to
meet one of the strongest arguments which is constantly quoted
against proposals for equalizing incomes, namely, that equal
incomes certainly would not produce equal enjoyment. This
seems to many thoughtful persons an obvious objection to
communism, from which they can see no escape. That it has
some degree of validity no economist would deny ; and yet the
truth may well be that communism, organized more or less as
outlined in this book, is nevertheless the best economic system
which it is practicable for mankind to attain within any foresee-
able period of time.

There are general laws in economic theory concerning the
relation of a person's enjoyment or satisfaction [1] to the size of

---

[1] There is no agreement among economists as to the term to be used to
signify the positive, i.e. desirable, state of feeling. *Welfare, satisfaction,
pleasure, pleasant state of feeling,* have all been used in much the same sense,
to mean reduction or avoidance of unpleasant feeling as well as production or
increase of pleasant feeling, produced by some thing or action which is transferable, or could be the subject of a bargain. I use the word *enjoyment* in a
slightly wider sense, as including both welfare or satisfaction, as above defined,
and the more highly emotional states of pleasant feeling which we call *delight*
and *joy*—the most important constituents of happiness ; and which are due,
to a large extent—at any rate, as regards their intensity—to that enlargement
of personality which results from education and travel, and association at an
early age with persons of refinement and culture. Such development of
personality is almost always the result of money or other resources having
been available for widening the education and experience of the man or woman

his personal income, to his innate and acquired characteristics, to the nature of the environment in which he lives and works, and the cost of living in his locality. The acquired characters of importance in this connexion are those due to social contacts, education and travel, and they increase in number and degree of development as the person grows older and habits of thought and action become fixed. The reader will find these facts and principles explained in those of the modern treatises on economics which devote attention to the theory of utility. Here it is only possible to state such of the accepted economic laws as bear directly on our subject.

It is characteristic of all men that the more they have of a thing in stock, or regularly available for use or consumption, the less intensely do they want more of it. In its formal statement this is known as the law of *diminishing marginal utility*. It applies to things individually, and also to the sum total of the things which a man possesses or receives, and thus also to the means of obtaining the things he wants, namely, his money income. Furthermore, as a rule, the decrease of marginal utility is not proportional to the increase of income, but less than in proportion. The intensity with which a man wants another shilling declines rapidly for the first hundred shillings received if he starts in a penniless condition ; but, if he becomes rich, and has £1,000 at his disposal at any moment, he cares but little whether he has a shilling more or less. So, also, £10 increase or decrease of income makes little difference to the man with £2,000 a year, but a big difference to one who earns but £100 a year ; and for incomes of intermediate size the difference of satisfaction is intermediate, though not in proportion. An increase of £10 per annum will afford a decided increase of satisfaction to any man with a small income. As we get up to £400, or £500, per annum, the increase of satisfaction which £10 will yield gets less and less, but more and more slowly so ; and thus, when we get to an income of about

in youth or early adult life. Occasionally it is the result of resources having been available to the parents, though not to their children. It is very rare to find a person with a fine appreciation of music, art, or books who has not benefited from expenditure on himself or a previous generation larger than a working-class family could possibly afford. In using the phrase *means of enjoyment* I have in mind that the means may refer to expenditure or utilization of resources at a time long preceding the enjoyment, the effect being, so to speak, stored up in the person, or even in his children.

£2,000 a year, each additional £10 added to the income adds comparatively little to the satisfaction—and still less, if the income be £5,000 or more. If a person cares for ostentation, however, the decline of the marginal utility of money with increase of income takes place much more slowly.

It would seem, therefore, that we could always increase human welfare—that is, add to that part of the happiness of the people in general which is purchasable—by transferring portions of their incomes from the rich to the poor. This would be true, however, only if all persons were exactly alike in their tastes and in the amount of satisfaction they could obtain from expending a given sum of money ; whereas in fact the reverse is true. People certainly do experience satisfaction with different intensities according as their power of appreciation varies, which may be due to differences of innate sensibility, to early upbringing, or to education and general culture. Education, social intercourse with cultured people, and foreign travel develop in a young person many new powers of intellectual exercise and aesthetic appreciation, thus affording unnumbered opportunities of enjoyment which the uncultured person will always miss. Hence, generally speaking, the more refined the person the greater the direct enjoyment which he gets from the wise expenditure of his income. The larger the income the truer this is. The poor man who has never had the desire or opportunity to acquire culture, if he gets suddenly rich, soon spends up to the limit of satisfaction on the pleasures to which he is accustomed ; and he knows no others. There remains as the object of further expenditure only the indirect, or subjective, pleasure of ostentation. Let him believe that other people will speak with admiration of his cleverness and wealth, and every expenditure which contributes to this idea is a further source of satisfaction to him.

The ordinary working man, however, who might suddenly grow rich would have neither the culture nor refinement for a substantial increase of true enjoyment, nor the knowledge and adaptability requisite for successful ostentation, if he were that way inclined. It may be taken as true generally, therefore, that an average working man who might suddenly inherit an income of £5,000 a year would get more satisfaction from it than he could from the £150 a year that he earned previously ;

but whether he inherited £1,000 per annum or £5,000 per annum would not make any great difference to the amount by which his happiness would be increased. On the other hand, it would make a great difference to a highly educated man, earning, say, £300 a year, whether it were £1,000 or £5,000 per annum that he inherited.

The psychic effects of a compulsory transference of income from the rich to the poor have been stated carefully by Professor Pigou in his authoritative work *Economics of Welfare*. He does not go so far as to assume equalization of incomes, but is concerned with social legislation for providing out of taxation State unemployment benefit, pensions for the aged and others incapable of supporting themselves adequately, and so forth ; that is, funds for preserving the poor in general from hardships. His statements and reasoning can be extended logically to the ultimate case of the equalization of incomes.

Basing his argument on the well-known law of diminishing marginal utility, Professor Pigou writes : [1] ' It is evident that any transference of income from a relatively rich man to a relatively poor man of similar temperament, since it enables more intense wants to be satisfied at the expense of less intense wants, must increase the aggregate sum of satisfaction. The old " law of diminishing utility " thus leads securely to the proposition : Any cause which increases the absolute share of real income in the hands of the poor, provided that it does not lead to a contraction in the size of the national dividend from any point of view, will, in general, increase economic welfare. This conclusion is further fortified by another consideration. Mill wrote : " Men do not desire to be *rich*, but to be richer than other men. The avaricious or covetous man would find little or no satisfaction in the possession of any amount of wealth, if he were the poorest amongst all his neighbours or fellow-countrymen." . . . The part played by comparative, as distinguished from absolute, income is likely to be small for incomes that only suffice to provide the necessaries and primary comforts of life, but to be large with large incomes. In other words, a larger proportion of the satisfaction yielded by the incomes of rich people comes from their *relative*,

---

[1] *Economics of Welfare*, Part I, Chapter VIII, § 3, 2nd edition, pp. 78–81 ; 3rd edition (1929), pp. 91–4.

rather than from their absolute, amount. This part of it will not be destroyed if the incomes of all rich people are diminished together. The loss of economic welfare suffered by the rich when command over resources is transferred from them to the poor will, therefore, be substantially smaller relatively to the gain of economic welfare to the poor than a consideration of the law of diminishing utility taken by itself suggests.

' It must be conceded, of course, that, if the rich and the poor were two races with different mental constitutions, such that the rich were inherently capable of securing a greater amount of economic satisfaction from any given income than the poor, the possibility of increasing welfare by this type of change would be seriously doubtful. Furthermore, even without any assumption about inherent racial difference, it may be maintained that a rich man, from the nature of his upbringing and training, is capable of obtaining considerably more satisfaction from a given income—say a thousand pounds —than a poor man would be. For, if anybody accustomed to a given standard of living suddenly finds his income enlarged, he is apt to dissipate the extra income in forms of exciting pleasure, which, when their indirect, as well as their direct, effects are taken into account, may even lead to a positive loss of satisfaction. To this argument, however, there is a sufficient answer. It is true that at any given moment the tastes and temperament of persons who have long been poor are more or less adjusted to their environment, and that a sudden and sharp rise of income is likely to be followed by a good deal of foolish expenditure, which involves little or no addition to economic welfare. If, however, the higher income is maintained for any length of time, this phase will pass ; whereas, if the increase is gradual or, still better, if it comes about in such a way as not to be directly perceived—through a fall in prices, for example— the period of foolishness need not occur at all. In any case, to contend that the folly of poor persons is so great that a rise of income among them will not promote economic welfare in any degree, is to press paradox beyond the point up to which discussion can reasonably be called upon to follow. The true view, as I conceive it, is admirably stated by Messrs. Pringle and Jackson in their special report to the Poor Law Commissioners : '' It is in the unskilled and least educated part of the population that drink continues to hold its ground ; as greater regularity of employment and higher wages are achieved by sections of the working-classes the men rise in respectability and character. That the drink bill is diminishing, while wages are rising throughout the country, is one of the most hopeful indications of progress we possess."[1] The root of the matter is that, even when, under existing conditions, the mental constitution of poor persons is such that an enlarged income will at the moment yield them little benefit, yet, after a time— more especially if the time is long enough to allow a new generation to grow up—the possession of such an income will make possible the development in them, through education and otherwise, of capacities and faculties adapted for the enjoyment of the enlarged income. Thus, in the long run differences of temperament and taste between rich and poor are overcome by the very fact of a shifting of income between them. Plainly, therefore, they cannot be used as an argument to disprove the benefits of a transference.'[2]

There are other well-recognized principles relating to a person's psychic income—that is to say, to his enjoyment of life resulting from his environment—which we may recall to mind here with advantage. The amount of his money is, of course, only a part of his environment, and the satisfaction he obtains from it depends upon its purchasing power ; that is, upon the prices of the things he wants most—in other words, the cost of living. There is the question too of the quality of the things he can buy : is the food unadulterated and nourishing ? Is the clothing which fashion or the shops compel comfortable and durable ? His rent may procure for him a dirty, dark, unhealthy and inconvenient house, or one entirely to his liking. Much of the enjoyment of life depends on whether the climate is suitable to a person's constitution, upon the absence of extremes in variation of temperature, and in rain or dryness. The natural and artificial amenities of the locality are of great importance. A person who could earn the same income in a dirty fog-bound North of England

---

[1] (Cd. 4795), p. 46.
[2] ' Similarly, of course, when we are taking a long view, the argument that a reduction in the real income of the rich inflicts a special injury, because it forces them to abandon habits to which they have grown accustomed, loses most of its force.'

industrial town or amidst the beautiful hills of Surrey would choose the latter, other things being equal, or nearly so—such as accessibility of family and friends and the manifold conveniences and pleasures of town life. Not only the layout and gardens of a town, but even the manners and customs of its people, may be an important factor for any individual in determining the sum total of his enjoyment. We have here to take a wide view of life. So doing, we find that any and every thing which affects a person's welfare, bodily or psychic, and is capable of being modified by him or by others, individually or collectively, is a cause which can be, and usually should be, taken account of, and if necessary modified, by organized authority in a state of communism.

EQUAL OPPORTUNITY OF ENJOYMENT

Perhaps it may be said that the two main objects of communism are, on the one hand, by universal co-operation greatly to increase the productive power of the nation, and, on the other hand, to introduce equality of economic condition amongst all men, both as an end in itself and as a means to realizing universal co-operation. It is this phrase 'equality of economic condition' which we have now to examine and define with as much accuracy as we can. Our object is to determine which are the experiences and means of life in respect of which equality may be conceived as possible ; and in respect of which of them it may be desirable and, if so, practicable. It is necessary first to obtain precise ideas which are sound theoretically, and then to consider by what measures the desired degree of equality can be most fully realized in a state of society the organization of which may be regarded as presenting no insuperable obstacles.

Equality of economic condition does not mean merely equality of incomes. A nearer approach to a precise definition of the idea would be to assume that it implies equality, not only of incomes, but of all other factors of the environment also. It would be impossible, however, to arrange equality of environment for all persons ; for obviously they must live in different places, some of which must be less desirable than others. We are thus thrown back on the principle of compensation. Those who have to live in unpleasant surroundings, or do objectionable work, must be allowed some special advantages or gratifications denied to those who live in pleasant places or have interesting and enjoyable work. Hence we see that the only principle which we can justify theoretically is that the aim of communism should be to secure for everybody equal enjoyment of life. That is the only principle which embodies fully the idea of fraternity, and satisfies every charitable impulse of brotherly love.

There is, however, an insuperable difficulty in using the principle of equality of enjoyment as a test of practical proposals ; for no method has been discovered yet of measuring and comparing the relative amounts of enjoyment which people experience, either as a whole or from a particular activity. Often we can tell from a man's or woman's looks, words or demeanour, whether he or she is leading in general a happy or unhappy life ; but, as a quantitative measure, that would be too vague, and opinions would differ so widely that we dare not attempt it.

We are driven thus to the conclusion that the only principle which the communist State can usefully adopt for regulating the distribution of wealth is that of endeavouring to provide for every person equal *opportunities* of enjoyment. This means trying to secure equality in the distribution of the *means* of enjoyment, so far as these are material and transferable ; to which must be added compensation for unavoidable inequality of an unusual degree in conditions of life or work. It will not be necessary perhaps in many cases to seek to counteract circumstances of life and work which are more than usually agreeable—a joyful person is indeed an asset to neighbours and associates ; but in the case of bad conditions which cannot be rectified, some sort of non-monetary compensation, of a kind to meet the wishes of the person concerned, might well be arranged. It was suggested in another chapter that, after the preliminary reorganization of industries following the adoption of communism, invention will be directed, and much expenditure of a capital nature be incurred, in removing unhealthy, disgusting or unpleasant conditions of work and in rebuilding homes on garden-city lines. Yet there must needs remain for many years a number of tasks to be performed the abolition

14

of which would involve inordinate capital outlay. Compensation, such, for example, as long holiday leave, could then be granted; but compensation may, perhaps, in some such cases, be automatically provided by the public esteem in which people who sacrifice themselves for the good of the community will be held. We may conclude that equalization of the opportunities and means of enjoyment or satisfaction is the general principle on which communism must be, and will be, based, and is the interpretation which we must give to the phrase ' equality of economic condition '. Let us proceed then to some studies of the applications of this principle in devising the organization of communism.

First, there is the technical question of prices. If in certain places certain goods are to be charged at higher prices than in other places, persons who rely largely on those goods will suffer in the places where prices are high as compared with similar persons in places where prices are low. Thus, theoretically, prices should be uniform throughout the whole area of the commonwealth, unless there is any counterbalancing advantage which goes with high prices or disadvantage with low prices.

Apart, however, from the question of prices of goods supplied through the general allowance, there are hundreds of circumstances which affect every person's enjoyment. His environment is made up of the character of the house and street or road in which he lives, the pleasantness or otherwise of the surrounding country, the purity, dryness, or bracing quality of the atmosphere, innumerable social contacts, and public facilities such as libraries, baths, theatres and organized sports. So important are the social advantages of town life that men of enterprise and education are loath to live in the depths of the country, and the agricultural population is constantly depleted of persons who can make their way in the cities.

A review of the actual facts should be sufficient, therefore, to convince any one that it would be impossible for the most efficient organization conceivable to give to persons in different places and occupations equal access to the means of enjoyment. It does not follow from this, however, that it is useless to attempt to make opportunities of obtaining enjoyment far more equal than they are at present. Such opportunities are distributed now with extreme inequality. The social conscience has been aroused sufficiently for social legislation and housing reform, and heavy income-tax and death duties, to do a little already in the direction of relieving this inequality. Socialistic legislation would continually lessen the inequality ; but communism, organized more or less as here described, would provide a form of distribution of wealth which would approach as nearly as can be to equality in the distribution of the means of enjoyment. It may be assumed that there will be a conscious endeavour to attain equality in this respect. The administrators of the time, guided perhaps by economists, will not rest content with providing every one with an equal credit income—the general allowance. They will realize that there are many other factors entering into the conditions of life which must be taken into consideration.

Besides the economic principles already mentioned, there are, for instance, at least three other general considerations which affect the problem of distributing equally the means of enjoyment, which I may now mention, the last of them being of importance only in the period immediately following the adoption of communism. There is first the fact that people may, and indeed seem to, differ innately in the facility with which they develop new wants in reaction to their education and environment. Two children of the same sex in the same family brought up in the same way develop quite different habits in regard to wanting things—one satisfied with the old toys, the other craving always for novelty, having an insatiable curiosity. To the former in later life saving is easy ; the latter tends to be a spendthrift. Difference in parental or other guidance or instruction may accentuate or lessen such divergencies in the growth of wants.

Secondly, there is the difficulty that different persons, having different tastes, are accustomed to consume different commodities in very different quantities. Furthermore, some dislike and avoid altogether things which others most desire. Obviously no system which did not cater for this variety of taste as well and as fairly as our present economy would survive a twelvemonth in a democracy like Britain. But beyond actually providing the goods and services needed to satisfy the inevitable variety of taste, there arises the question of relative prices. When these are to a large extent arbitrarily arranged by predetermined policy it may become a difficult question to decide whether the resources at the disposal of the community should be directed towards cheapening one product or another. Are those who live on nuts and apples to be given preference over those who consume meat, eggs and dairy products? Is a fish diet to be encouraged, and is the eating of bread of ultra-white flour to be discouraged? Should efforts be made to cheapen woollen garments, or should it be cotton or artificial silk that is to be favoured? General inquiry from store committees, as well as statistics of actual demand, might indicate what was the general desire; but whatever decision was made would result in inequality of benefit to persons having different tastes. This would be no worse, however, than at present, when our customs and excise duties penalize those specially fond of tobacco, spirits, cigars, tea, sugar, silk, and several other things. The only possible conclusion is that in the application of capital and labour to improvements of supply the interests of persons with different tastes would have to be kept in view.

Thirdly, there is a principle which is of considerable importance in the initiation of communism. If the new standard of living which is equal for all is a high one, those who were formerly well-to-do and had a high standard of living will feel the change much less than if they were to be forced down to a much lower standard of living comparable with that of the working classes to-day. I can best express what I mean by hypothetical figures. Suppose there were two men, A and B, whose family incomes before the change were respectively £5,000 and £150 per annum. If the standard of living after the change is equal for both A and B to what £600 per annum net [1] would have represented before the change, A will feel the hardship much less than if the new standard of living were to correspond with what £200 per annum would have represented before the change. Hence, so far as the aim is to realize equality of enjoyment as nearly as possible, the change should be postponed until the £600 per annum standard is assured.

It may be observed that the question of the realizable standard of living after the change has also a political aspect.

[1] By ' net ' income is meant after payment of income tax.

There being a large percentage of the population which would have already an income of about £200 per annum before the change these would gain nothing by it, if the new standard of living were to correspond with only £200 per annum. The rich and well-to-do would expect to suffer hardship and would bitterly oppose the change, and only the very poor would gain. The conclusion from this is that a country is not ripe for the introduction of communism unless there has been already a great industrial development which has created a considerable *rentier* class living on rent, profit and interest ; for this means a considerable surplus of the national dividend above the standard of living of the working classes, and also so large a body of skilled organizers and technical experts that the introduction of universal co-operation would be practicable and would result in a great increase in the efficiency of industry, This explains why real communism cannot possibly be successfully established in Russia, and why it is likely to be realized first in England, Germany, America or Australia. Russia must be content for several decades with State socialism : an intermediate phase which has its own difficulties, especially the continuance of money in circulation and of private enterprise in agriculture.

The problem of realizing equality of distribution of the means of enjoyment is, as I have shown, theoretically insoluble. Nevertheless, by keeping this aim steadily in view, a fairly close approximation thereto could be achieved which would be of immense benefit to the mass of the people.

The theoretical conclusions to be drawn from a discussion of the problem of equality in the distribution of wealth may appear disconcerting at first sight. Yet they are not so when considered in their true perspective. It is important to distinguish the temporary aspect of the problem during the period immediately following the realization of communism from its permanent aspect for all succeeding time. Throughout most of the former period a large proportion of the population will have been educated under the old economic system, with its distinctions of wealth and class. It is true, as Pigou states, that equalization of incomes might mean an actual reduction of the sum total of enjoyment, or welfare, as he prefers to put it, because the poor would gain less enjoyment by increased income than the well-to-do would lose. I do not say that I would subscribe to this statement, when relative numbers are considered ; but it is possible. Let us assume that it will be as Pigou describes. Is that any reason for denying or delaying the realization of communism ?

We have to consider whether communism as the ultimate state of society is desirable or not, and to set against the net advantages we may find in it the losses which must be incurred during the transition and early period of realization. The first generation of children growing up under communism will not have the marked differences of standard of life and culture existing amongst their parents ; though parental influence will undoubtedly differentiate them to some extent. Their children, however, that is, the second generation brought up under communism, are likely to differ amongst themselves but little according to the economic status of their grandparents. All will have had the same opportunities of education and cultural experience ; and nearly the same level of refinement will have been reached everywhere through longer stay at improved schools and colleges. This does not mean that there will be any attempt to turn out young people educated according to a uniform pattern by a kind of mass production in teaching. That indeed is what State-provided and inspected schools tend to do now. It will be realized that variety of knowledge and personality is highly desirable ; that only essential ideals and standards of morality must be common to all.

Within two generations, therefore, the population is likely to have become nearly equalized throughout as regards standard of living and capacity for wise enjoyment of income. For a much shorter period only would the hardship on the former well-to-do be severe. One or two generations is but a short time in the life of a people ; and there is not the slightest reason why we should not plan a change which might involve some regression of happiness for a brief span of years in order to realize a clear progression to last for ages thereafter.

The principle underlying the establishment of communism may be put in this way : that it is right to afford all the people as nearly as possible equal means of enjoyment, in the belief that the people will adjust themselves to the system, rather than to retain in existence an evil system of distribution in order that the distribution of incomes may accord with the present composition of society. The progress of civilization has frequently affected adversely the interests of large classes of people, as, for example, workers deprived of their livelihood by the introduction of machinery, and bondholders ruined by devaluation of the currency; but such have been the inevitable results of economic and social progress, of war and of the safeguarding of democracy, and must be yet again.

Turning now to consider what are likely to be the practicable measures for securing as nearly as may be equality in the means of enjoyment, we may be sure that equality of the general allowance for all adults of both sexes would be its foundation. For children the allowance would be less. It might start during infancy at one-eighth of the adult allowance, and rise gradually to half at the age of eighteen, from which time it would be put at the disposal of the young person, instead of being drawn on by his or her parents. By further annual increases the allowance might reach the full amount for adults at the age of twenty-five.

As between persons in different occupations, and living in different places, every endeavour would be made to provide equally pleasant and healthy conditions for home life and for work. The policy would be to provide equally good housing conditions for all in garden-city environment. All rural workers, men and women, might have telephones and wireless receivers, and be allowed special privileges in transport, such as a motor-cycle each and a car for the family, horses for riding when wanted, travelling lecturers, cinemas, libraries, and so forth. By these and other privileges a rough equalization of means of enjoyment could be sought, and a result incomparably better than the present system of inequality would be attained.

IMMIGRATION AND EMIGRATION

Questions of practical importance which cannot fail to need careful adjustment from time to time will be the rights of immigrants and emigrants, and the provision necessary for the convenience of travellers. There must be definite laws as to who shall enjoy the privileges of citizenship—the unlimited and the measured services, the right to housing accommodation, and to the travel and special allowances. All persons born in the country, or both of whose parents were citizens, would doubtless, on the analogy of the present-day law of domicile, be accounted citizens of the commonwealth provided they resided in Great Britain ; but how would a foreigner, or a resident of one of the British countries overseas, be treated if he desired to live for a period, or settle permanently, in England ? What would be the fate of an English citizen who desired to live abroad temporarily or permanently ? Would he lose all rights in his own country ?

These questions are more difficult to answer than they would be if there were money in circulation, which could be saved and taken with one. But it is of the essence of communism that there should be no money in circulation. Hence adjustments in respect of any person entering or leaving the country must be made by credit arrangements ; and, to secure uniformity of treatment, such arrangements would have to conform with rules having the force of law. The general idea of the rules would be to secure a business arrangement fair to both countries and to the individual.

Let us take first the case of travellers. We may suppose that an English citizen is sent abroad on business. How, then, would he finance his travelling expenses ? He might be going to a country which had adopted communism, or to one still under the competitive system. In the former case he would take with him a letter of recommendation, which would be honoured by giving him all the privileges, other than political, of the country he was visiting. He could thus live and travel where he liked during the period covered by his official letter of recommendation ; and on his leaving a debit note against England would issue from the country he had visited, calculated merely on the time he was there at the rate corresponding with the computed monthly value of the allowance enjoyed by every citizen of that country. For travelling in a non-communist country he would simply take with him a letter of credit issued by the British National Bank. For persons desiring to go abroad for pleasure the arrangements would probably be similar ; but, as under present-day immigration laws, there would be a limit (six months perhaps, or twelve) after which a tourist would become subject to the rules on immigration.

I think communist countries would afford mutual hospitality to travellers, subject to the person's country of domicile being debited for the value of the services and allowance which he would enjoy in the foreign country. For travelling in money-using countries the Englishman, as above suggested, would take a letter of credit ; but it might be that his expenses would be such that he would require more than the equivalent in the foreign currency of the general allowance which England would be saved for the time he was absent. This contingency would be to some extent provided for by the rule that the general allowance could for any purpose be saved to an amount not exceeeding one month's credit ; and for travelling abroad the amount permitted to be saved might be increased to three months' credit. He would thus have the opportunity of spending abroad the equivalent of five months' general allowance in two months, of six months' allowance in three months, and so on. For a longer stay abroad where foreign currency was required much in excess of the equivalent of the general allowance, some special reason, usually of public interest, like geographical exploration, would have to be shown, as his excess expenditure would have to be met from public funds, and would be a charge on this country's command of foreign exchange resources.

Visitors from other countries to England, if they came from communist countries, would be put on the same footing as our own people (except political rights) for the period for which their own country granted them leave. A visitor from a money-using country would be obliged to produce on landing either a passport and a declaration of his intention to remain no more than forty-eight hours in the country and to leave by the same port, or a letter of credit or cash in foreign currency of the prescribed total value for a certain period of residence, or evidence of a deposit already transferred to his account in this country. The formalities would not usually take longer than it commonly takes a foreign visitor now to have his passport examined and get through the customs, which annoyance would have been abolished, unless smuggling of harmful drugs were suspected. The letter of credit, cash or deposit he would hand over in return for the right to enjoy for a specified period all the usual services and allowances of the country. Probably there would be a maximum period for which a visitor or tourist could stay as such—six or twelve months—after which period he would cease to have the right to housing and the general allowance in return for an income derived from abroad ; and, if permitted to stay longer, would be required to work. This would apply only to visitors below the retiring age—probably fifty-five. It would be against public policy to allow an idle class of foreigners of working age to be living in the country permanently on incomes derived from property in capitalist countries ; but elderly foreigners might be welcomed.

Immigration with a view to permanent settlement would not be encouraged unless the person concerned had special ability, in view of the liability which would be imposed on the country for maintenance of the immigrant when sick and after his retirement at the age of fifty-five or so. Migration from one communist country to another would involve the recovery by means of a capital payment, or an annuity, of a credit equivalent to this liability. Hence objection might come from the country he proposed to leave. An immigrant arriving from a capitalist country would have to bring with him sufficient money to enable him to purchase the right to naturalization and all the privileges of citizenship. Such payment would be like a single premium which nowadays can be paid to an insurance company to purchase an annuity for life. The amount payable by the immigrant would vary from quite a small amount at twenty years of age up to the maximum (quite a large sum) on nearing fifty-five, the retiring age, as from the age of fifty-five he would enjoy the general allowance and all benefits without having given any work to the country.

The right of emigration would be recognized in general, though in some cases there might be conditions to satisfy. For instance, if a man had been at a university and had spent four years thereafter in special training as a doctor or electrical engineer (all necessarily at the country's expense), leave to emigrate might be withheld for a period of ten years, unless the country to which he proposed to go would be ready officially to guarantee refund of the cost of his training. In normal cases, that is to say, of men and women who had begun work in public service at the age of nineteen or twenty, the tendency would be for England to be glad enough to let them go—at any rate, after they had given the country a few years of work. Such persons having no exceptional knowledge or experience, the country would stand only to gain by the lightening of the contingent and probable future burdens on the national dividend for sickness and retirement which their permanent emigration would entail. For the same reason, from the opposite point of view, the country which an English middle-aged emigrant proposed to enter, if it had adopted communism, would probably object to receiving him without the credit of a capital payment or an annuity as a set-off against this liability. The question of the amount to be paid would therefore become a subject of negotiation between countries ; but only rarely in respect of particular persons. Scales of payment graduated according to age and intended to meet all ordinary cases could probably be mutually agreed on between pairs of communist countries, each country having its own scale against immigrants. It is improbable that there could be one general scale applicable as between all communist countries ; because, for a century or more, differences in the standard of living would persist in different countries. Only when the prosperous countries had reached such a high level of material welfare that they ceased to desire further progress in that respect would the poorer countries have a chance of catching up with them.

Ordinary people who had not had a long special training would be allowed to emigrate freely at any age to a capitalist country. If in the twenties, they would have earned no stake in their own country, but, from the age of thirty upwards, a person leaving the country permanently might be thought to have a claim on it for some *quid pro quo* for the privileges which he would surrender. It is possible the country might agree to pay to the individual who emigrated in middle-life an annuity for life similar to, but slightly less than, that which would be paid in his behalf to a communist country if he went there.

The right of a person who had emigrated to return and resume citizenship would, no doubt, be recognized, though the practice would probably be discouraged. As between communist countries the necessary adjustment would be simple enough. If a capital sum had been credited when he went, the sum corresponding with his age would be credited in the reverse direction on his return. If he proposed to return from a capitalist country, and had been absent more than, say, two years, he would have to bring with him a cash or credit payment like a new immigrant; but if he were charged at the same rate as an immigrant, he would not be called on to repay any of the annuity he might have been receiving.

The protection of the country against interlopers, by which I mean persons who evaded compliance with the immigration conditions, would be no more difficult than the enforcement of immigration laws by the United States or Australia is now; in fact it would be easier. Any person who landed irregularly, or any member of the crew of a foreign ship who deserted, could not exist in the country for more than a few days without seeking the hospitality of an hotel, hostel or lodging-house, or getting supplies from a store. In either case he would have to give his number. If fictitious, this would be discovered within two or three days; if he were impersonating some one else, discovery would arise when it was noticed that the person appeared to be in two places at once, judging by vouchers arriving for debit of his account. If the real owner of the number were abroad, that fact would, of course, be known at his store; because he would have to apply for his letter of recommendation, or letter of credit, through his store, and his return to the country would be notified direct by the port immigration officials to his store.

Nevertheless in all probability there would be frequent attempts made by ignorant foreigners to enter the country illegally. One of the few remaining duties of the police, all motives for theft having been abolished, would be patrolling docks and river landing-places to see that rules in regard to landing were obeyed. Captains of ships would probably be required to provide their crews with landing passes on standard British forms, and containing a brief description of the physical characters of the person, such as the American immigration practice has for long required. I have given these details merely to show that a communist society would easily find ways of protecting itself when necessary.

DELINQUENTS

One of the glaring wastes of the modern industrial State is the impossibility of making any economic use of the labour of prisoners and of mental patients who would benefit by doing interesting and useful manual work. It is an inevitable consequence of the competitive system that both employers and organized workers object to the products of jail and asylum labour entering into competition with the products of free labour. Thus there is the loss to the community of the labour of many thousands of able-bodied men, and to the patients and prisoners of the consciousness of doing useful work, which might in many cases help to regenerate them. In India the competitive system is not yet strong enough to prevent the use of prison labour for doing printing and other kinds of work for the Government, and in making carpets, furniture and many other products for sale to the public. Besides this, most of the prisons are provided with extensive fields for cultivation.

At present the average cost of our prisoners, allowing rent for prisons, exceeds what the average workman can earn. Instead of contributing to the national dividend, the prison population is a dead weight charge on it, even worse than the cost of the physically and mentally unfit. Under communism one of the essential principles in dealing with persons whom it may be necessary to detain will be that they should earn their keep ; and that too by means of labour in no way degrading, but such as ordinary members of society have to do.

Crimes against property will have almost completely disappeared, and all those arising from poverty and despair. Every other sort of crime would also diminish, we may be sure ; but there could not fail to be occasional cases of fraud against the public, and of violence due to passion or culpable negligence. In the early years of communism there might be cases of downright refusal to work ; and at all times there would be cases of persistent irregularity and gross negligence. I am very doubtful whether fines, by way of deduction from the general allowance, should be utilized as a penalty. This would retain the commercial idea. To be successful the new economic system must be consistent, and abhor every kind of transaction capable of being treated as a bargain or offset in money.

Most probably no penalty would be imposed for the first offence in the case of all misdemeanours, except negligence which endangered life. Repetition of the offence would involve sentence to a short period of restraint ; and a third occasion of wrongdoing to a much longer term of restraint. This ' restraint ' is my conception of a substitute for imprisonment which could be adopted under communism, and would be designed to have both deterrent and reformative effects. It would mean detention in a colony situated somewhere in Great Britain and covering a large area—anything from four to fifty square miles of country. Therein work would proceed under strict discipline, and for longer hours than in free industry. Agriculture would be the main occupation of such a colony ; but there would be also factories and workshops for making various kinds of goods, so that a man might work with efficient machinery at the occupation to which he was accustomed, or one similar in the skill required. A person under restraint would receive no general allowance during the period of his detention, and the rules of the colony would enforce plain living, with no luxuries.

Each colony could, I think, with advantage be run as a small commonwealth in itself. The total value of the produce of industries during the month would be ascertained, and an estimate would be made of the value of work done in agriculture on the basis of a normal crop. From the total of these would be subtracted the cost of raw materials, depreciation, etc., the debits for time of officials and guards, and the cost of food and other living expenses. The excess of the value of the month's work over all these expenses would be divided up between all the detenues who worked. On release each would find his share of the colony's net earnings placed to his credit at his store in lieu of the general allowance which was suspended. But it is not likely that this would be too large a sum, for the monthly dividend of a colony could hardly amount to more than 5 or 10 per cent of the general allowance, the living expenses of the detenues having been already met in the colony before calculating the dividends. One advantage of this system of self-supporting colonies would be that the community at large would neither gain nor lose economically by the restraint of erring individuals. The detenues themselves would see the justice of the arrangement, and would probably work well with a view to having some dividend.

Each colony would as a matter of fact be a small unit of communism organized in much the same way as the big unit—the country as a whole. Every detenue would learn to understand the working of his colony as a co-operative unit ; and this might well give him more respect for the laws made for working the country as one co-operative unit. In order to secure suitable division of labour the colonies should be large, and four or five for the whole of Great Britain ought to suffice. There would no doubt be a classification of the detenues according to their previous history and present character, with a view to avoiding demoralizing contacts. Education and cultural influences would be made available, and serious cases would come under the examination and observation of psychologists and mental specialists. Continuous research might lead to the causes of some kinds of deliquency becoming understood, and to the protection of young persons from influences which had been shown to have vicious results on certain temperaments. The hereditary, instinctive or pathological origin of certain kinds of antisocial behaviour would become thoroughly known, and cases would be watched accordingly. We may well believe that in course of time scientific, preventive and remedial measures—the teaching of self-control, sensible education, the growing freedom of self-expression in work, and the gradual disappearance of intolerant control in industries—would reduce so greatly the number of second offences that but a single small colony of detention would serve for the whole country.

CHAPTER XII

THE FIXING OF PRICES

GENERAL PRINCIPLES

IT was stated in the last chapter that the prices at which goods will be debited to the general allowance will be arbitrary ; but this does not mean that there will not be principles upon which rules for calculating them will be based. These principles, which may be regarded as an extension of the existing theory of monopoly price, are indeed an essential part of the economic system of communism ; and, through their effect on relative prices, they might conceivably affect to an appreciable degree the distribution of the means of enjoyment. The theory of monopoly price in the case of a monopolist not working for profit (usually a public authority) has been adequately dealt with by Marshall ;[1] and the communist organization of industry as outlined in this book may be regarded as a national, or at least public, monopoly which does not work for profit of each and every kind of goods and services—for private production with a view to sale for profit will be strictly prohibited.

The central price-fixing authority, probably the Council of Supply, will be confronted with two different aspects of the problem of determining the current prices of goods and services. It will seek always, we must assume, the greatest good, with reference to the future and present needs of the whole community, seeking always to balance as nearly as may be the application of additional resources to the satisfaction of the varied tastes of different persons. Thus its main problem will be the consideration of the prices which should be fixed for different goods and services relatively to one another, with special reference to the cost of production, but also taking other factors into consideration. The other aspect of the

---

[1] *Principles of Economics*, Bk. V, Chapter XIV, especially § 8 ; see also A. C: Pigou, *Economics of Welfare*, 2nd ed., p. 373.

problem of price fixation above referred to is the question what is to be the general price level; for obviously, whilst the relative magnitude of prices is fundamental, it is essential, if the economic organization is to work smoothly, that the price level shall have the proper relation to the annual quotas of goods produced and the amount of the general allowance credited to each person.

The principle of seeking the greatest good of the greatest number, combined with the necessity of having an equal general allowance for every adult, must lead to certain rules for the fixation of prices, amongst which, I think, the following will be found to be important : (1) In the first place, the price of every commodity and service must be uniform for all persons throughout the commonwealth. (2) Secondly, the price must be fixed *with reference to* the cost of production, which is mainly labour time. For this purpose the average cost of production in all the producing units throughout the country for a year's working must be used. (3) Lastly, the prices of certain kinds of goods may be fixed purposely higher or lower than the actual average cost of production (thus yielding profit or loss respectively), with a view to influencing the consumption of those goods.

Various reasons might indicate a departure from the cost of production as being immediately or ultimately beneficial ; but I think that most of them will fall within a simple classification. It is likely that the price would be raised above the cost of production in the case of goods the production of which involved any process considered physically or morally deleterious to the worker, e.g. certain chemical manufactures and perhaps the slaughter of cattle for meat ; also in the case of goods which may be considered to be deleterious when consumed in excess, such as alcohol, drugs, and to a small extent tobacco. On the other hand, the consumption of goods the production of which has an educational or physically beneficial effect on the worker, as hand-made house furnishings, might be stimulated by selling at less than the cost of production. So also the prices of art wares, household medicines, health-giving foods, gardening implements, and so forth, might be fixed at less than cost. Considerations of demand and supply could not fail to affect the prices of many kinds of goods from time to

15

time. If stocks accumulated owing to falling demand for a commodity, its price would be reduced temporarily until production could be conveniently adjusted to the reduced demand ; and even more frequently the price of an article might be raised to meet a growing demand until the supply could be increased, though in the case of necessary goods this situation might be met more advantageously by rationing. In the case of perishables—fruit and agricultural products harvested but once a year, and certain imported goods—a shortage or surplus might be dealt with by variation of price. The standard price for the present and the ensuing year would always be known, however ; and, in the case of these temporary variations, both producer and consumer would be influenced by the knowledge that the accepted economic policy involved efforts being made to return to the standard price at an early date. During the period in which foreign trade would have to be carried on mainly with countries which had not yet adopted the economy of communism, probably the fluctuations of prices would occur most frequently among imported goods— tea, coffee, cocoa, rubber, a variety of clothing materials and semi-luxuries.

COST OF PRODUCTION

We may now proceed to consider the principles upon which the cost of production of a unit of a commodity should be determined for the fixation of the standard price as above described. The subject can be approached best by considering first the components of price in the present competitive régime, with a view to seeing how far they will exist as real costs under communism, or may appear in modified form.

The economist is accustomed to distinguish the following elements of price in goods which enter markets under competitive conditions :

Prime Costs—
    (1) Raw materials, stores, etc., and power.
    (2) Labour.
    (3) Repairs and replacements.

Supplementary (or Overhead) Costs—
    (4) Supervision or management.

(5) Rent of land.

(6) Interest on all capital employed in buildings and plant, and as working capital.

(7) Depreciation of buildings and plant.

(8) Insurance, and average profits (in restricted sense) which in reality are compensation for risk.

Distribution Costs—

(9) Expenses of selling, wholesale and retail.

(10) Cost of transport to market or shop.

The heads under which the cost accountant divides expenses do not correspond exactly with the above, which are based on theoretical considerations ; but it would not be difficult to introduce a system of factory and distribution cost accounts to classify expenditure under the ten major heads set out above. We now proceed to consider each of these heads so as to discover its meaning or applicability in the economics of communism.

The cost of raw material is a question of quantity and price, and the latter will be determined in the general manner now under discussion ; or, if the raw material be wholly or partly imported, then according to the method to be detailed in the next chapter on foreign trade. The same applies to the cost of stores, and of fuel or electric power. Repairs must be charged according to labour time and the cost of material used, and replacements according to the price of the new machine or tool, less the value, if any, of the old machine in another use or as scrap.

Labour as a prime cost means manual labour, usually measurable or accountable in terms of output ; and it may be paid by the piece or by time. In either case the cost per unit of output can be calculated, however much the work may be sub-divided. Prime costs are those which are incurred only when the concern is actually producing ; so that the total expenditure on each of the items of prime cost varies in close proportion with the total output. Hence in the total cost per unit of produce the amount of each item of prime cost remains nearly the same whether the total output be great or small. This statement is true generally of capitalist industry, because it is the custom to engage or discharge labour according as the state of business enables a larger or smaller output to be sold. If, however, the number of workmen was fixed, and they were engaged permanently, like the managing staff, manual labour would have to be treated as a supplementary cost. That would be the position under communism; for each industry would be held liable to account for the whole working time of every worker assigned to that industry, manager and workmen alike, irrespective of whether the total output demanded were sufficient to keep all the workers fully employed or not. In practice, the industry having a permanent staff, the tendency would be, so far as possible, to adjust the output to the fixed number of workers, so as to keep all occupied. An increase or reduction of numbers would be made gradually as recruits came forward or as retirements occurred, or opportunities offered of securing transfers from or to other occupations. It is clear, therefore, that in the analysis of costs under communism manual labour must be placed along with supervision among the supplementary costs.[1]

[1] In order to make this important principle appear in concrete statement, I give here an example of how the labour and supervision costs would actually appear in the cost sheet of some one department of a factory. The assumption is that the department is making, by special machines, a section of the complete article which the factory turns out. This department only makes three parts, which I call A, B, and C; but of part C two are required for every one of A or of B. The department as a whole turns out parts for 320 complete sections of the article per hour, but does not assemble them. There are twenty-one persons employed on the machines; and the department has its own foreman and one routing and costing clerk keeping account of raw materials received, of output and waste. The department shares a mechanic with another; and the factory manager may be estimated to give one-fifth of his time to it. We can thus set out the cost of labour and supervision per article (i.e. per unit of produce) in making this section of the article in detail as follows :

Work.	Output per Hour	Cost per Unit (in Decimals of 1 Hour of 1 Worker).
10 persons working Part A ..	320	·03125
6 ,, ,, ,, B ..	320	·01875
5 ,, ,, ,, C ..	640	·01563
1 foreman	320	·00313
1 costing clerk	320	·00313
Half time of mechanic	320	·00156
One-fifth time of manager ..	320	·00062
Total labour and supervision cost	..	.. ·07407

The unit of cost—one hour—might also be written as £1. I merely give this amount of detail to emphasize the fact that the foreman, clerk, etc., each cost

The rent of land always enters into industrial costs under the capitalist system, though in the accounts often wholly or partly included in interest or profits, or rent of buildings. It cannot be said, however, that rent of land is a real cost from the point of view of society as a whole. Ground rent is a diversion of part of the produce of labour from the group actively engaged in production to the passive owner of the land which happens to be fertile or well situated for the particular work in hand. The fact that real costs are lower on certain lands or sites than others need not lead us to the conclusion that rent must be charged. There are in fact ' producer's surpluses ' in regard to machinery and buildings, and to management, in an industry at any given time, so that the average cost per unit of produce of different mills or factories in an industry varies considerably. At present the firms with highest manufacturing costs are eliminated by competition in a time of trade depression, and the firms which just survive are those which have costs which are marginal as regards the industry as a whole in its then condition.

It was stated above (p. 224) that the communist organization of industry might be regarded as a public monopoly not working for profit ; and the policy of such a monopolist would be to average the cost of production of all plants producing a given article. If this were not done there would be a profit or a loss. If profit were made, part of it might be regarded as arising from the advantages of certain sites, and would be of the nature of rent ; but it would be a useless calculation to find out how much. Moreover, if any profit were made, it would usually be made deliberately for specific reasons, as indicated above. On the other hand, if it were thought desirable to charge rent, this would simply swell the average cost of production of the whole industry, and the ' rent ' would be indistinguishable from profits. Charges of rent on works and factories would in fact be merely book debits, and the corresponding credits to national income could have no real meaning. Under communism there will be no need for the nationalization of land

in their time exactly the same per hour as the workers on machines. Exactly the same result could be quickly got by dividing 320 into 23·7, the total of persons employed in the department. Under present (capitalist) conditions the cost would have to be calculated at a different rate of wage per hour in each of the lines in the above table.

as commonly advocated by socialists and others, in the sense
that the State would become the rent-receiver for all the land
of the country. It must not be forgotten that there can be no
such thing as public revenue, or even public finance, under
communism : only public economy—the planning of the use
of all man-power and resources of the country to the greatest
advantage. The setting of persons to work at tasks of public
administration constitutes the equivalent of public finance.

It might be argued, however, that there are two grounds
on which rent should nevertheless be charged : (1) on the
ground that the true cost of a commodity in any place can
only be determined if the rent appropriate to the locality be
charged, (2) because the omission of rent may unduly affect
the relative prices of different commodities. Let us consider
these objections.

It will be observed that the first has no validity if the
principle held to be necessary earlier in this chapter be adopted,
namely, that the price of each article should be uniform
throughout the commonwealth, as one of the essential conditions of securing equal means of enjoyment. Thus the cost
of production would be averaged for the whole country, and
the charging of rent would have no meaning. If, however,
we assume that the principle of uniform price throughout the
country will not be adopted and that rent will be included as
an item in the cost of production, we shall find that the determination of a fair rent charge would be no easy matter. In
the first place the rents which actually prevailed under capitalist
conditions might be taken as the basis for fixing arbitrary
charges of rent in the costs of manufacture. A factory situated
near the centre of a large town would then, as now, have its
costs weighted by a heavy rent as compared with a factory
situated in the country. If that were a real cost it might be
a good reason for closing the town factory and moving it out
into the country. But under communism the public would be
both payer and receiver of rent ; and a charge of rent on the
capitalist basis would be stereotyping the results of competition. If competitive rents were always the result of
avoidance of real costs permanently unavoidable by other
means, that would not be unsound. But, in fact, the kinds of
costs, the lowness or absence of which leads to the emergence

of rent in competitive conditions, are very largely those which a better organized society would be rid of, or would greatly modify. Availability of transport, or of labour, and proximity to markets for raw materials and finished produce, will bear a wholly different aspect under communism. The Industrial Planning Commissions will take direct account of the costs of bringing raw materials and delivering finished produce to the great consuming centres or ports of export. Availability of transport will naturally be carefully considered, and proximity to the homes of the workers will be arranged to the best advantage, either by moving the factory or by building new houses.

The second objection, that the omission of rent may unduly affect the relative prices of different commodities, has a certain validity, particularly as to the costs of production of agricultural products relatively to factory products. Under present conditions the cost of production on marginal land [1] approximates to the average price prevailing over a period of years, so that little or no rent can be paid for such land. But the great bulk of the produce marketed has been produced at lower cost and has paid rent, amounting sometimes to as much as 40 or 45 per cent of the price. The proposed rule of determining prices with close reference to their average cost of production over the whole output might lead, therefore, to the prices of agricultural products being unduly low. As they are so largely foodstuffs, this would not seem to be a disadvantage ; but a difficulty might arise from the necessity of drawing on foreign supplies of foodstuffs and agricultural raw materials. If the cost of imported wheat, butter or sugar exceeded the average cost of the British product (which at present seems unlikely), there must either be a loss incurred on the quantity imported, or the price must be the average of the cost of the home production and the amount imported. How far the cultivation should be pushed in England on the more unsuitable lands would be a question of policy. It would be wasteful to continue cultivation year after year on lands which resulted in a marginal cost higher than the price at which the product could be imported, unless there were some offsetting social advantage. The conclusion which will be drawn, I think, from

[1] That is, the cost of production on those of the lands on which the crop is actually raised on which the cultivation of that product is most expensive per unit.

such considerations as these, is that an actual debit of rent in the costs of agricultural products would have no more meaning than in industries.   What the price-fixing authority will require to know is the average cost of the whole harvest, and the marginal cost—in each case the average of the results of the previous three or four years.   It would, of course, be necessary to know the average annual cost on every farm approximately ; and if regular cost accounts were not kept by every farm, special investigations would have to be made on sample farms in each district.

INTEREST

We may pass on now to a consideration of the next item of costs—interest.   To exclude interest from the cost on which price would be based would accord with that school of socialist thought which sees in labour the only real cost of production, and with the writers who have advocated the use of ' labour notes '.   A charge for the depreciation of capital—tools, machinery, buildings, etc.—of such amount as would recover their cost in their presumed lifetime, would be allowable ; for capital goods are only ' crystallized ' labour, the result sometimes of several stages of accretion.   They are used up like raw materials in the process of production ; but, instead of serving once only, they last for a thousand or ten thousand, maybe a million, repetitions of service—or until deterioration by weather or other causes renders them useless.

Interest stands on quite a different footing from depreciation. It cannot be said to embody labour, but merely represents on the one hand the reward of the sacrifice made by postponing the enjoyment of the fruits of labour, and on the other hand the productivity which labour, indirectly applied and suitably embodied as machines and so forth, acquires by reason of the postponement.   There would be no fundamental inconsistency in omitting interest from cost as the basis of price were the results of so doing deemed expedient.

It is important to realize that under communism interest would not be required in order to secure the accumulation of capital.   The whole labour power of the country would be under the control of the Council of National Economy ; and it

would be a matter of administrative decision from time to time
what proportion of the total labour force should be applied to
making capital goods. The existing population might decide
to sacrifice itself for the future : to live for ten years on the
bare necessaries of life, so that, say, 80 per cent of the entire
labour-power of the country might be devoted to producing
fixed capital goods in the shape of engineering works, ships,
electrical and mechanical plant of all descriptions of greatly
increased efficiency. On the other hand, the population might
decide to live riotously and devote but a small fraction of its
labour to increasing the capital fund. The decision as to which
industries should be furnished with additional capital would
rest with the Council of Equipment.[1] They would be guided
on the one hand by the needs for reducing or avoiding onerous
or disgusting labour, and by the demands of consumers for
increased quantity or for a reduced price, and on the other hand
by their information as to the most promising fields for reduction of costs, and thus ultimately of prices, in the light of the
latest technical achievements.

It might even be argued that the exclusion of interest from
the cost basis of price would act as a stimulus to saving, that is,
to devoting a larger part of the total labour force of the country
to augmenting the capital fund. It might be that an intelligent
and highly educated population, understanding the working of
the national economy, might deliberately choose to adopt the
policy of cheapening goods, or making them more abundant.
It might gain such confidence in its technical advisers as to be
quite ready to make a sacrifice for a few years in order to reap
a substantial advantage which would accrue to the great
majority within their own lifetime.

The question of whether interest should be reckoned or not
turns in reality upon relative prices. In our present industrial
equipment very different proportions of capital to labour are
found in the production of different commodities and services.
Take, for instance, the products of the distillation of petroleum
—petrol, paraffin, etc.—and of coal-tar ; a modern plant
requires an enormous outlay of capital, but needs no more than
a few skilled workmen. Perhaps the cost of labour and supervision at the refinery runs to about a halfpenny per gallon.

[1] See Chapter IX, p. 160, and Chapter X, pp. 178–9.

Compare the making of felt hats, or ready-made clothing, in which much labour is employed assisted by simple machines ; or, better still, the building of houses, where the interest on the capital employed in plant is negligible in comparison with the direct expenditure on wages. Assuming for the moment that no interest will be charged, it is evident that the prices of goods which are produced by methods requiring a great investment of capital, and but little labour, will be unduly low as compared with the prices of goods manufactured with the aid of a small capital investment. Thus the consumption of such goods will be stimulated by the low prices. The reorganization of an industry by means of a great investment of capital in entirely new plant, which resulted in the reduction of labour costs per unit of output to one-fourth of what they were, would bring the price down also to a quarter of what it was, instead of to about one-third, as it might be if interest were charged. In the case of commodities for which the demand was elastic the resulting increase in quantity demanded would probably prove embarrassing, requiring a further enormous investment of capital to meet it.

Such stimulation of the consumption through lowering the price by the whole cost of the saving in labour due to a large investment of capital might, of course, be desirable in the case of certain commodities considered specially beneficial to the consumer (e.g. bifocal lenses for spectacles), or to the worker producing them ; but these considerations are extraneous to the theory of interest under communism, and have been mentioned above amongst the reasons for varying the price away from the cost of production.

When I first considered the question of interest in relation to price my opinion was that it should not be charged. I am inclined to believe now, however, that the results of not charging interest would in the great majority of cases be inconvenient, perhaps highly undesirable. Amongst other results, the public might, for instance, vociferously demand the diversion of capital resources into cheapening the production of motor-cars, television sets, and innumerable novelties, whereas a more conservative policy would require the greater part of those capital resources for improving and cheapening basic services like transport and power-supply. The work of the

Council of Equipment would, I think, be simplified by adopting an interest charge as an item of cost. The rate at which the interest would be reckoned would be arbitrary, depending on the presumed intensity of the adverse forces which it was intended to counteract. It might be 5 per cent at the commencement ; and it might be lowered to 4 per cent, 3 per cent, and 2 per cent, in successive decades, and perhaps ultimately be abolished. The rate would be the same for all industries, as it is pure interest, the factor of risk being accounted separately.

REMAINING SUPPLEMENTARY COSTS

When introducing the subject of interest in the preceding section it was convenient to refer to depreciation of buildings and plant. We saw that such fixed capital goods may be regarded as ' crystallized ' labour, and that the service they render is the gradual using up of the stored labour. This continues for the whole of the ' life ' of the machine or building : that is, whilst it remains serviceable. The useful life of a machine may be terminated by obsolescence long before it is worn out ; and then so much of its cost as has not been recovered already by debit against the produce, must be carried forward to be added to the depreciation fund of the machine which replaces it. Depreciation which involves scrapping a machine or building (and not merely loss of market value) is a real cost, and must be provided for in the cost basis of price.

The last item of supplementary costs in the capitalist system, as stated above on page 227 is ' insurance and average profits' (in restricted sense).[1] In practice, of course, insurance and average profits are separately stated. I have linked them together because, as is well known to economists, the profits (in restricted sense) of a normal firm averaged over a number of years—or at least the *anticipated* average profits—constitute a compensation for the commercial risks unavoidable in the business. Thus a charge for average profits (*sensu strictu*) is like an insurance premium for commercial risks of a kind which no outside agency would insure.

[1] The term *profits* in its restricted sense, as used by most modern writers on economic theory, does not correspond with net profits in the commercial sense. It may be defined as the remainder of the net profits after deducting from the latter so much as represents interest on capital, rents of land and buildings owned, and remuneration of management.

The risks which industrial enterprises incur under the capitalist system are of two kinds. There are the natural and the human risks which are inseparable from industry however organized—of damage by fire, flood and tempest, and of accidents to men and to machines, however carefully guarded against. Nowadays these are usually covered by insurance. In certain industries—for example, agriculture—the ' natural ' risks are great : drought, too much rain, an epidemic of plant or animal disease. In many industries the raw material and even the finished product is more or less perishable, and in spite of care quantities must from time to time be thrown away. All these are risks of one kind—those over which the manager of the undertaking can have little or no control.

The second class of risks is that called ' commercial ', using the term in a wide sense. It includes all the chances of loss from bad buying and selling, from fluctuations of prices, from competitive bidding and from mere bad management of production in the factory or works.

The risks of the first class would still remain under communism. There would be no actual insurance, for the whole industry—the whole community—would be bearing the risk ; but an allowance to cover the average risk in making particular goods must be charged in the cost per unit so as to arrive at the true cost. The allowance for average risk will necessarily be different in different industries—particularly heavy in agriculture, fruit-growing, the manufacture of paints and varnishes, rubber goods, and so forth. Of commercial risk there would be none, except a very slight chance of over-production, and the likelihood of occasional wasteful management in the works. The last would be revealed by the cost accounts, and be rapidly remedied as a result of the external inspection to which every works and factory would be subjected.

DISTRIBUTION COSTS

Under the heading ' Expenses of Selling ' (p. 227) there should be included the cost of the sales department and of commercial travellers and the entire cost of retail sales to the public, including advertising. Many factories sell direct to retailers ; but often there are wholesale dealers intervening. The host of people who are employed in bringing to the consumer's notice and hands the goods he requires, or is made to want, is so expensive that the retail price may be any amount from 15 to 300 per cent above the factory cost. It is usually from 30 to 50 per cent above for articles of daily use in wide demand. Contrast with this the small expense of distributing goods under communism, with its exact organization directed to doing just what is necessary. There would be the time of the manager and assistants of one of the retail stores (each replacing dozens of shops), and of the staffs of the Commissions of Supply. The latter would have a branch compiling requisitions from the stores—a trifling job on listing and adding machines ; another branch would be forwarding orders to the local factories or to the import offices or supply offices of other divisions ; and a third branch would be dealing with the goods received and warehoused for dispatch to stores as required, and checking invoices of goods delivered direct from factory to stores. All transactions would relate usually to large quantities of goods ; and so the entire cost of man-power engaged in securing the distribution of goods, other than furniture, into the hands of consumers could hardly run to more than from 5 to 15 per cent of factory cost—say, perhaps, 10 per cent on the average.

The cost of transport from factory to retail establishment is the last item of cost on our list. This is real, and must appear in our cost basis of price. It may be observed, however, that the cost of transport would be reduced to a quarter or a third of what it is now by (1) improved railway organization, particularly the handling of goods at terminals, (2) the use of co-ordinated road transport, (3) the avoidance of cross routing, i.e. obtaining goods usually from the nearest source of supply.

SUMMARY OF COSTS FORMING THE BASIS OF PRICE

The results of this discussion may be gathered in a list of items of cost comparable with that given on pages 226–7 for the capitalist system. In order to show clearly which items of cost will be entirely excluded the same numbers are given in each list to the corresponding headings.

Prime Costs—
  (1) Raw materials, stores, and power.
  (3) Repairs and replacements.

Supplementary Costs—
  (4) Labour, manual and supervisory.
  (6) Interest on capital cost of buildings and plant.
  (7) Depreciation of buildings and plant.
  (8) Allowance for average risk.

Distribution Costs—
  (9) Costs of staffs of Commissions of Supply and retail stores.
  (10) Cost of transport to retail stores or place of consumption.

THE PRICE LEVEL AND THE GENERAL ALLOWANCE

It was stated at an early place in this chapter (page 225) that, if the economic organization of communism is to run smoothly, it is essential that the price level shall have the proper relation to the annual quotas of goods produced and to the amount of the general allowance credited to each person. If the conditions assumed be accurately apprehended by the reader, he will find this relationship extremely simple—a mere matter of arithmetic.

In the preceding chapters [1] I have explained that many kinds of goods should be available free to an unlimited amount, e.g. water, electricity, matches, pencils, etc., and services such as local transport ; and other goods and services in limited amount, such as newspapers, long-distance travelling, and perhaps those staple foods which everybody requires. These would not be priced ; they would be available to everybody in such quantities as were needed, subject to a generous maximum, which would not come into operation except for people of unusual voracity. The assumption is that there would be no house-rents to pay, and no rates, taxes, school fees, doctors' or hospital charges, or charitable subscriptions.

Thus about two-thirds of the ordinary middle-class family's expenditure of to-day would be provided for otherwise than by

[1] Chapter IX, p. 162, and Chapter XI, p. 198.

the general allowance. The object of the latter is to enable people to provide themselves with clothing and house furnishings, and all the miscellaneous comforts and luxuries we need for pleasure and the growth of our individuality. All these goods would be stocked by, or be obtainable through, the retail stores by debit against the general allowance ; and it is the prices of all these miscellaneous goods in particular which form the subject-matter of this chapter. The goods which would be distributed through the general allowance form only a part of the national dividend as defined in Chapter X, probably less than one-third.

Of all the workers of the country, men and women, perhaps no more than one-fifth—indeed I should think only one-sixth—would be employed in the manufacture of goods to be supplied through the general stores, including, in respect of imported goods, the equivalent labour on exports. The remainder would be working in the railway, steamship and other transport industries ; in mining, agriculture, and engineering industries ; in State and municipal administration ; in education, or the newspaper press and cinematograph industries ; and in countless direct and professional services. In all these latter industries and services there would be no price to the consumer. They would be producing either raw materials or goods and direct services on a full or measured basis of quantity.

The amount of the general allowance will obviously be determined by the total value of the annual production of the kinds of goods which are to be purchased by means of it. I use the word ' value ' here in the business-man's sense, to mean a quantity of a commodity multiplied by its price. Divide the grand total annual value of the goods produced for supply through the general allowance by the estimated population, and the quotient is the general allowance in terms of the same ' money ' units as were used to calculate the total value of the goods produced.[1] If everybody were to spend the whole of his general allowance, and no more, in a year, the whole of the year's production of ' stores ' goods would be exactly

[1] It will be remembered that in making the estimate of population for the divisor, children and young persons up to twenty-five years of age are to be counted as various fractions of an adult, corresponding with the fractions of the adult's general allowance to which they will be entitled. (See Chapter XI, p. 215).

balanced by the consumption. In practice it would be impossible to forecast accurately the distribution of expenditure over the wide range of goods made available through the stores. Hence large stocks of most articles would be carried forward from year to year (as in shops and warehouses now), and a considerable margin of error would be allowed in calculating the total value of production to be divided. A budget estimate, or final program of production, as I shall call it, would be made for each kind of goods in the autumn of each year for the ensuing year. The price would be settled according to the estimated cost of production, based upon existing experience, modified in accordance with any changes of plant or personnel which had been arranged ; and the quantity would be fixed according to the estimated demand. Such estimates, approved by the council of each industry, would be totalled by the Council of Supply, which would ascertain, and recommend to the Council of National Economy for announcement, the general allowance for the ensuing year.

The relation of the price level and the general allowance is clearly a simple one, about which only two or three generalizations need to be made. The unit in which prices would be stated would be quite arbitrary, as already mentioned : just a mere sign for the product of an hour's labour, with interest and allowance for risk calculated in the same unit. I have suggested that from habit the unit would probably be called £1 ; and it might be divided as now into shillings, or decimally. The price level depends upon the ' money ' value, i.e. number of units of the general allowance, assigned to an hour's labour.

Although the amount of the general allowance and the unit in which it is stated are quite arbitrary, and therefore prices also, it seems likely that the price-fixing authority, guided by the habits and convenience of the public, and its own convenience, would maintain a relationship once established, and allow the amount of the general allowance, the price level, and individual prices, to vary only on account of definite causes which the public could understand. For instance, on the assumption that each unit of the allowance represents a man-hour of labour of any kind applied to producing goods supplied through the general allowance, a reduction of working hours per annum in all or any of the industries supplying such goods would operate to decrease the general allowance ; but the employment of a larger number of workers in proportion to the population would increase it. A larger volume of goods available as the result of improved machinery or organization, without change of the number of workers, would not alter the general allowance, but would decrease prices inversely as the increase of output per worker, except for the amount of the increase of the percentage added for interest, if new plant more costly in labour time to produce were employed.[1] The general allowance might be varied slightly each year to adjust consumption to a surplus or deficit of production in the preceding year, and to allow for fluctuations in the prices of imported raw materials and the prices realized for British goods exported.

On the assumptions stated above it seems highly probable that there would be two general tendencies manifest : the one a gradual lowering of the price level, the other a slow but steady increase in the amount of the general allowance. The first would be the result of reduced cost of production, due to reorganization of the industry and individual plants, and the further adoption of labour-saving invenions. We may well believe that drastic reorganization of industries one after another would be undertaken, and that improvements would be made continuously in all industries. Hence there would be reductions of the prices of practically all goods produced within the country from time to time, and hardly any increases, except when the prices of foreign raw materials rose.

A tendency for the general allowance to increase, although prices were being reduced, might be expected to arise from the gradual abolition of much clerical labour, and from the reorganization of transport and other industries supplying direct unlimited or measured services ; for these changes would set free additional labour-power for the expansion of the industries providing goods obtainable through the general allowance. The increase from year to year of the general allowance in ' money ' units would probably be small, but the increase in purchasing power would be substantial.

---

[1] If the same volume of goods were produced by a smaller staff, the workers released being transferred to making a new article, it might be considered expedient to maintain the price in spite of the reduced cost of production, and to increase the general allowance by the value of the annual production of the new article ; for a reduced price would usually result in a larger consumption.

CHAPTER XIII

FOREIGN TRADE

ORGANIZATION AND FINANCE

A FEW words as to the conduct of foreign trade and its effect upon prices must find their place here; and if my treatment of the subject seems inadequate, this is due rather to the abstruse character of the economic principles which would be involved in a full treatment than to any failure to recognize its importance. Indeed, my own opinion is that overseas trade will be almost as necessary for the prosperity of the country under communism as it is now, and that no scheme for a unified economic system for the country could be worth considering for practical adoption which did not contemplate the interweaving of the business of export and import with the routine of production and distribution for the home demand.

In an earlier chapter [1] it was suggested that the organization and general control of foreign trade will be entrusted to a Council of Foreign Trade, under which there would doubtless be separate councils for export and import trade, and committees in charge of each section of these, according to commodities, and sub-committees dealing with each foreign market. In general the members of these committees would be the chief executive officials, with representatives of the executives of the corresponding industries and of the Council and Commissions of Supply. We could not expect to sell our goods in other countries without sending representatives abroad; so probably there would be a British Trade Agency in every important commercial centre of the world, holding large stocks of our principal manufactures, ready for immediate delivery, a facility which British exporters now cannot afford to give to the requisite extent. On the other hand, some countries, particularly those, I think, which had adopted communism, might prefer to send buyers to us. As regards imports we

[1] Chapter IX, p. 155.

should probably have our own agents abroad for purchasing certain raw materials, particularly from Asiatic and tropical countries; but for raw materials originating in Europe, America and the British dominions, and for most imports of manufactured goods, we should rely mainly on foreign co-operative organizations, and on the trade representatives of other countries established here, sending abroad only occasional missions of inquiry.

The finance of foreign trade would have to be organized in two sections : the one for settling mutual indebtedness with other countries organized on a basis of communism, or having a government foreign trade monopoly, and the other for financing trade with countries in which the competitive system still prevailed. For the first a clearing-house only would be required ; for the second there must be a National Exchange Bank, having its branches in all parts of the world, always ready to buy and sell foreign currencies, and to give credit to foreign customers.

Many commodities—for example, tea, coffee, cotton, rice, raw rubber—we must import at whatever price it is necessary to pay ; but the greater part of our foreign trade will require a continuous and careful study of prices. I think that each section of trade will have its own statistical and research bureau for investigations of prices and qualities, ascertaining and comparing the prices of goods available abroad with the costs of production of similar goods in England. This study is fundamental, and I shall try to indicate briefly the economic theory on which must be based the policy of foreign trade.

COMPARATIVE COSTS

The doctrine of comparative costs tells us that trade between any two countries will arise and be advantageous to both when the costs of production of the commodities bear a different ratio to one another in each of the respective countries. The absolute cost of production in hours of labour per unit produced may be less in one country, say, America, for practically all commodities than it is in another country, say, India ; yet it pays America to import from India (chiefly raw materials) and India to import from America (manufactures).

Each country tends to specialize on producing those goods for the production of which it has advantages, such as natural resources, climate, skilled labour, or capital, and for which the cost of production is low, and to export those kinds of goods. It imports in exchange commodities for which it has fewer or relatively smaller advantages, and thus a higher cost of production, than some other countries.

Exactly the same principle would apply between two countries which had adopted communism. An example of the usual kind will help to make the theory clear. Suppose that in country A it requires a total of six hours labour (of many persons) to make a unit of commodity P (say, a ton of pig-iron), and three hours labour to make a unit of commodity Q, whilst in country B it requires sixteen hours per unit of P and twelve hours labour per unit of Q. It would then be advantageous for country A to specialize in making commodity Q, and country B to make only commodity P. Within each country the amount of one commodity produced by an hour's labour would ordinarily exchange for the amount of any other commodity produced by an hour's labour. This is the same thing as saying that their prices would be proportional to the number of hours labour needed to make a unit of the commodity.

Country A could devote twenty-four hours' labour to making either two units of P and four of Q, or eight units of Q only. If trade were opened between the countries, the latter would be the more advantageous, because four units of Q exported to country B would be exchangeable there for three units of P. Thus in country A the result of twenty-four hours' labour is now three units of P and four of Q; and country A will cease to make P. Similarly, going back to the original assumption that each country was producing both commodities, we see that country B could spend ninety-six hours' labour in making three units of P and four of Q, or in making six units of P only. In the latter case three units of P exported to country A would bring back six units of Q, at the original ratio of exchange when country A made both commodities; and the six units of Q would compare with only four units which she could make with the same labour herself. To simplify the demonstration we have assumed all the gain to go first to one country and then to the other. In reality the gain would be divided; and we should have to take cost of transport, customs duties, if any, and merchants' expenses into account.

The actual result can be conveniently illustrated by displaying the price changes by means of the percentages which the price of Q would bear to the price of P taken as 100 under the different assumptions. Thus, before trade was opened, the prices of P and Q would be in country A as 100 to 50 ; in country B as 100 to 75. After trade was opened, if there were no cost of transport, duty or other expenses, the ratio would become the same in both countries, probably between 100 to 60 and 100 to 65, though it would be impossible to say at what figure exactly without knowledge of numerous other factors. Admitting costs of transport, etc., as necessary impediments to trade, equilibrium would become established with the prices having different ratios in the two countries, as, for example, in country A, P : Q :: 100 : 62 ; but in country B as 100 : 68.

In beginning this exposition the assumption was tacitly made that the cost of production per unit remains the same in a country whatever be the total volume of production. In reality such a case of 'constant returns' would be extremely rare. It is only possible to increase the total output by drawing on resources of land and labour which are less efficient, or by trying to 'squeeze' more out of the existing resources. In both cases the *marginal* cost, i.e. the cost per unit of the *additional* units produced, is higher. Hence the marginal cost is always higher than the average cost per unit. This must be so permanently in the case of the agricultural, mining and other industries subject predominantly to the law of diminishing returns. In all kinds of manufacturing industries, however, the economies of large-scale production and of the reorganization of the industry as a whole, may be so considerable that a reduction of the *average* cost per unit accompanies an increase of the total volume of production of the industry. We have seen striking reductions of the prices of bicycles, motor-cars, electric light bulbs, vacuum flasks, and many other articles for this reason. In these industries, which are said to be subject predominantly to the law of increasing returns (which includes decreasing costs both internally and externally to the producing unit), an exceptionally large and well-planned new factory will have a lower cost of production than any other concern in the industry. It takes its place, not at the margin, but at the centre, the safest position in the whole industry ; and old establishments, small and ill-equipped, become marginal, that is, they now have the highest cost which the prevailing market price of the product will support. Some of the badly-equipped or managed factories will probably go out of business altogether ; and the marginal ones, which just keep going, will be forced into liquidation by any further reduction of price resulting from increased output by the new low-cost large factories.

COMPARISON OF MARGINAL COSTS WITH FOREIGN PRICES

We are now in a position to take a complete view of the problem of prices in foreign trade under communism. In present-day competitive trade the equilibrium of prices of two commodities in a country and between two countries illustrated on the preceding page is also an equilibrium of marginal costs. The marginal cost is the highest cost which any portion of the country's total output actually bears ; and, if the marginal (or highest) cost is less than the prevailing price, there will be profit in enlarging the total output, even at higher cost, until the cost of additional units of product shall have risen to the price, though the latter will fall more or less to meet the rising marginal cost, since the demand price for a larger quantity per annum is lower.

Rents and high profits arise from the difference between the cost in a favourably situated or managed establishment and the marginal cost, which is equal to the market price. It is for this reason that *internal* prices under communism will be fixed with reference to the *average* cost of production over the whole output of the country. The price will thus usually be less than the cost of production for a considerable part of the total output, the loss on that part of the output being made up by the profit on the rest which has cost below the average to produce. In foreign trade under communism, however, it is the marginal cost—the cost at which an increase of the home country's total output could be secured—which is to be compared with the price at which the same article could be purchased abroad. When considering whether more potatoes should be imported, or the needed addition to the supply should be obtained by extending cultivation in England, the cost of cultivation per ton in labour, and capital, must be computed, to which must be added a charge of the nature of rent based on the loss which would be sustained by having to import the wheat, oats, beans or butter, now being produced on the land proposed to be turned over to potatoes. It might be found that it would pay to import more wheat, oats or butter, and to grow at home more potatoes ; but if the foreign price of potatoes fell decidedly and the prices of other agricultural produce rose or remained stationary, it would be found profitable for the country to contract the area under potatoes.

At any given moment an increase of the country's output of any product, whether in agriculture, mining, fisheries or manufacturing industries, can be obtained only at a higher cost per unit. This is true permanently of the first-named industries, which are subject predominantly to the law of diminishing returns (or increasing costs) ; but it applies to manufacturing and other industries which obey the law of increasing returns (decreasing costs) in the *short period* only. That means for the time within which it would not be possible to obtain an increased output from new large-scale plant. We see, therefore, that the business of the statistical bureaux of the foreign trade departments would be to be constantly collecting from the industries concerned information as to the marginal costs of producing various kinds of goods commonly available abroad. These costs they would compare with foreign prices, so as to find out which goods could be most profitably exported and which imported ; and operations would be carried out after consulting the industries concerned as regards increase or decrease of output. Care would have to be taken to balance the exports and imports ; or, rather, to see that the total indebtedness each way would balance. It would seem probable that British capital abroad (which would have become, of course, a State asset, unless the owners had exercised their option to emigrate permanently) would still be considerable, and that British shipping and insurance business might still be in operation in most parts of the world. If so, we should have then, as now, an excess of imports over visible exports, in order to secure an equilibrium of total indebtedness.

The industries, in making plans for future production some years ahead, would take the possibilities of the export trade into consideration ; for it might be possible, if there would be an assured foreign demand at reduced price, to reorganize the manufacture of an article by mass production on a large scale which the home demand alone would not justify. Countries under communism might very well consult with one another, so that each might specialize in the manufacture of certain articles or products. The present-day concentration of the aniline dye production in Germany and of typewriter manufacture in the United States indicates how a world-planning of the location of the manufacture of particular goods could be arranged, once private vested interests had been eliminated.

CYCLICAL FLUCTUATIONS OF TRADE

The alternation of depressions of trade and industry with periods of activity in cycles usually of seven, ten or eleven years in duration, is a phenomenon dating back to the early eighteenth century, if not earlier. There is a school of thought which supposes these to be due to alternations in the psychological state of the business world, whereby confidence develops into undue optimism, and so business develops into speculation, which overreaches itself. The resulting collapse induces caution and pessimism, and consequent depression of trade and severe unemployment. The effects of this supposed 'natural' sequence of psychological states are held to be accentuated by our system of credit, which has the vicious habit of expanding credit freely whilst prices are on the upgrade, and of unnecessarily prolonging a depression of trade by deflation and senseless restriction of credit when prices are low or falling. It is held by this school that by means of national regulation of bank credit, or the complete nationalization of banking, these fluctuations of prices, and thus of the state of trade and employment, could be abolished, and industry be kept always in a healthy state of activity with a full load and no unemployment. The majority of socialists regard this as one of the earliest benefits obtainable by the establishment of a socialist régime.

On the other hand, a school of economists, amongst whom

I claim a place, believe that these fluctuations of trade have their prime cause in actual changes both in the cost of production per unit, and in the quantity produced, of the principal commodities of commerce. These changes arise from two quite distinct causes. The first is the result of invention and the extended application of power in one industry after another. The second is an actual variation from year to year of the harvests of the great agricultural countries of the world.

In one industry after another for the past 150 years mechanical engineers have been improving the machinery employed and introducing new mechanical processes. Improvement of quality has been a subsidiary object. Always the chief aim has been reduction of the cost of manufacture, mainly by saving labour. Large-scale organization, and plant constructed on a larger scale, have also been important means of reducing costs. In any period when trade is active and money is available for investment it is easy to raise capital to apply these improvements in practice ; and the prospective profits are usually large enough to induce many firms and companies to build new mills and factories or extend existing ones. When the products of this new machinery are on the market the supply very soon exceeds the demand. The price falls suddenly and the old mills and factories fail to cover expenses, but yet continue working for some time. Overproduction causes a temporary depression of trade, which is ended only by one or both of two changes. The first of these changes is the going out of business of the least efficient producers and the restriction of their production by others, so that when stocks are reduced supply becomes again equated to demand on a profit-making basis. The second change is an increase of demand for the products of the industry, which may arise at home or abroad. In three or four years after the slump usually industry has become normal again. Gradually profits accumulate, and a year or two later another period of active trade begins, leading to another period of investment of capital in new mills and factories, thus beginning another cycle of over-investment, over-production and slump of prices, followed by depression, passing into a gradual revival of trade.

There is, indeed, an inevitable tendency to fluctuations of trade and prices in an industrial country ; but some further explanation is needed of two important features of the trade cycle. The fluctuation of trade exhibits a curious irregular periodicity, the most frequent lengths of the cycle having been, as above mentioned, seven, ten or eleven years. Secondly, these fluctuations of trade occur almost simultaneously throughout the world in all industrial countries. These two peculiar features suggest that, whilst industry naturally moves through a cycle of activity followed by depression passing into revival, some special cause is at work helping to determine the time when active trade begins and the time when the collapse of prices begins, especially because these happen throughout the world at the same time. The explanation appears to lie in actual changes of supply and demand caused by variations of the harvests throughout the world. If the cotton crop is good in America and Egypt, the cost of yarn in Lancashire is reduced, and trade is stimulated by the larger quantity demanded at home and abroad when the price of cloth is reduced. Moreover it is well-known that good harvests in agricultural regions having a large trade with industrial areas cause a great demand for the products of industries : agricultural machinery, jute sacks, railway wagons, and so forth, in anticipation of the harvest, and more agricultural machinery, and the clothing, comforts and luxuries wanted by the farming population, after the harvest.

There is statistical evidence that nature is more bountiful in some years than others in her return for the labour of cultivation, taking the world as a whole. The causes of the variations of the harvests are by no means fully understood, though it is obvious that they depend mainly on the difference of weather conditions from year to year. These latter have not been fully explained, but they seem to be due to a great extent to more or less rhythmic fluctuations in the radiant heat which the earth receives from the sun,[1] acting indirectly, perhaps, through the alternate warming and cooling of the oceans, as well as the atmosphere. There is discernible a fluctuation of harvests in variable periods which average about three and a half years, and accord with the fluctuations of certain solar phenomena. Allowing some influence to wars,

[1] See C. G. Abbott, ' Weather Dominated by Solar Changes ', in *Smithsonian Miscellaneous Collections*, Vol. 85, No. 1, 1931 ; and Abbott and Bond, ' Periodicity in Solar Variation, ibid., Vol. 87, No. 9, 1932.

and to the results of unusual over-investment of capital, it may be said that the trade cycle appears to correspond approximately with either two, three, or sometimes four, of these three-and-a-half-year periods.

Doubtless the full truth embraces the psychological and credit theories, as well as the over-investment and harvest fluctuation causes. The spontaneous increase of demand arising from good harvests renews confidence and starts prices on the up-grade. A second succession of good harvests may turn active trade into a boom. Then optimism prevails, with speculation and over-investment of capital. The first year of bad harvests in the great continental countries of the world breaks the spell. Confidence is shaken, prices begin to fall, and finally the credit structure collapses like a house of cards. A consumers' strike against the high prices of the boom period is not in itself a sufficient explanation, except perhaps for the collapse following an after-war boom ; but in some cases a break of prices from over-production may be the main cause of the slump, as in 1929–30. My own view is that the *impulse* of the special demand created by good harvests, and of the sudden cessation of demand caused by widespread bad harvests, acts upon the business organism with its tendencies to psychological states and to inflation and sudden deflation of credit in such a way as to start, and set a time limit to, the ' swing ' of business and industry. An economic system, prone to alternating periods of confidence and expanding credit and of over-investment followed by collapse and pessimism, is (it seems) reacted on, and kept swinging, by a physical cause, which probably has a cosmic origin. Human causes like war and revolution also have their effects in producing or modifying the cyclical fluctuation of trade ; and this constitutes the great difficulty in isolating the effects of the important physical cause, so as to obtain conclusive proof thereof.

Believing, as I do, that the trade cycle is to some extent the result of the fluctuation of harvests on a world-wide scale, due to causes over which man can never hope to have control, I cannot believe that the national regulation of credit, or even the nationalization of banking, would wholly prevent alternations of industrial prosperity and depression. The change of foreign demand from year to year is real, and is something over which one country, or even a group of countries, can have no control. As demand grows it must be met to some extent by a rising price ; and a reaction with falling prices must follow when foreign demand falls off. A national system of credit could greatly mitigate the evil results of fluctuations of foreign demand, but it could not wholly abolish the industrial cycle. Neither would the industrial structure under communism be free from the impact of the cyclical changes of foreign demand. Provision would have to be made for meeting this in two ways : partly, and so far as possible, by building up stocks of commodities usually in demand abroad, so that the surplus carried over from the years of slack demand would meet the shortage in busy years ; and partly, so far as stocks were not available, by working overtime in the industries concerned, because caution would be exercised as regards laying down additional plant for what might prove a merely temporary increase of demand. There being no possibility of additional payment for overtime, as the general allowance would be the same for every one, whatever his work, those who worked overtime would probably be compensated by additional leave, to be taken at their pleasure after the busy period was over.

PART III
REALIZATION

CHAPTER XIV

PREPARATION FOR THE CHANGE

A NEW SOCIAL MORALITY

COMMUNISM being the regeneration of society presupposes the regeneration of man. No violent revolution could accomplish this. Violence at best could only clear away privilege and vested interests and thus leave the field free for the unimpeded growth of progressive ideals and institutions. The character of the English people is such that they will avoid violence if another road to the objective is open ; and my business in this chapter is to indicate that road. I hope to show that a moral reawakening is beginning, and that it can be stimulated and eventually developed into a social purpose almost universally accepted. I shall maintain that this purpose can be fulfilled without violence if the intellectual work of planning the successive stages of advance be efficiently performed, and if a propaganda of enlightenment of all classes be systematically organized by the party of progress.

Any one who reads the signs of the times cannot but be impressed with the advance in positive morality which has taken place in the present century. Discussions of social justice are of everyday occurrence, and legislation has marked every stage of advance by some act recognizing the responsibility of the State for the welfare of all its members. Old age pensions, health insurance, unemployment insurance, their great extension after the War, and the grant of pensions to widows, no less than the great sums voted as subsidies for improved housing, are indications of the general recognition, even by the Conservative Party, of social responsibility to a degree unthought of amongst practical men during the nineteenth century. The organized Churches, established and dissenting, have at last begun to interest themselves closely in labour problems ; and the intervention of the bishops and Nonconformist leaders in the coal strike of 1926 was a striking example of the recognition that industrial and social problems have a moral basis.

Socialist propaganda and the demands of the Labour Party in Parliament, backed by the efficient organization of the trade unions, are largely responsible for the advance hitherto realized towards a higher plane of social morality, because they have forced the ruling and middle classes to think seriously about social problems. Progress could, I think, be still more rapid if the writing, teaching and propaganda in favour of socialism and social justice were to be systematized with a view to the gradual attainment of a recognized ideal state of society. Those who are convinced that the ultimate ideal involves economic equality, the public ownership of all the means of production, and acceptance of the doctrine of service to the community in all work, could most fruitfully at the present stage devote their energies to converting people to a belief in these fundamental principles. I must again emphasize the view that a new social order can only evolve out of the acceptance of new moral ideas.

The desire to see social justice realized seems likely to continue growing amongst the middle classes ; and a definite acceptance of the ideal of economic equality may be expected amongst a small, but ever increasing, section of the same class. The principle that all work should be regarded primarily as rendering service to the community is likely to gain effective expression and almost universal acceptance ; for the doctrine was widely taught by Ruskin, and has been emphasized by R. H. Tawney in his *Acquisitive Society*, his later book *Equality*, and by many other recent writers.

In no true sense are these doctrines new. They are all explicit or implicit in the teachings of Jesus Christ. This suggests that the most powerful stimulus to the acceptance of a higher social morality will be a reinterpretation of the teachings of Jesus. This will come about, I think, through an increasing impatience at the meek and hypocritical toleration of social evils by those who most loudly profess themselves Christians. There will arise a direct, frank search after truth and simplicity of Christian doctrine, a determination to be rid of hypocrisy in the individual interpretation of religious truths, and finally a wave of thought freed from the intellectual domination of the ecclesiastical tradition, which upholds the sanctity of class privilege and property.   This movement, of which the Oxford Group Movement now widely in action may be a forerunner, will, I hope, be greatly stimulated by socialists themselves.   They can advise people to seek for themselves the essence of Christian teaching, and honestly try to apply it to the conditions of modern civilization.   With the heart searching which must accompany this there will surely grow the desire to create the conditions in which the brotherhood of man can be fully realized.

A SOCIAL PURPOSE

The growth of the higher moral conception of social relations just indicated will create the desire for conditions in which the brotherhood of man can be realized, but will not, of itself, do much to break down the existing economic system and establish another.   A motive for combined action will arise only when there has been formed also in men's minds a clear idea of a state of society which would fulfil the new and higher moral conditions.   A definite social purpose cannot exist unless there is a clear perception of the end to be attained.   It is the work of Christian teachers and moralists to create a desire to apply in practice a higher positive morality ; but it is the work of economists and technical men, and those with wide experience of public administration, to define the objective.   A proper exercise of the imagination combined with social studies and research will enable them to present a clearer and more practicable view of the desirable future state of society than any yet presented.   When books in popular style describing the England of the future and the means of attaining it, become widely diffused, knowledge of the ideal will be widespread, and the first stage in the creation of the social purpose will be accomplished.

The next stage will be to persuade a majority of the people that what will be regarded still as an ideal state of society can, in fact, be materialized at no distant date by a consistent series of measures of reform.   Once this idea of progress in a defined and orderly manner from stage to stage towards the new social system has entered into the minds of the people and has been

17

accepted as desirable by most, and inevitable by others, the social purpose will have been fully formed, and progress will be rapid. Ancient shibboleths will be scornfully rejected ; and the rising tide of hope and desire for the new state of freedom will abolish peaceably, because irresistibly, one after another, every privilege and vested interest, however strongly they may seem to-day to be entrenched.

PRELIMINARY RESEARCH

As the new social purpose begins to inspire the great majority of the people, so will their interest in the means of realizing the ideal develop. There will, of course, be varieties and fluctuations of opinion, both as to the exact character of a communistic society and as to the means and stages by which it can be reached. Considerable research will be necessary for both these purposes. It is impossible that a safe and gradual evolution to communism can take place unless close and detailed study be given to all aspects of the proposed changes. I think the research necessary may be divided roughly into two stages which I shall denote : ' preliminary research ' and ' organized research '.

The preliminary research should be undertaken in the near future, during the early stage of propaganda and enlightenment. It would be carried on necessarily by non-Governmental agencies : partly by private persons, no doubt, but mainly by various organizations connected with the Labour movement ; perhaps also under the auspices of, and with the assistance of, two or three learned societies. Organized labour, and the Parliamentary Labour Party, seem likely to become more and more the focus of the progressive social purpose. It may be hoped that the Trades Union Congress will be willing to contribute funds to research work, supporting and developing work undertaken by organizations in which it has confidence. It is quite conceivable that members of academic institutions like the Sociological Society, the Royal Economic Society, the Royal Society of Arts and the British Association will be stimulated by the growing interest in defining the path of progress to a new state of society to undertake inquiries on their own account. There are many indications that engineers are becoming increasingly interested in the problem of planning a more efficient economic system.

In the preliminary stage which we are now considering I do not think that research definitely tending to the realization of a socialist or communist state of society will be undertaken at the expense of universities or of the State. That is a later phase, which will be reached when the majority of electors in the country are convinced that the change must come. In the period of preliminary research the contributions of work likely to be made by State agencies will be confined probably to the collection and publication of accurate information about the industries and trade of the country. Royal commissions and committees will be appointed from time to time, each to make an inquisition into some important industry. With the growth of trade union combination and monopolistic combination among employers, industry after industry will be finding itself in difficulties in each succeeding period of trade depression. In recent years we have had two commissions inquiring into the coal mining industry.[1] The building trade has been the subject of inquiry in relation to housing ; and both the building trade and the ship-building industry have been investigated by joint committees of employers' and workers' representatives ;[2] and the Lancashire cotton industry is in such a condition that a public inquiry has been demanded. The Ministry of Labour has conducted a number of inquiries into wholesale and retail trades in foods, drapery, etc., and certain branches of production ; and the Committee on Industry and Trade has published a number of volumes describing the condition of British industries and markets, and industrial relations. The railways have been the subject of two official inquiries. The Agricultural Marketing Act (1931) provides for the appointment by the Minister of Agriculture and Fisheries of committees and commissions of inquiry into the marketing of any

[1] The Coal Industry Commission, 1919 (Sankey Commission), and the Coal Industry Commission, 1925 (Samuel Commission).

[2] Report of Departmental Committee on High Cost of Building Working-class Dwellings, 1921 ; Inter-Departmental Committee on Prices of Building Materials, 1923, etc. The reports of the non-official inquiries were published under the titles : *Report of the Industrial Council of the Building Industry on Organised Public Service in the Building Industry*, 1919 ; and *Report of Joint Enquiry by the Shipbuilding Employers' Federation and the Shipyard Trade Unions into Foreign Competition and the Conditions in the Shipbuilding Industry* (1925 *and* 1926).

specific agricultural or horticultural product, and articles of food and drink manufactured or processed therefrom, and for drawing up schemes for the re-organization of marketing. The Minister is required to present a report to Parliament annually on schemes submitted and on the working of those in force.

The frequent repetition and extension of official and semi-official inquiries, and the periodical collection of detailed statistics of labour, and detailed censuses of production of the principal industries, will provide a mass of information on which the non-official research agencies above mentioned will be able to work. The secrecy which has hitherto shrouded the operations of our great industries is rapidly passing away. It will soon become possible to know the costs and working conditions of every great industry throughout the country.

Probably also there will be inquiries into the operations of rings and price associations and other monopolistic combines in various industries when the public begins to realize how widespread are their activities and believes that the interests of consumers are affected seriously by the limitation of output and the artificial maintenance of prices. The economic conditions governing each industry will thus become known ; and in course of time statistics will be regularly compiled for the purpose of testing the cost of production and other aspects of the productive efficiency of each of the great industries. To meet a growing demand these statistics will be made readily available to the public in intelligible form.

So much we may confidently anticipate the State will undertake in the near future. As the demand for the nationalization of mines and railways becomes more insistent, so will the State be obliged to undertake specific inquiries into the methods of organization of nationalization and the effective operation of nationalized industries. Detailed knowledge will be required as to the methods of the public operation of transport and industries in other countries and as to the problems to be dealt with in this country in the successful establishment of non-profit-making management on a large scale. Probably it is only by means of the resources at the disposal of the State that the great mass of information needed on these subjects can be accumulated. It is highly important to observe that such inquiries, and particularly the collection of information, its

classification, and the drawing of deductions therefrom, should
be undertaken under the direction of the men who are likely
to be called upon to play an important part in the task of
organizing and managing the nationalized industry ; or at
least with their constant advice. Otherwise much labour might
be wasted ; for the results might not be such as would be
regarded as reliable and useful by the executive and technical
officers in whose charge the nationalized industry would be
placed.

ENLIGHTENMENT

The development of a defined social purpose into a constructive policy may be said to depend upon society as a whole
learning to know itself. Just as an individual finds himself
strengthened in achieving his purpose by having acquired a
knowledge of his capacity—his weaknesses no less than his
abilities—so does a people or nation move more swiftly and
with harmony towards an accepted goal the more fully it is
aware of itself as a body politic. The economy of the country
as a whole should therefore be widely known and understood,
before any great change is attempted. How the people are fed
and clothed, how coal is raised and ships are built, the nature
of our foreign trade, the intricacies of finance—all these must
be widely studied. In recent years there has been already a
remarkable extension of the teaching of economics. Numbers
of text-books on the subject have been published, and—
equally important—a variety of books devoted to particular
industries. A further extension of instruction in economics is
necessary, until no person can be accounted even partly educated
unless he understands the causes underlying the operations of
business, the sources of wages, rent, interest and profits, and
the nature of the national dividend.

The education of the public must be extended to a wider
field than an acquaintance with the theories of capitalist
industry, trade and finance. All parts of the social organism
are interdependent ; and the subject-matter of the early
chapters of this book indicates the importance which I attach
to studies in sociology as the basis of ordered progress to the
new society. Our universities should give as much attention
to sociology as they do to economics by the foundation of

chairs, readerships and lectureships, and by making it a subject co-ordinate in importance with history or economics for a degree. It should be popularized by university extension lectures and the adult education movement generally. Economics is favoured because it is felt to be an important study for the understanding of business and the national economy. Socialists should realize that for the cause they have at heart the diffusion of a knowledge of sociology in its various approaches and branches is even more important.

From the branch of sociology which studies the social organism in its modern form there is a logical transition to the study and understanding of the movements of reform now in progress. Amongst these the more constructive, such as the consumers' co-operative movement, and town and regional planning, should receive the support of socialists ; and an understanding of their principles should be widely diffused. Such subjects furnish the ideas which will lead people to accept the proposal for an entire replanning of society in all its activities on principles of social justice. It is important to accustom the public to think in terms of industry and the distribution of goods being carried on for service rather than for profit, and of that ordering of social activities which it is the object of town planning to achieve.

The study of Utopias, and other complete schemes for the regeneration of society is a fascinating subject, having a close bearing on the object of this book.[1] Utopian dreams are not helpful, however, by way of education or propaganda, unless they have been brought into close relation with existing progressive social movements, for without interpretation they do not carry conviction to persons who have not accepted the socialist viewpoint. A critical analysis of More's *Utopia*, a search for the true principles of a new society in Cabet's *Icaria*, Fourier's *Philansteries*, or Comte's *Western Republic*, a study of modern syntheses like those of Bellamy, William Morris and H. G. Wells would be a highly interesting and instructive way of approaching the problem of the actual future society of England.

Together with enlightenment as to the existing social and

---

[1] A brief bibliography of Utopian literature, including books descriptive of the literature, will be found in Appendix III.

economic order and present progressive movements, the public must be instructed as to the precise nature of the communistic society which it is proposed should be established in England, by those who have accepted it as the ideal and actual objective of social progress. Communism in England cannot be founded on anything else than democracy, meaning by this the will of the majority of the people, and not any particular form of constitution devised for realizing that will. The adoption of communism should be, and will be, based on the assent of the great majority of the adult population ; hence the people at large must have a more or less clear conception of what is proposed. I am convinced that when the social objective comes clearly into view in every man's imagination, controversy will rage only over the best and quickest means of realizing it. A wide knowledge of present economic conditions will be indispensable if this controversy is to be fruitful. I emphasize again, therefore, the desirability of inculcating amongst those classes having industrial and political power, especially amongst organized labour, a knowledge of the existing structure of society.

The party of progress who accept the social objective as outlined in this book, or some equivalent thereto, will need to formulate their ideal clearly in simple language and to carry on an extensive educational campaign amongst the middle classes as well as the workers. Whilst explaining attractively their ideal and the methods of attaining it, they must adhere in their statements to the real facts about the existing social order and be sure that they teach the truth in all the fullness in which they have been able to discover it. The repetition of stock phrases of Marxian doctrine should be avoided. That social thought owes much to Karl Marx no sensible person will deny ; but to quote his dogmas, in several respects patently erroneous, as if they were the final revelation of socialism, is a hindrance to actual progress.

SOCIALIST PROPAGANDA

The diffusion of correct ideas regarding the national economy of Great Britain, and how it would work when transformed into a system of general co-operation under communism, is an indispensable preliminary to propaganda in favour of actually attempting to realize the new state of society. Brainwork is necessary, and must not be shirked—by socialists especially. Assuming, however, that the groundwork of informing the public through books, periodicals and lectures is well and truly done, the field will be clear for an intensive propaganda in favour of taking the first steps towards nationalization of industries and preparatory measures towards the ultimate adoption of communism.

Socialist propaganda is at present far too vague. As was indicated earlier in this chapter there are numbers of intelligent people in the middle classes, mainly in the professional and salaried posts, who are sympathetically disposed towards the general principles for which socialism stands ; but their reason is never convinced that socialists can propose a workable scheme of society. To a large extent they will take no trouble either to read what socialists have proposed or to attend lectures. The first stage of organized propaganda, therefore, must be to combat this apathy. It can only be done, I feel sure, by a general claim which appeals to the highest emotions.

What higher appeal could be made than to religion and to patriotism ? At present we are rather accustomed to think that patriotism and true Christianity are mutually exclusive ; but are they ? Does not the socialist believe that he is proposing a social and economic system which will conduce in every way to the benefit of his country ? The people well cared for and happy, healthier and physically stronger ; wealth production immensely increased under communism—the complete co-operation of all : will not these conditions enable England to hold her great place amongst the nations which now she seems in danger of losing through the relative decline of her great industries ? There is no need for the socialist to be a ' Little Englander '. He ought not to be ; and in this respect might well take a lesson from the ruling party of Soviet Russia, which, by forming semi-autonomous republics, has maintained as Russian territory the full extent of the old empire, except in the West, where nationalist aspirations amongst non-Russian peoples prevented it. If socialism is good for England, it will be good for each and every part of the British Empire when it reaches the right stage of economic and political development.

Socialists, therefore, may appeal to patriotism. They may also appeal most strongly to religion. I sometimes think that socialists would be more sincere, and would be recognized as such, if, instead of carping at and criticizing the organized Churches, they took up a positive attitude towards Christianity and became teachers themselves. Does not every thoughtful socialist believe that he could offer purer, simpler teaching of the gospel than can be heard from *bourgeois* pulpits in church or chapel ? Then why shrink from going to the very fundamentals of life and claiming allegiance on the basis of these ? Let socialists have the confidence of their convictions and their teaching will be listened to. So long as socialism is regarded as a matter of class interest, even class warfare, so long will the intelligentsia of the nation regard it with suspicion, and the trading class with open hostility. Such is the prestige of a high moral conviction, however, that even the hostility will be weakened by a demand for social change explicitly based on the profound but simple truths of Christian life and thought. By direct personal study of the gospels socialists can evolve their own simple Christianity.

There are other directions also in which, as it seems to me, the moral basis of effective propaganda could be strengthened. It is never too early to begin practising what one preaches ; and those who believe not only that all men are of equal worth in the sight of God, but that they should be so also in the estimation of men, may advocate the adoption even now of reforms and social customs tending to recognize equality. Propaganda is particularly needed amongst the working classes to give them self-respect. If they do not claim equality in a thousand and one social ways they will never get it in the economic domain. A title, evidences of wealth or position in society, even arrogance of manner in a ' well-bred ' person, still make the average English workman behave obsequiously. He has not the self-respect and spirit of independence of the poor of America or the British Colonies ; even of some of the European republics. It is amazing to me in how many occupations the worker is still willing to demean himself by accepting tips as a normal part of his remuneration for his ordinary work.

In all these respects America has for a century been far in advance of us. Egalitarian thought, inherited partly perhaps from the Levellers of the seventeenth century, grew in congenial soil during the eighteenth century in a new country with a sparse population, and gained expression in the opening sentences of the Declaration of Independence. The French Revolution, in spite of its excesses, spread the ideals of Liberty, Equality, Fraternity in a great wave throughout Europe ; and the Jacobins, for a time, demanded economic equality. If French proletarian thought was influenced by the American Declaration, it again reacted on America, and strengthened the hold of egalitarian principles there.

In America, therefore, the industrial classes have grown up owning a spirit of independence, based on the idea of equality, which has many practical manifestations. On the American railways, for instance, it has never been the custom for employees, other than negroes, to accept tips ; nor was it the custom, until recent years, for hotel employees to accept them, except in the Atlantic coast towns where for the most part newly arrived European immigrants have been employed. The railways theoretically provide one class only, and on local trains actually so. The provision of Pullmans and parlour cars for long journeys is a recognition of economic inequality, but does not suggest a stigma of social inequality. So also it will be remembered that the Government of the United States confers no titles or orders, and that everybody is plain ' mister ' ; there are no ' esquires '.

' Why call attention to these trivial matters ? ' some readers may think. I assure my socialist friends that they are not trivial ; and that socialists, by condoning the continuance of social customs which originated in class privilege, weaken most seriously their moral and intellectual appeals. I should like to see socialists follow the Quakers and refuse to use the designation ' Esq.', unless used for all, which, historically would be absurd. The railways should convert their carriages to one class only, which is the practice already on the tubes and omnibuses. The trade unions concerned should start a movement for the abolition of tips. It appears to me that it should be an essential part of the early stage of socialist propaganda to create a public appreciation of the dignity of all useful manual labour honestly and efficiently applied. This propaganda cannot be merely general ; it must be directed specially against any indignities which the workers actually suffer.

The propaganda on these basic principles, together with the progress in organization, which will be discussed in the next chapter, would, I conceive, prepare the middle classes, and the cautious element amongst the workers, to listen to definite socialist teaching ; and then would arise the opportunity of gaining wide acceptance for the idea that a big economic change must come at no very distant date in the direction of equality, and the organization of all work as service to the community. People would then be eager to discuss the economy of the country in a socialistic or communistic régime. The pros and cons of public operation of essential services would begin to interest the ' man in the street ' ; and the more intellectual amongst the middle classes would be drawn to study the principles and working of the proposed society of equality, and the preparatory stages of the transition. Propaganda, which is now so largely sterile, would fall then on fertile ground, and before many years had passed actually bear fruit.

CHAPTER XV

PROGRESS IN ORGANIZATION

A GRADUAL SOCIAL REVOLUTION

THE advancement of thought in favour of socialism, the formation of a social purpose, and the means of undertaking all the necessary research in economics and administration, were the subjects of the last chapter. Our inquiry can be carried a stage further in the direction of initiating fruitful research by considering in this chapter the actual organization by which the stages of advance to socialism, and ultimately communism, may be achieved. After some further analysis of the social and psychological factors influencing a change of opinion we shall survey existing institutions with the object of reviewing those which have been founded to diffuse its ideals, or are working in accordance with the principles of socialism, and may be regarded as the seeds from which, by intelligent expansion, the institutions of the new order of society may develop.

To imagine that the establishment of socialism in other countries must follow any such course as the Russian revolution is the result of ignorance of the economic and social history of Europe. Russia has attempted to achieve five great revolutions which England, when socialism is established, will have taken over four centuries to complete. Russia has gone through a great agrarian revolution, a closing of monasteries and disestablishment of the church comparable with our reformation, the establishment of political democracy, and an important stage of the industrial revolution, and has attempted the establishment of socialism : all in fifteen years. England began her agrarian changes in the fifteenth century, the reformation came early in the sixteenth century, political democracy slowly in the seventeenth, eighteenth and nineteenth centuries, and the industrial revolution slowly in the eighteenth and nineteenth centuries. We, in Great Britain, do all things by gradual changes ; but the process of realizing socialism may perhaps be hastened and eased if we fully understand whither we are going, and how we may advance towards that goal of social welfare. A peaceful change to a socialist régime is not merely practicable : it is essential for the well-being of the country. The way of achieving the change by constitutional and legal means can be, and must be, devised.

In a democracy this obviously requires the education of public opinion ; and this will have to be undertaken in two ways, neither of which without the other is likely to achieve the desired effect. The first way is by the written and spoken word. The second is by the actual establishment of industrial and commercial concerns to be operated on a non-profit-making basis. The advantage of starting these would be that the technique of the incentives of administrative control could be worked out. Some might be started mainly with the object of giving employment to the people of a locality ; but it would be important to demonstrate that public service can be effectively rendered by non-profit-making concerns, even though working amongst existing capitalist businesses and forced to share in the wastes inevitable until competition is replaced by a planned scheme of service in every branch of production and distribution.

The peaceful change to socialism would be facilitated by the gradual growth of institutions organized and working in accordance with the principles of socialism which would carry over into the new state of society. Some perhaps, when the State has passed a general law abolishing or limiting profit-making business, will enlarge their functions. Others will serve as models for other professions and industries. Thus the change to socialism is not to be thought of as a sudden revolution. The social revolution will be a change to a new moral and psychic basis of industry taking place slowly like the industrial revolution. The final change to communism must, however, take place at a given moment, as we shall see in the next chapter, by the coming into force of a carefully prepared set of laws. This does not mean that violence is likely ; for the laws will only be passed when the great majority of the population understand and feel themselves ready for the culminating phase in the evolution of socialism.

DISTINCTION BETWEEN SOCIALISM AND LABOURISM

An essential preliminary to any real progress in the formation of opinion in favour of socialism is the recognition of the fundamental difference between labourism and socialism, which should be clearer than it is to socialists themselves. The Conservative press persistently calls the Labour Party ' the Socialist Party ', probably with a view to prejudicing it in the eyes of readers, and to creating confusion of thought. The editors are well enough aware, on the one hand, that many influential trade union officials and prominent members of the Labour Party are not socialists, and, on the other hand, that the tacit assumption that socialism teaches approval of the seemingly absurd rules of trade unions, and of taxing the rich to maintain a growing army of unemployed and to subsidize rents, will tend to prevent acceptance of socialism by the middle classes. For the prevailing confusion of thought English socialists are, however, to some extent themselves responsible. Several well-known socialist writers are members of the Labour Party, or of the Independent Labour Party, and write not only on socialism, but on immediate political and industrial issues from the labour point of view.

Logically there is a fundamental distinction between socialism and labourism. The latter is the advocacy and supporting of the interests of the organized wage-earners. Socialism, on the other hand, is the theory of a possible organization of society in the interests of all. The fundamental point of view in the case of socialism is that of the consumer. There is to be no propertied class—distinguished as such from manual and other wage earners. The new state of society which it is the object of socialism to create aims at securing the welfare of the whole population : of the professional intelligentzia and administrative officers in industries and public services quite as much as of the manual and clerical workers.

The antiquity of the doctrines of communism, and the fact that a school of thought in favour of a society organized on some system of state or co-operative socialism (though not at first so named) has existed in Europe ever since the publication of More's *Utopia*, are proofs that the theory of socialism arose independently of the Labour movement. The latter, in so far as it had men of imagination, like Keir Hardie, who could escape partly or wholly from the immediate business of settling wage-rates and securing by legislation improved conditions for the working classes, naturally adopted socialism ; for socialism alone inspired such men with hopes of a better world.

Trade unions arose as the result of the factory system, and grew in membership, extent and power concurrently with large-scale organization in industry. Legislative care for the workers was in the hands of philanthropists, mainly of the Liberal Party, until electoral reform and the better education and wider outlook of trade union leaders, and the availability of political funds, brought the movement for direct representation in Parliament to fruition. The Labour Party in Parliament, quite as much as the trade unions, has been occupied with countering the results of the growth of the capitalist competitive system. The Labour movement is therefore the antithesis of the capitalist movement. Consequently, the mentality of the efficient trade union officer is that characteristic of the business man in the capitalist system. He is out to drive a hard bargain on behalf of his fellow-workers : to sell labour as dearly as possible per unit of work, and to buy food as cheaply as possible. His idea of administrative efficiency is formed by his observation of how a large and successful business is run. The mentality of the rank and file of the workers is likewise affected by their being the human units of a profit-making machine. The habit of responding for years to egoistic incentives not only develops their egoistic attitude to their employers and to the public as consumers of their services, but leads them to regard the idealism and altruism of socialism as something unreal and visionary which does not concern them as practical men.

The confusion of socialism with labourism is retarding the acceptance of socialism by the middle class. Many trade union practices are widely believed to be antagonistic to national prosperity. It is thought that trade unionists usually restrict their rate of work ; and the leisurely ways of plumbers and decorators when they are needed in middle-class homes are taken as evidence. The strictness with which a man is confined to his own trade, with resulting waste of time, and the effects on our export trades of the unwillingness of British workers to accept conditions of hours and of manning of machinery which prevail in competing countries, are other examples. It cannot be denied that the practices of many trades unions in protecting their particular group of workers do involve waste in one way or another and consequent higher costs. It is essential to disabuse middle-class opinion of the idea that socialism involves the general acceptance and perpetuation of trade union practices, of the ' dole ', of ' lavish ' pensions for the aged and disabled, and subsidies for housing, all provided out of taxation of the wealthy and middle classes. These expensive ameliorative measures are the inevitable result of widespread education and adult suffrage grafted on to the capitalist-competitive system ; which latter arose because it was the most efficient in production with an ignorant proletariat. Obviously such trade union practices and measures would not be necessary in a socialist society, because the evils of unemployment, destitution and bad housing, against which they are directed, would be prevented from arising by proper planning in advance.

THE PRESS AND THE FILMS

The written and spoken word is the essential way of converting the public to socialism ; though, as stated above, it will need to be supported by the actual achievements of non-profit-making industries. The visual story, in a thoughtfully prepared film, can also help to prepare the ground.

There is already a voluminous output of socialist literature in Great Britain in the forms of books, tracts and periodicals, weekly and monthly, the periodicals being mostly issued by societies and organizations which will be mentioned below. No one could read them all ; and if he confined himself to current literature he would be bored by constant repetitions and depressed by a feeling that nine-tenths of what is written brings us no nearer to the realization of socialism. Nearly all of it, whether issued by the Labour Party or by organizations with views further to the left, suffers from being condemnatory and assertive rather than intellectual and argumentative or quietly persuasive. Such writing, however much it may please the writer and ardent supporters of the cause, does not carry conviction to non-socialists. The circulation is almost entirely confined to the converted, with the exception of the *New Statesman and Nation*, which is a mild advocate of socialism. Moreover, the modern tendency in English socialist and labour literature is to assume that readers dislike anything which demands the slightest intellectual effort. I believe this to be an error of judgment, and that the professional class and educated wage-earners want thoughtful articles taking them over new ground in sociology, history, politics, art and science, written from the progressive and, where appropriate, the socialist point of view ; and with them studies of the moral, economic and administrative aspects of socialism and communism. Relaxation there must be ; but this may be full of interest. Jejune articles savouring of the popular magazine, literary ' criticism ', or inaccurate diatribes, are waste of space, or worse, in a socialist paper.

Unfortunately there is no socialist daily, if we exclude the communist *Daily Worker* and the *Daily Herald*. The latter is a labour paper which supports trade unionism and the Labour Party, but does not advocate socialism. It is not hostile : merely indifferent ; but reports speeches of labour men in favour of socialism. The old daily papers which aimed primarily at furthering the public good and supporting a cause are gone, with the notable exceptions of *The Times* and the *Manchester Guardian*. The capitalist press exists partly to further business interests, but mainly to make profits like a manufacturing concern. For this purpose it aims either at a large or a select circulation, with the sole object of maximizing advertisement revenue. Since the progress of socialism and of the co-operative movement are judged likely to diminish advertising revenue they are ignored, ridiculed or treated briefly with ignorant hostility.

The popular dailies make a business of providing sensation and excitement ; they appeal to one of the primitive instincts, which finds least satisfaction in civilized life in times of peace. Many persons have found distraction from their personal worries or disgruntlement due to the evils and injustices of our economic system in alcohol or drugs. The daily press, cheap periodical literature and the cinemas have in recent years increasingly supplied the wanted pleasant distraction without intellectual effort. They act as a sedative and tend to allay social unrest. Life is presented in its rosiest hue. Vice and misery exist only to be banished by the hero ; and after adventures there is always the happy ending. Several novelists, of course, have given us true pictures of the tragedy of the economically unfit. The foregoing refers to the commercial press, daily and periodical, and to the films. The cinema trade knows well that the majority of people do not want to have the evils of the world forced on their attention, and that stories based on the conditions of work and life of the poor and suggesting the possibility of a better state of society would stir unrest and be disloyal to the profit-making business system. The British Broadcasting Corporation to its credit allows more latitude. The social problem may be stated frankly and the need of a new economic system indicated. ' Talks ' on this subject are anaemic, however ; for a definite solution or particular plan may not be presented, for such would be controversial, or have a party aspect.

It is essential to the formation and ripening of opinion that there should be a good socialist press with wide circulation. There ought to be at least two socialist dailies, whereas now there is none ; and weekly and monthly periodicals more informative and intellectual, though simple in style and easy to read, and of wider general interest.

Some of the cardinal principles of journalism seem largely to be overlooked by the editors of existing labour, socialist and co-operative newspapers and periodicals. To begin with, the reader must be given value for money. This does not mean that periodicals must be cheap, but that they must be alert and interesting, with subject-matter different from the usual run of existing and widely circulated journals.[1] A socialist daily must provide the public with general news as efficiently as any other paper, give news of special interest to socialists and be generally bright and interesting. A paper issued by a party or organization, be it socialist, co-operative or any other, must be free to criticize and not regard itself as a propaganda agent to sing the praises of that organization and push its ideas. To achieve a large circulation it must be

---

[1] Comparison of the Co-operative movement's *Reynolds' Newspaper* as regards general information and entertainment with, say, the *Observer* and the *Sunday Express*, will indicate my meaning, for they all cost the same. The *Millgate Monthly* is an attractive co-operative magazine.

bought by the members of that organization. They will always constitute the majority of its readers ; for a solid and secure foundation for the circulation can be made only by obtaining their patronage. To appeal to the loyalty of members of the party is the weakest and most uncertain way of maintaining or increasing circulation ; for why should members buy a paper if it does not interest them ?

People like a journal which echoes their own views, perhaps expressing them better than they could do, and at the same time gives news and interesting information. Newspapers supporting the Parliamentary opposition usually increase their circulation ; for it is easy to blame the Government for economic and other ills, and people like to read public expressions of their own feelings of dissatisfaction. Co-operative newspapers are not read widely by co-operators. They soon would be, however, if they adopted an attitude of independent criticism, and gave vent to members' grouses about the policy and management of their own societies, the productions of the wholesale societies, and co-operative services generally ; and this not merely by publication of members' letters, which they sometimes do now, but by well-informed editorial and other articles. A running fire of constructive criticism gives life to any institution or movement ; and the freedom of the Press within a movement is something to be established and jealously guarded.

Almost as necessary as a press full of life and leadership is the development of a film art which depicts life as it is seen by socialists and actualizes in scene and speech their ideals of a better social order. It must depict faithfully, not without humour, the present life amongst the workers, and delicately but clearly point the moral of socialism. The films must be such as will fill cinemas at remunerative prices ; but they must also stir the audience with generous emotion and effective thought. Recent Russian films suggest various lines of approach ; but in this country at least such obvious propaganda as some contain defeats its aim. Sincerity of purpose and expression and the beauty of true art will claim attention and carry conviction.

A moment's thought should be sufficient to convince any one that a film art favourable to socialism can only be developed by socialists. Some who are ardent believers and have artistic gifts must study the technique of the films and master it as thoroughly as the profit-makers. We have in England novelists and dramatists who have done much to stir thought on social questions, to advance positive morality and to diffuse the ideals of socialism ; but their works are too intellectual for the masses. A popular socialist press and art is yet to seek. If rightly conceived and well executed success is certain.

But the need for consistency must not be overlooked. A socialist must not set out to make large royalties or profits out of composing or producing films, nor yet out of showing them. He is entitled to his living like every professional person, and to terms or earnings which give him reasonable security for the future ; but no more. Though self-appointed, he works for the public service, and must claim no privileged position. The actual organization and capitalization should follow the principles of non-profit-making industry.[1] The 'trade' will not show such films. There must be special cinemas owned either by co-operative societies, formed perhaps for the purpose, or by associations not working for profit and paying only a fixed interest on capital.

EXISTING SOCIALIST PARTIES AND ASSOCIATIONS

The existing organizations which have as their only or principal object the realization of socialism may be divided first into the political and non-political, and secondly as to whether they hold views of the right and believe in gradualism, or of the left and belong to the Marxian school, believing in the class struggle leading inevitably to revolution, for which the way must be prepared.

Of the political parties the Labour Party is, of course, the most important. It is committed to a general support of socialism as the ideal aim of labour policy, to be realized some time in the distant future. This was clearly stated in 1928 in the elaborate manifesto *Labour and the Nation*, and adherence to this was reaffirmed at the Labour Party Conference in October 1932. When the Labour Party is in office, however, socialism recedes into the background as the pious hope of

[1] Mainly the payment of a fixed rate of interest only on the capital employed.

theoreticians, and labourism tinged with liberalism holds the field. The characteristics of the Labour Party in relation to the realization of socialism need close examination, and this will be attempted in the next section.

The other party of the right is the Co-operative Party, first organized in 1917, but of no importance until recent years. Its funds are raised by contributions from the retail and wholesale distributive societies ; and in the Parliament of 1929-31 it had twelve members, one of them a Cabinet Minister. These members identified themselves closely with the Labour Party, the policy of which they hardly influenced. Neither were they successful in inducing the Labour Government to meet the special needs of the co-operative movement, e.g. to raise the legal limit of share-holding from £200 to £300. The party is now being actively organized and intends to make itself a factor of importance in national politics. Its platform includes the gradual realization of socialism, partly by the steps advocated by the Labour Party—nationalization of land and of banking, and transport, power and fuel supply (mainly coal-mining) and the heavy industries to be operated by public boards—and partly by the voluntary method of extending the existing co-operative movement. This already embraces societies with 6,590,000 members, representing, with their families, over one-third of the population of Great Britain. In London and other areas the number of members is rapidly growing ; so that the enlistment of almost the entire population in certain areas is by no means an impossible objective. The Co-operative Party assumes that, concurrently with the growth of membership, the production of consumers' goods, including house-building, would be organized more and more completely on a co-operative basis by the wholesale societies or otherwise.

The political parties of the left are the Independent Labour Party, the Social Democratic Federation, the Communist Party, and the Socialist Party of Great Britain, the last having but a small membership. The first, usually referred to as the I.L.P., was affiliated to the Labour Party until recently. It has always sponsored the socialist cause, and for the past ten years has been pressing on the Labour Party its ' Socialism in Our Time ' policy. In the Parliament of 1929-31 it had forty-three members, and some of these were thorns in the side of the

Labour Ministry. In spite of the vagueness of its plans for socialism, it has been, and still is, the 'spearhead' of the socialist movement, the majority of socialists amongst the working classes being its members, in spite of recent secessions to the Labour Party. A statement of the policy of the I.L.P. will be found in the Appendix to the report of the Conference held at Blackpool in March 1932. Prior to this conference the I.L.P. might for some years have been classed as Centre rather than Left; for it had ceased to hold its belief in the class struggle and revolutionary method which it has now resumed.

The Social Democratic Federation was before the War the chief exponent and guardian in this country of Marxian doctrine. The growth of the I.L.P., on the one hand, and of the Communist Party on the other, has sapped its membership, so that it has now no political importance. The Communist Party has an extensive literature and organization in this country, and its membership has been growing of recent years amongst the working classes, stimulated by the increasing trade depression; but it has never had more than one member in Parliament. Most of its energies seem to be devoted to the discussion of the means of organizing the overthrow of the capitalist system. It is a sterile subject, because capitalism will not be overthrown until the majority clearly apprehend the character of the system which it is proposed to set up in its place, and are convinced that it will be better.

The non-political organizations devoted to the study of, and the propaganda for, socialism are numerous and varied. First in time and importance stands the Fabian Society, the chief centre of English socialist thought during the past forty years. It has advocated chiefly State and municipal socialism to be attained by the evolutionary method; has published a long series of books and pamphlets and arranged courses of lectures; and in these and other ways has promoted study and research in social economics and the problems of socialism, mainly in questions of administration. The New Fabian Research Bureau, established two years ago on the initiative of Mr. G. D. H. Cole and Major Attlee, is organizing research amongst several groups of its members, who have come into voluntary association for the purpose. Membership is confined to members of the Labour Party; and it has to some extent undertaken to carry out the work originally intended to be done by the Labour Research Department, the complexion of which has entirely changed of recent years by its membership coming to include a majority holding views of the Left.

The New Fabian Research Bureau has an ambitious program of work, as may be seen by perusing its *Memorandum on a Plan of Research into Economic Policy*.[1] Some eight or ten committees are at work, and some preliminary reports have been prepared on certain subjects proposed in the Memorandum ; for instance, on Wage Theory in relation to socialism, staple Commodity Control in Foreign Trade, the

[1] Issued in May 1931. The Committee which prepared the Memorandum proposed that the field of research be divided into eight sections, as follows :

'1. Form and scope of State control and socialization of industry, rationalization, and the reform of commercial law.

'2. The Machinery of Economic Planning and the problem of Capital Supply, including, e.g. (a) the Inter-relations of Socialized Industries, Financial Organization, the control of prices and wages ; (b) the supply of Capital for Investment, Control over the Export of Capital and the problem of " The Flight from the Pound " which a Socialist Government may have to face ; (c) State Planning.

'3. Economic and Technical Research, in their relations to economic development, State organization and control and working-class conditions.

'4. Appointment and dismissal of manager's and staff in socialized or State controlled enterprises, questions of wages, hours and conditions, and the problem of workers' control in industry.

'5. The Standard of Living in relation to wages and social services. The promotion of economic equality on these lines, including the problems of taxation and taxable capacity.

'6. The Theory of Socialist Economic Policy, including the problem of price regulation and the distribution of productive resources.

'7. Foreign Trade, including the question of control of imports and exports, the problem of State or collective trading, and the question of Protection v. Free Trade.

'8. Finance and Industrial Fluctuations, including the causes of trade depression, banking policy and the price level, and the possible socialization of the banking system.'

Subdivisions of these sections are given and discussed in detail. For instance, Section 1 includes the question of what enterprises are ripe for socialization under the headings : Transport (road, rail, shipping, air, cables and wireless) ; Power (coal, electricity, gas, water) ; Industrial Production (mainly the heavy industries and building) ; Finance (banking, investment, stock exchanges) ; Distribution (including the position of the co-operative movement in relation to a policy of socialization) ; Import and Export Trade ; Land and Agriculture ; State Control of above services. Section 1 also includes : Forms of Socialization ; State Control of Marketing ; Compensation to owners ; Rationalization (the question of State encouragement or compulsion) ; Mixed enterprises (partly State and partly private owned) ; the Law relating to Trusts and Companies.

Details of proposed research in the other sections are also given. A later re-draft of the Memorandum (Nov. 1932) has further defined and added to the above subjects, especially in politics, international relations and colonial policy. (For some studies already published, see Appendix III.)

Theory of Price in a Controlled Economy, and Price Level Policy. Others are in preparation ; and a number of pamphlets have been printed and published. The Bureau is sadly handicapped for lack of funds ; and thus in permanent staff and office facilities. The impression given by the first annual report and other documents is that a number of young economists are undertaking in their spare time the investigation of extremely important aspects of socialism ; but that these activities of what appear to be more or less independent groups of members will need careful co-ordination if they are to effect any substantial progress in the theory of socialism. The field· is so extensive and the subjects so difficult that a staff of wholetime economists is necessary, with suitable statistical and office assistants. Organization in the form of an Institute, the governing body of which would not be subject to frequent or irresponsible change by members' votes, would seem to be desirable in order to secure continuity of work and policy and that degree of centralized control which would make proper co-ordination possible.

The Labour Party headquarters has a research department, and so has the General Council of the Trades Union Congress, both being situated at Transport House, Westminster. Only indirectly and occasionally do these turn their attention to questions connected with the realization of socialism. Naturally they are concerned mainly with economic issues of the near future in their political and industrial aspects. Such proposals as nationalization of transport, coal-mines and power-supply, and their operation by public boards, have been investigated and advocated.

There are no other organizations in this country known to me concerned with research relating to the realization of socialism under the control of persons holding views of the Right or Centre. The Labour Research Department, now controlled by sympathisers with the Communist Party, is, I believe, the only centre of research in which opinions of the Left find expression. Besides a number of pamphlets of varying value, it issues a monthly circular. The articles in this frequently contain useful information and statistics, and it gives an interesting survey of current events from the Labour point of view.

Associations of a non-political character engaged in education and propaganda in socialism are not so numerous as might be expected. The Fabian Society has been mentioned already. Its membership, distinguished and influential, remains comparatively small, probably because it is too academic and cautious for the great majority of socialists. The most active and numerous body is the Socialist League, which was formed in 1932, the occasion being the split in the I.L.P. caused by its decision to disaffiliate from the Labour Party. Those socialists who desired to remain or become members of the Labour Party agreed with the members of the Society for Socialist Inquiry and Propaganda, which was established two years previously, partly by the same persons who started the New Fabian Research Bureau, that the former be merged in the new association called the Socialist League. Members must also be members of the Labour Party. It has issued several pamphlets, has arranged an extensive program of lectures and conferences, and has a number of active branches in the principal towns of England and Wales. In Scotland the Scottish Socialist Party, formed on the same occasion, and affiliated with the Labour Party, takes the place of the League.

There are socialist societies, or Labour clubs with strong socialist tendencies, amongst the undergraduates at Oxford, Cambridge, Manchester and other universities ; and an interesting recent event has been the formation of a society by a group of young Liberals said to be inspired by the teaching of Keir Hardie. In some provincial towns the Trades and Labour Council, and in many the local Labour Party, is strongly socialist ; and these are to some extent agencies for education and propaganda in socialism. There are also local associations in London, such as the Promethean Society, and in the provinces, which include socialism in a wider field of cultural studies, or whose members are mainly socialists. The small provincial socialist societies which used to exist seem to have disappeared since the Labour Party in all centres soon after the War admitted to membership individuals as well as organizations ; for meetings of the local Labour Party have served for lectures and discussions on socialism, as well as on political questions of immediate interest to labour.

In the trades unions there exists what is known as the Minority Movement. From about 1911, when the miners in the Rhondda were preaching syndicalism in their own and the other principal coalfields, there has developed amongst the younger trade unionists in most of the great industries a school of militant socialism, which is largely Marxist and revolutionary in character. They are in general sympathy with the communists, but do not care for their extreme views and Russian doctrine.

The principal non-political organization of the Left is the National Council Labour Colleges, which issues the monthly magazine *Plebs*, and with which are affiliated ' Labour Colleges ' in several provincial towns. These are centres for evening classes and lectures, where the principles of socialism and economics are expounded, the defects of the capitalist system analysed and social reforms and legislation discussed.

Of quite a different character from the foregoing associations is the British Llano Circle, formed some ten years ago with the object of establishing in Great Britain a co-operative colony on the basis of the economic and social equality of all the members. It is named after the successful communistic colony at New Llano in the State of Louisiana, U.S.A., which calls its economic system ' integral co-operation.' The history of the Owenite co-operative colonies established in England a century ago is not encouraging ; but one founded at Ralahine in Ireland had a successful career for a few years, and came to an end only through the sale of the estate it occupied owing to the bankruptcy of the landlord.[1] In America several communist colonies existed successfully for a long time ; but most have been dissolved, usually because the younger generation, out of sympathy with the religious teaching and puritan practices of their elders, sought education and occupation in the great cities, and the communities became practically land owning corporations.[2]

NEED FOR A CONSISTENT ORGANIZATION OF POLITICAL ACTIVITIES

Political thought must be well organized in its expression, if it is to bear fruit in actual results. For the necessary propaganda to be successful, in the sense of leading to definite action

[1] For a brief account of this colony, see "Industrial Co-operation," by Catherine Webb. (Manchester: Co-operative Union, Ltd.), pp. 60-4.
[2] For references to literature on co-operative or communist colonies, see Appendix III at the end of the bibliography.

towards the desired objective, a carefully thought-out organization must be built up which will work consistently to secure
agreement as to ideals and methods, and general acceptance
of a policy to be elaborated. It is also important that the
organization should secure agreement as to the successive steps
which must be taken towards the realization of the objective.
It is the problem of rendering progressive thought and propaganda consistent and then effective, by linking it, on the one
hand, with political action in Parliament, and, on the other
hand, with suitable industrial measures, which should now
occupy the attention of socialists.

The activities of trades unions are, at present, directed to
improving the condition of their members in three distinct
ways : by industrial means, by political activities, and by
schemes of prudential benefits of the nature of insurance. The
last has always been an important part of the work of the
great craft unions—the engineers, carpenters, printers, and so
forth ; but many of the big unions of more recent origin,
such as the miners and the transport and general workers,
have never undertaken the provision of benefits for their
members.

This field of activity does not seem likely to expand. As
socialist doctrines come to be more and more widely held
amongst the working classes, members of trade unions will
realize that their best hope lies in concentrating on industrial
and political action : the former for the welfare of the workers
of their own industry, though with due regard to the interests
of workers in other industries ; the latter for the benefit of
the working classes as a whole. It is already understood that
friendly benefits have little or no constructive value. In the
existing economic system they serve to strengthen the union
by binding its members more closely together ; but to those
having a wide outlook they appear merely as an incident of
the capitalist competitive system.

The Parliamentary Labour Party is weak in action and
deficient in prestige with the other parties in the House and
with the electors. It is too heterogeneous in respect of the
opinions of its members ; hence the party as a whole has no
very clearly defined program—certainly nothing which strikes
the imagination. The party concerns itself largely with

issues of the near future of the ameliorative type, e.g. unemployment benefit, pensions, minimum wage legislation, regulation of hours, factory conditions, improved housing, and so forth. All members of the party, whether advanced socialists, Fabians, or of the ' Liberal-Labour ' type, can support these. The majority of members of the party, however, are or were socialists ; hence the party has adopted a rather vague program of steps towards socialism, e.g. the nationalization of land, of the mines, of the railways, and of docks and ocean shipping, and aid for agriculture by public organization of marketing. There is still a good deal of difference of opinion as to the method by which these measures of nationalization should be carried out, what amount of compensation, if any, should be given, and as to the nature of the controlling public authority. In some quarters the view is expressed that the leaders of the Labour Party are not over-anxious to have before them the task of putting into effect the principles of their party in respect of nationalization when first they come into power with a clear Parliamentary majority, and that this is the reason why little attention is given by the party to the elaboration of really practicable plans for nationalizing mines and railways, and why the propaganda of labour amongst the middle classes in favour of nationalization remains too feeble to have any effect. A source of weakness lies in the divisions of opinion amongst socialists themselves, each school of thought being reflected in the composition of the party in the House.

A fundamental cleavage of opinion remains in the Labour Party, even though the I.L.P. members have left it, between those who favour progress by the old system of piecemeal reforms and those who hold that no substantial or permanent benefit to the working classes is possible except by a radical alteration of the whole social and economic system, and that the party should occupy itself with fundamental measures. The former, who constitute the right wing, or Liberal-Labour, section of the party believe in a policy which may be called ' incoherent opportunism '—opportunist, because they would press for or support any scheme of reform intended to benefit the poor when a favourable combination of circumstances seemed to assure its passage through Parliament ; and ' incoherent ' because such reforms—e.g. improved poor-law administration by county councils, extension of the period for which transitional unemployment benefits may be paid, with increase of the State contribution, adequate pensions for widows, and so forth—are unrelated and involve but little progress towards a new social system. Indeed, it may be argued that, in so far as such piecemeal reforms do in fact alleviate the condition of the poor, they actually delay the true realization of social justice in the economic system, and would be more fittingly left to the initiative of the Conservative Party.

The latter section, comprising the left wing of the party, and more and more the centre also, believe in a policy of advance, guided throughout by the deliberate object of achieving socialism at the earliest practicable moment. They believe in progressing by a series of co-ordinated reforms directed to realizing step by step the new social system. They may be opportunists, but theirs is at least ' coherent opportunism '. As they make no secret of their intention radically to change the existing economic order, their every move necessarily incurs the suspicion and veiled or open hostility of the capitalist parties—Conservatives and Liberals.

Just so long as the Labour Party consists of two sections —those who take the near view and those who take the distant view—so long will it be ineffective for any function but criticism. At present it can give no lead to the country with a constructive and practicable program of immediate progress in accordance with the principles of socialism, because the large minority of non-socialists, and some cautious Fabians of the centre, hang back. The very name of the Party was adopted so as not to offend the susceptibilities of non-socialist labour representatives. A section of the Conservative daily press has dubbed it the ' Socialist Party '. Why not take up the challenge and officially re-name it the Socialist Party ? The loss of the members wedded to liberalism of the radical description would be more than made up in a few years by large gains at the polls on a logical and consistent socialist program. The Englishman's love of compromise and opportunism is characteristically revealed in the composition and proceedings of the Labour Party. Both are futile from the point of view of the socialist ; for the public can only be stirred by uncompromising leadership and a plan of action which appeals to the imagination and drives men to love or hate. Rapid progress towards socialism by non-violent means waits merely for tireless agitation and bold constitutional leadership.

THE INDUSTRIAL POLICY OF ORGANIZED LABOUR

Turning our attention now to trade union policy, this too should be conceived on a logical and consistent plan. Here, as in the political sphere, the present tendency is to fight for immediate advantages, to the risk of, and sometimes actual loss of, strength and strategic power. A union efficiently organized and possessing substantial funds can gain much with few actual strikes ; though if and when they do occur the struggles will be long and bitter. It is not mere brute ' striking power ' that is required, however ; for capitalists, if driven to fight for their ' lives ', even for their freedom (which they value), can outstay the men in numbers sufficient to be victorious always as a class, though individual firms or companies may go under. Trade unions ought, therefore, to have a clear, well-thought-out and consistent strategy : one which, whilst protecting members in their present status, lays out a scheme for steady progress to a higher standard of life, and by means which are in accordance with the permanent principles of socialism.

This is a big subject which cannot be followed here in detail ; but I shall try to suggest the main features of such a policy, for I believe that trade union pressure for the adoption of logically conceived industrial measures will prove to be a fruitful and indispensable aid to political action in realizing the social objective. When a long-term policy leading to socialism has been worked out and accepted, the immediate action of every trade union should be considered in relation to it.

There would seem to be three main directions in which the policy of organized labour could be shaped so as to conduce to the realization of socialism, and at the same time improve, or at least safeguard, the welfare of the workers. The first is the regulation of industry with a view to raising the standard of living, which can only be done by developing the productivity of labour and securing more economical distribution of the goods produced. The second is to agitate and press for the elimination of the profit-making incentive in the provision of capital ; in other words, the conversion of shareholders into holders of fixed interest-bearing securities, the workers, managerial and manual, to benefit in wages up to the accepted standard of living, and further advantage to go to the consumer. The endeavour should be to establish a regulated industry, controlled in the interests of the public and the workers. The third is to develop amongst the workers consumer-consciousness to replace the employer-consciousness which now prevails.

Trade unionists are not as a whole constructive thinkers, and yet they have to face the incredibly difficult problem of raising the standard of living of their members, and at the same time guarding them from displacement by labour-saving machines or the substitution of semi-skilled labour. They find themselves in a very real dilemma. The General Council of the Trades Union Congress advocates the reorganization of industries, and their re-equipment with the most modern and efficient machinery, because it is convinced, on grounds of economic theory, that only by increasing the productivity of labour and reducing costs per unit of output can the worker obtain higher real wages and increase the total volume of production, which would be necessary to avoid a serious reduction in numbers employed. Yet the trade unions concerned are frequently unwilling to agree to this policy, because their members have learnt by bitter experience that ' rationalization ' of plant, or merely allotting more machines to each man, leads to unemployment or working short time, or to irregularity of employment.

To the workers in the unsheltered industries it does not seem fair that they should be called on to endure these hardships, even if it be only for a few years, when the standard of living of the workers in other occupations has been maintained or advanced with comparatively little effort or sacrifice on their part. The increase of the national dividend which has arisen from the greater productivity which has been realized during the present century in many industries has made higher real wages possible for all ; but the actual gain has been unevenly distributed. The almost continuous fall of prices and the cost of living since 1920 has benefited all workers in sheltered occupations, unless the demand for the commodity produced was falling off, as in the case of coal-mining. The great number of Government, municipal and other public employees, and certain other classes like railwaymen and insurance clerks, have benefited by the fall of the cost of living being greater than the reduction of their wages.

Various other classes of workers have benefited too because they are in sheltered occupations, although in their industries there has been no increase whatever in the productivity of labour. An interesting example is the making of bricks by the ancient hand method, which may still be seen in numerous small brickfields in country districts in England. Without any increase of skill men so employed earn about twice what their fathers did in the eighties and nineties of last century; and the cost of living having risen less, they have a higher standard of living, besides shorter hours. So also agricultural labourers have benefited in less degree, and many hundreds of thousands of others in the catering and distributive employments and workshop trades, by the general increase of the productive efficiency of labour in industries, arising from improved plant and organization, their wages being protected in one way or another.

The problem of how to reorganize industries subject to intense foreign competition in our foreign and home markets, so as to protect and, if possible, raise the standard of living of the workers, is one of extreme difficulty. The only solution I can offer, after considering and discarding several others, is the establishment of a statutory national Board of Control for each industry, with almost unlimited powers of interference to co-ordinate marketing, secure the reorganization of plant and prescribe conditions of employment.

Briefly, the powers of such a Board of Control would be : to establish a central selling agency for all or some of the products of the industry ; to advise upon and when necessary prohibit, or require, alterations of plant ; to make regulations having the force of law regarding the conditions of employment and dismissal of labour ; to determine the total output of the industry and of each section ; to fix quotas, for periods up to a year, at a time of temporary over-production or reduced demand ; and to make a levy on the industry for its own expenses in research and administration, for compensating (if thought fit) owners of undertakings compulsorily closed on account of excess capacity or otherwise, for compensating work people thrown out of employment by the technical changes, and for granting a subsidy on exports.

Probably its policy would be to use these powers first to secure orderly and economical marketing, and then to adjust production to demand, in whatever kinds or qualities of goods increases or decreases of demand had been experienced. The powers above described would enable the Board to prohibit the opening of a new mine, mill or works if it thought such prohibition advisable in the public interest, or to attach any reasonable conditions to the establishment of any such new undertaking in its industry. For instance, a firm which proposed to erect a large new mill for the mass-production of some textile, and which could obtain its market only by undercutting existing small mills, might be required to make a substantial contribution annually for a few years to compensate the capital and labour rendered idle, such contribution being treated as part of the cost of production for income-tax purposes.

The most difficult and the most important work of the Board would be that connected with endeavouring to secure regularity of employment for the workers in the industry and to minimize hardships due to displacement of labour through introduction of new processes or labour-saving machinery. It is only a body which has resources for investigation, and the desire to negotiate and conciliate, with the power of compulsion in the last resort, which can solve this problem under present conditions and those of the transition to socialism.

The constitution of the Board and selection of its members might present some difficulties. It should certainly not be composed mainly of employers in the industry serving on a voluntary basis like the Central Council which regulates the quotas and minimum prices of coal under the Act of 1930. The divergent interests of the coal-owners paralyse the Council when proposals are made to initiate constructive reorganization. The Board of Control here proposed must be completely independent, and its members must have no interest in any companies or firms in the industry. Probably it should consist

19

of eight or ten members, most or all of whom would be whole-time salaried officials. All, or nearly all, of them should have had experience in the productive or merchanting branches of the industry, or be specially qualified by professional attainments in technology, engineering, finance, and so forth. It is probable that the appointments would have to be made by the Government—possibly from a number of candidates nominated by organizations in the industry. The term of office should be sufficiently long and the tenure secure enough to induce men in the prime of life to relinquish their existing occupations. The Board would naturally consult the trade associations about measures it proposed to take, and the latter might appoint committees to advise and negotiate with it.

Such Boards of Control are not likely to be established unless they are vigorously demanded by organized labour. They would be a first stage in the direction of the nationalization of the industries concerned. The Board of any industry would have no power itself to operate mines, mills or factories, but it would be able to bring into existence a public board to work any section of the industry on a non-profit-making basis whether for supplying raw materials, for extending employment, for meeting a new demand, or any other purpose. It would also be able to organize finance and credit facilities for the industry, and might find this a useful way of guiding its growth in accordance with an accepted plan of development. Nationalization of a great and complex industry like the cotton or woollen textiles by a single act at a given moment could only end in disaster. The process must be extended over fifteen or twenty years, and the operations of such a Board of Control, which would investigate the whole industry, and publish information and reasons for its decisions, would prepare the way.

The second of the three main approaches to socialism towards which organized labour might well shape its policy was stated above to be the elimination of the profit-making incentive in the provision of capital. An essential feature of the capitalist-competitive system is risk-taking by capital in the hope of a high return. Except in mining and farming, the risk is mainly commercial risk due to competition at home and abroad. The object of establishing a new industrial undertaking is to make profits beyond the ordinary.

On the other hand, in any socialist system of national economy industries are planned, established and operated to provide the goods needed in the country, and for sale in foreign markets in order to purchase foreign goods, especially raw materials. Service of the consumer is the end for which industries are organized ; and when socialism is fully established the duty of seeing that necessary and suitable industries are established in the country and equipped in the most efficient manner will devolve upon the State.

A first stage towards socialism is to secure the operation of industries whilst still in private ownership so as to meet consumers' needs with the utmost degree of efficiency in service and cost. This will be facilitated if the directors and managers do not have to keep constantly in mind that their duty is to earn as high a dividend as possible for the shareholders. If the latter were to be converted into holders of fixed interest-bearing securities with a low rate of interest, a tradition of service to the public would be more easily established, and at the same time the prosperity of the industry would be promoted.

It is curious how little attention has been given to the importance of the psychological changes which have come over the personnel of the older British industries during the last sixty or seventy years, and to the consequent changes in industrial organization which are necessary to restore prosperity to those industries. The workmen of to-day are educated and thoughtful, and many of them form definite opinions about industrial policy. Men of the younger generation have been much influenced by socialist propaganda ; and their general attitude to their employers has become of primary importance. The thought that more careful and assiduous work merely leads sooner or later to higher dividends to be enjoyed by shareholders whom they never see is not encouraging to manual workers, nor indeed to members of the managing staff.[1] This feeling could be removed by giving the salaried staff and manual workers an assurance that increased profits would not go to

---

[1] In industries other than coal-mining and cotton manufacture a piece-rate may after a time be reduced as the result of workmen's earnings being high owing to working faster ; and this is one reason for the words ' or later ' in the foregoing sentence.

the shareholders in higher dividends or bonus shares, but would be used first to build up reserves and thus provide security for capital, and every prospect of continuing employment for the staff and workmen, and secondly to increase the remuneration of all the workers in the undertaking. The *modus operandi* is extremely simple : it would be necessary only to convert all share capital into cumulative ' preference ' shares entitled to a fixed dividend, and no more under any circumstances, even on winding up. They would not, of course, really be preference shares, because there would be no ordinary shares. Dividend would be due on them at a fixed rate, say 5 per cent ; and arrears caused by profits falling short in any years would be paid when possible with interest at the same rate on the deferment.

The rate of dividend to which capital would become entitled under such reorganization, or in a new company formed on this plan, is crucial. Given adequate security, large amounts of capital are forthcoming in this country at 5 per cent from investors large and small, or at 4 per cent free of income-tax. Assuming that all the capital invested in a large industrial undertaking is to be remunerated at no higher rate and to have no claim to reserves other than for depreciation, it becomes to the advantage of the managing staff and workmen to work together and assist one another in every possible improvement to increase the profits of the undertaking. This is obvious when it is considered that there is no way of disposing of large profits in excess of the fixed dividend on capital and an adequate fund for depreciation and obsolescence except by either (1) accumulating them as a reserve or (2) paying them to all or some of the employees. To pay to some and not others would create jealousy and dissension, and reduce the profits to be disposed of. The increased profit which they jointly realize by assiduity and collaboration must therefore be enjoyed by all members of the managing and clerical staff and workmen. I do not suggest that this be done by a profit-sharing scheme. It is not a case of sharing extra profits with capital, but of those actively engaged in running the industry taking *the whole* of the profits after guaranteeing to capital its fixed remuneration. Hence the simple and proper course is to use the whole of the extra profits to pay higher salaries and wages to all members of the staff. If first accumulated as a reserve invested in extending the business, that reserve would in effect belong to the workers, mental and manual, who had created the profits, because they alone could enjoy the additional profits it should bring if wisely invested.

Concerns which have been paying no dividend for many years seem to present a difficulty. The shareholders would have to agree to a drastic writing down of capital. It would be in their interest to do so, and thus be at least assured of receiving 5 per cent on what remained. A more serious objection is that in a régime of free competition the powerful stimulus to exertion and improvement here proposed would soon reduce the profits ; and might ultimately turn them into losses, because the system would spread from one firm to another in the industry, and the increased output could not be marketed except at a greatly reduced price. This indicates the necessity of some regulation of the increase of producing capacity, either by voluntary agreement or by the establishment of a statutory Board of Control as proposed above. Voluntary combination to limit output might, of course, develop into a policy of squeezing the public by obtaining a high monopoly price, and thus exceptionally high remuneration, for both managing and manual workers in the industry. This would not be a step in the direction of socialism. The only means of preventing or ending this would be the growth of public opinion, which, if its expressions of resentment were insufficient to prevent exploitation of the consumer, would demand legal action and perhaps a Board of Control. The cure in fact would be a step towards socialism ; but probably no such situation would arise, for the public is already beginning to recognize that rates of remuneration in industry, transport and agriculture should be ' fair '—neither too low nor too high. It is realized that an industry must be organized or protected so as to provide the workers with a decent standard of living, and conversely that high salaries or wages not due to special ability in any occupation are anti-social, as leaving less of the total product of all industries for other classes of workers.

This brings us to the third of the main directions in which the policy of organized labour might be shaped so as to conduce to the realization of socialism, namely, to develop amongst the workers a consumer-consciousness. Indeed that is the desirable way of preventing the situation just considered, in which managing staffs and workmen might combine to exploit the public. Socialism will not be realized until workers are ready to regard themselves as having a definite responsibility to the public at large immediately they are freed from the incubus of capitalist shareholders.

At present the workman is ' employer-conscious '. In most industries no work is offered except by employers, small or large, working for profit. The wage-rate and conditions of work are a bargain made individually or collectively strictly on a business footing. For any improvement of his position he is dependent on the employer's policy and the good will of the latter's representatives. He knows little or nothing of his employer's ways of disposing of the product, and certainly is not consulted. Hence the wage mentality, which tends to ignore the public, and concentrates the attention of the workers on the technique of trade union organization and action for improvement or maintenance of their wage-rates and conditions of employment.

Yet it is impossible that the industrial activities of the trade unions in the great industries shall be devoid of political significance; because they affect the interests of large classes of people favourably or unfavourably. When organized labour undertakes propaganda in favour of advances towards a new economic system, and combines it with industrial action, seeking to remedy some present grievance,[1] there is every likelihood of alienating still further the middle class, commercial and clerical, and the intelligentzia. Every measure needs to be considered in the light of this danger, for there can be no question but that communism will be realized much sooner, and by peaceful means, if the middle classes are largely won over to support the movement. This will be possible only if trade union action is not anti-social, as it often is when resort is had to limitation of output and to sympathetic strikes and embargoes.

This leads me to emphasize the very important political principle that the people as a whole will always acquiesce in

[1] As, for instance, in the miners' national strikes and the general strike of 1926, and on every occasion when the ' Minority Movement ' influences workers on strike.

the assumption and exercise of power by persons who show that as a rule they use it rightly for the common good. For this reason a benevolent autocracy has always been one of the most secure types of government. This principle accounts for the endurance of British rule in India, and for the power of the Bolsheviks in Russia. If the trade unions will carefully study the public good as well as their own they will not only be tolerated but encouraged.

Another obvious deduction from this principle would seem to be the drawing of a clear line of distinction between men working in the service of the State, or any public authority, and men in the employ of profit-making firms or companies. Workmen have an inalienable right to strike in protest against bad conditions in their own employment, whether they serve a public authority or a private employer, if proper representations have failed to obtain redress ; but as regards sympathetic strikes the case is entirely different. I would urge the view that a distinction ought to be made between public and private employment with reference to sympathetic strikes, although this may seem difficult in certain circumstances. Persons in public employment are already serving the community under conditions similar to, if not so good as, those which will exist when the preliminary régime of socialism is established. Public employees ought, therefore, to free themselves from a merely wage mentality and give proof now to the consumer, especially the middle classes, that they have a keen sense of duty towards the public at large. It is only logical that they should behave now as they will do when socialism is realized. The middle class will be impressed more by finding that it gets better service from employees of public authorities than from the employees of companies, than it will be by public employees showing fight.

EXISTING INSTITUTIONS OF SOCIALIST CHARACTER

The realization of socialism in this country will be a gradual process ; and the usual English plan seems likely to be followed of cautious and tentative beginnings, which will be developed as they prove successful in meeting the needs of the public. In characteristically British fashion we have, in fact, already made a beginning in the establishment of socialistic institutions.

A felt want and a new sense of social justice have led to innovations for particular purposes, with no perception on the part of the initiators or the general public that the principles they involve belong to a new era and a wholly different economic system.

The importance of these experiments in their relation to socialism, passing, as some of them are, beyond the purely experimental stage, has not been sufficiently recognized, even by socialists. I propose therefore to make my meaning clear by briefly describing some of them. General recognition and acceptance of the principles of service to the consumer and welfare of workers cannot but lead to the growth and extension of the institutions in question and the foundation of others. There will thus be opened a wide field for the development of socialist industrial establishments, initiated in many cases by private enterprise. Co-ordination by State planning and control is likely to be a later development.

Various classifications of commercial and industrial enterprises, including ' public utility ' services like water and electricity supply, are possible ; and two of them are of special interest for our present purpose. The first will classify such enterprises according to the motive which led to their establishment, or, if originally profit-making, to their present control and form of organization ; and the second according to the character and authority of their administrative control.

The motive for establishing practically all producing units in our great industries, and most of the newer industries, was profit-making, whether under competitive conditions or a title conferring monopoly, as in the case of water supply and gas companies. The profit was for the benefit of the promoter, who often expected lucrative employment in the business, and of capital, i.e. passive shareholders, who had to be induced to invest by the hope of a return above the normal. But there are in Great Britain many industrial establishments, businesses, and public utility services which were initiated for other reasons. Three distinct purposes may be recognized : (1) To meet the needs of the consumer—whether the general public or a particular group, like a co-operative society or the inhabitants of a particular estate or area ; (2) in order to provide employment to unemployed persons in a particular trade or locality ;

(3) for some philanthropic purpose such as benefiting morally or physically a particular class or group of persons on account of their poverty or of their being afflicted by some abnormal condition.

Of these purposes, other than profit-making, 'the first and third are the more important and have given rise to the most numerous and important enterprises. Those which are operated to meet the needs of the general public are : the postal services, telegraphs and telephones, wireless telephony and broadcasting, Government printing works, river conservancy and harbour development and management, drainage, water supply, gas and electricity supply, local transport by trams and motor-bus services, including parcels delivery, milk supply, banking facilities (Birmingham), provision for sports, including horse-racing (Doncaster), and a few others.

Business and industrial enterprise established on a non-profit-making basis to meet the needs of a particular group of persons is well represented in this country by the consumers' co-operative movement. The earliest co-operative societies a century ago established corn-mills, and workshops for making boots and shoes and clothing ; but the movement in its modern form may be said to date from the commencement of manufacturing by the Co-operative Wholesale Society (English) in 1873, nearly ten years after its formation. The Scottish Co-operative Wholesale Society began manufacturing in 1884. During the present century the number of members of retail distributive societies in Great Britain has been increasing rapidly, and reached 6,590,000 at the end of 1931. Allowing for some duplication of membership in the same family, it is probable that the total number of persons who subsist, at least partly, on supplies from co-operative sources is not less than 18,000,000, or over one-third of the population. The total sales of retail societies during 1931 amounted to £207,888,385. The English Wholesale Society has 110 mills and factories, large and small, and employs 33,400 workers in its productive and service departments, as against 8,000 in its distributive business. The total value of its manufactures in 1931 was £25,670,000. The Scottish Wholesale Society has 16 mills and factories and a number of workshops, and employs 8,200 persons in productive and service departments ; whilst about

800 more work in the joint English and Scottish tea, coffee and cocoa warehouses and works. The value of the manufactures of the Scottish Co-operative Wholesale Society in 1931 was £5,053,000. To this class of non-profit-making enterprises belong also some ventures in drama and opera, e.g. the Sadlers Wells and Old Vic Trust, and the recently formed National Opera Council; subscription concerts; circulating libraries, like the London Library; and some truly mutual insurance societies and building societies.

The second of the purposes other than profit-making above mentioned for which industrial enterprises have been established was to provide employment in a particular trade or locality for unemployed persons having no other prospect of being employed. Numerous attempts have been made in centres in depressed areas to provide occupation for men who have been out of work for a long period, in some cases for years ; and besides recreations a number of workshops have been started, allotments have been cultivated on a large scale, and outdoor work of public utility has been carried out. In the workshops boot-repairing and making, and furniture making are the commonest trades, the articles being made for presentation to hospitals, schools and institutions which could not afford to purchase them, and for the use of the unemployed themselves on payment of the cost of the materials. Only in a few cases does a workshop group sell to the public the furniture or other articles produced, mainly because the men are mostly in receipt of transitional benefit, but also from the desire not to compete in the open market and thus perhaps throw other men out of employment. This difficulty is being met by the Production for Use League, which is a federation of a number of unemployed men's workshops and occupational centres. The League proposes to organize the interchange of the products of different groups, so that the unemployed may produce fruit and vegetables, bread, tools, boots and shoes, clothing, furniture, etc., for each other, each man working at the trade in which he is skilled if there is a demand amongst the unemployed for his work. The difficulty in making this a national scheme is to effect interchanges between widely separated groups.

Other examples of industries operated for giving employment

are those established for enabling persons suffering from some form of bodily or mental weakness to earn their living, or at least to contribute to their keep, and for giving them the benefit of having an occupation. St. Dunstan's is well known ; but there are more than twenty other workshops for the blind in this country producing furniture, baskets, brushes, woven and knitted goods, and many other articles, which are sold in the open market. Notable amongst such enterprises are Papworth Industries and Enham Industries. The former was established to give employment under conditions of fresh air and short hours to men and women who have been cured of tuberculosis at the Papworth Village Settlement (near Cambridge), because return to their old work and city environment usually entails relapse. The industries are joinery, furniture making, leather and cane trunk and bag making, printing, and poultry rearing ; and efficient machinery and plant is installed. The goods are marketed, mainly through the trade, strictly on business principles on the merit of the goods, and without appeal to sentiment. Enham Industries provides work for disabled ex-service men. After inspecting the balance-sheets of several of the older workshops for the blind and disabled, I estimate the total annual value of the output of industries established to provide employment at more than £500,000.

The third of the purposes for which non-profit-making enterprises have been established is for benefiting morally or physically a particular class of persons needing assistance on account of poverty or some abnormal condition. We at once think of housing the poor, and setting a higher standard of housing, for which there exist numerous trusts, such as the Rowton Houses and Peabody Trust in London, Bourneville, Earswick, and others, established by wealthy men, and many public utility societies which limit the dividend on capital to 5 per cent. Housing has, of course, long been a field of municipal enterprise. Hospitals must also be classed here, whether run on charitable funds or by county councils in connexion with public assistance.

There do not seem to be many instances of industries conducted to benefit poor people morally or physically ; but perhaps those of the Salvation Army should be classed here. Its business and industrial enterprises fall into two distinct groups established with different objects. The first was to provide for the needs of Salvationists, and of their Army as an organization, using the profits for its general revenues ; the second in connexion with rescue work to provide regular employment under the best conditions for men whose moral fibre had deteriorated in the slums through unemployment, imprisonment, or drink.

The first class of undertakings includes a printing establishment at St. Albans, which prints most of the Army's literature, music, and periodicals issued in this country, and profits by doing a good deal of outside commercial printing, a musical instrument factory, also at St. Albans, and a bonnet factory at Luton. ' Salvationist Publishing & Supplies, Ltd.' is a distributing concern with its chief depot in London, near King's Cross, which buys the Army's requirements wholesale for all parts of the country, carries on a mail-order business and an export trade. The Army has also its own bank (The Reliance Bank, Ltd.), an industrial and ordinary life insurance company, a fire and burglary insurance corporation, and an approved National Health Insurance Society, all doing business with the general public as well as Salvationists.

The second class of industrial enterprises are the ' elevator workshops ', which include waste-paper and rag sorting, salvaging of old furniture, and such like. Laundry work, box-making and wood-working in London, and various small trades in provincial towns are also carried on.

There is also a Land and Industrial Colony of about two thousand acres at Hadleigh, in Essex. Its main object is reformative and curative. It was designed also to form a training ground for home colonization, and overseas settlement. Much of the land acquired, all of which had been out of cultivation for many years, is now a large and flourishing market garden and fruit farm. General farming, brick-making, and other industries are carried on. During recent years, the Colony has been much used as a training centre for boys for emigration.

Several philanthropic industrial enterprises of the Army have been closed for various reasons. General Booth established a match factory to demonstrate that matches could be made without risk to the workers of the horrible disease, ' phossy jaw ', and was largely instrumental in securing the legislation which has entirely abolished the disease in this country. A brush factory and mat factory were run for some years to employ ex-convicts, also wood-chopping, carpentering, and cabinet-making workshops ; but all these were closed for business reasons, largely owing to protests by employers and trade unionists against competition by prison labour and a philanthropic organization. These protests led to the abandonment for sale to the public of brush-making and mat-making in prisons, and thus rapidly diminished the number of ex-prisoners who could support themselves by either of these trades whilst settling down to a new life as honest workers.

Another philanthropic purpose which has led to extensive non-profit-making business enterprise and a State undertaking is the cause of temperance. The Peoples Refreshment House Association, Ltd., owns or leases and manages about 190 public-houses and inns in all parts of the country, giving its managers an incentive to sell non-alcoholic refreshments ; and Trust Houses, Ltd., has about 220 houses. Both of them limited the dividend payable on share capital, the former to a maximum of 7 per cent, the latter to 10 per cent (though only 5 or 6 per cent is paid). There are a number of smaller trusts and associations in various parts of the country running refreshment houses with the same object. The Government has entered this field in the State Management District, in and around Carlisle, where the Government has a monopoly of the supply of alcoholic liquors and works a brewery—one of the few examples in this country of a State commercial undertaking, and one which is successful and profitable.

It would take too much space to examine and classify in detail commercial undertakings not for private profit according to their control and method of administration. The table on the next page contains the principal categories of such undertakings :—

COMMERCIAL UNDERTAKINGS NOT FOR PRIVATE PROFIT

PUBLIC ENTERPRISES

State Management

Post, telegraphs, telephones.

Stationery Office, printing works.

State Management District, Carlisle.

(In other countries, e.g. in India : State railways, mines, and industries, such as tanning, boot and harness making, brick making, etc.).

Public Boards

(a) Nominated by the Government :—

British Broadcasting Corporation ; Central Electricity Board.

(b) Appointed by a body of seven ' Appointing Trustees ', being persons holding public or recognized offices named in the Act :—

London Passenger Transport Board.

(c) Partly Nominated ; mainly elected by local Authorities and interested bodies (trade associations) :—

Metropolitan Water Board and numerous provincial water boards.

Port of London Authority, Southampton Harbour Board, and other harbour boards and commissions.

London and Home Counties Joint Electricity Authority.

Local Authorities

Mainly County Borough and other Municipal Councils and County Councils, elected by the public :—

Water, gas, electricity, and tramways undertakings, bus services, milk supply, race-course, bank, housing.

Relief schemes and work centres for the unemployed.

NON-PROFIT-MAKING PRIVATE ENTERPRISES

Associations of Consumers with democratic control :—

Co-operative movement : Co-operative Wholesale Societies of England and Scotland. Productive departments of retail distributive societies. Co-operative housing : co-partnership tenants societies.

Associations of Producers with democratic control or partially so :—

Productive co-operative societies. Agricultural co-operative purchase and sales societies. Actors' Guilds. National Opera Council.

Philanthropic Associations and Trusts, the administrative control usually settled permanently by the founders :—

Housing Trusts and public utility societies for housing, the capital of which is not owned in part by the occupiers.

Workshops for the blind and the disabled.

Industrial colonies, e.g. Papworth.

Work centres for the unemployed. Salvation Army schemes.

The foregoing review of non-profit-making industrial and business enterprises brings out clearly the fact that the present century has already seen opinion grow in favour of steps being taken to meet an unfilled public need, either by governmental or municipal action or by the enterprise of a group of persons not seeking profit, willing to take some financial risk, whether for their mutual benefit by co-operation or philanthropically in the interests of others. In such undertakings the motive usually is either to meet a want which private enterprise does not supply because profits are too small or uncertain, or to supply goods or services of a better quality than competitive traders offer, especially in cases where quality affects health, as in water and milk supply and housing. In the case of municipal gas, electricity and tramway undertakings the principal aim has been cheaper services, and secondary objects a better service and profits in reduction of rates. A distinct movement to free educational and cultural activities from commercialism has also been growing. Only a minute fraction of the children of this country are now educated in profit-making schools, the tendency of the last twenty years having been for all large schools for middle-class boys and girls to be converted to a non-profit-making basis. A beginning has been made in freeing music and the drama from dependence on capitalistic enterprise ; and interest in this reform seems to be growing rapidly.

These observations suggest that there is a large field for associated private enterprise of non-profit-making character in this country, and that the practice of such association for purposes which would clearly enhance material or cultural welfare is likely to grow. Such voluntary association on a business footing, whether it be of consumers for their own benefit or of philanthropically disposed persons for the general benefit, or in aid of the poor, is a stage in the realization of socialism. When new ventures on the non-profit-making basis have proved successful, and have been extended and generally recognized as the best way of meeting a widely-felt need, public authorities will begin to supply the same need, utilizing the resources of public finance ; and governmental aid and co-ordination will follow.

There are some enterprises of this kind the starting of which in the near future would be welcome. For instance, a non-profit-making trust or co-operative society is wanted which would own or lease a chain of cinemas and exhibit films of artistic and educational value besides the best commercial films. There is an opening also for certain productive co-operative societies to be started by consumers, such, for example, as one to manufacture household medicines. Many of the widely advertised patent medicines are absurdly expensive, and some of them are positively injurious if taken frequently as recommended. A non-profit-making society would place equivalent medicines on the market at cost price, publishing the formula of each, and giving directions for proper use and avoidance of abuse. The formation of a business society would probably be assisted in each case by the prior existence of a propaganda society. This was the method adopted in the successful establishment of garden cities. The Garden Cities Association organized public interest in the first garden city at Letchworth and the second at Welwyn. The Film Society might, for instance, initiate the formation of the non-profit-making Cinema Operating Society ; and the New Health Society, or a ' Better Health Society ', might start a co-operative society for manufacturing household medicines.

There is room for both co-operative and philanthropically established industries in many directions ; and, as these grow, large-scale employers may see the advantage of converting their companies to a non-profit-making basis with fixed interest on capital. Although private enterprise may in these ways realize some of the principles of socialism in industry, the intervention of the State is necessary to secure the full advantages of socialism as an economic system, including the abolition of unemployment. Non-profit-making enterprises in the same industry might, of course, federate to co-ordinate their marketing and production and adjust the latter to demand ; but, since profit-making concerns are sure to linger in competition, State planning of the industry is likely to be necessary, through a Board of Control or otherwise, after which the State would initiate or finance a reorganization of production. State planning and organization of producers' selling is indeed already beginning in the marketing of milk, pigs, hops and other agricultural products under the Agricultural Marketing Act of 1931.

CHAPTER XVI

THE TRANSITION

THE INSTABILITY OF A SOCIALISTIC SYSTEM

IT is by no means difficult to imagine what this country will be like when most of the great industries of the country have been nationalized, or are under investigation for the purpose. Perhaps that will be some thirty or forty years hence. With continuous progress in this direction the country will reach in course of time an economic system based on the public ownership of land, and the national operation of banking, of fuel and power supply, and of transport of all kinds. Some of the great industries will be nationalized, others operated by huge monopolistic companies, working under partial State guarantee and control. The smaller industries will be socialized, that is to say, they will be organized nationally or locally in some non-profit-making or co-operative form, with or without State interference, and with the workers largely represented in the ultimate control.

The difficulties inherent in the smooth functioning of a non-competitive economic system in which the workers are closely organized in a trade union in each industry, but different rates of remuneration prevail in different occupations, have been discussed in an earlier chapter.[1] Inequalities of earnings will exist partly as a legacy from the capitalist competitive system of the present day and partly from the conditions of supply of labour in different industries being restricted or unrestricted, and from varying degrees of regulation of the demand. In the nationalized industries and public employments of a local character there will be high minimum wage-rates, and these will cause the skilled occupations under the same control to be remunerated on a correspondingly liberal scale. Trade-union combination will maintain high wages in the sheltered industries ; but in those subject to foreign competition, abroad or

---

[1] Chapter VI, pp. 104–8.

at home, lower rates of wages are likely to prevail, causing much unrest.[1]

In Chapter VI (p. 107) I have given reasons for believing that any scheme for determining wage-rates officially on a scientific basis would break down in a few years, because the principles and methods of such determinations of wages, even if understood by the workers, would be regarded with suspicion in their application to individual cases. It is, in fact, quite probable that their validity would be openly challenged. Jealousies as between different classes of manual workers would be serious ; but more intense would be the growing envy of persons enjoying the relatively high salaries which would still be considered necessary for intellectual and organizing work.

Whether official wage determination be introduced or not, the discontent of those who consider themselves underpaid will grow. No agreement will be possible as to what should be regarded as appropriate rates of pay for different occupations. Hence the idea will begin to find acceptance that all must be equally remunerated. The socialistic system with unequal earnings which will be created by successive steps in the transference of industries to a basis of public service will necessarily prove unstable ; and a growing body of opinion, soon to become a large majority of the people, will demand economic equality. When circumstances and educational propaganda have forced this conclusion on not only the great majority of manual workers, but also the intelligentsia and a substantial number of business organizers, the advance to some

[1] Inequalities of the kind referred to have arisen already, and are attracting attention. This may be illustrated by a quotation from an article entitled ' Some Problems of Wage Fixing Methods ' by Mr. P. J. Pybus, which appeared in a supplement on ' Industrial Relations,' published by the *Manchester Guardian* on November 30th 1927. He writes : ' This kind of discussion may end by clothing in a new garment a most deep-seated grievance amongst the manual workers of this country. I refer to the inequality of remuneration not only between the employee in the sheltered and unsheltered industries, but also between the workman employed in one industry and the man of the same trade employed in another. The problem can be simply stated. The wage discrepancies between the sheltered industries, such as the railway service, or the building trades, or municipal employment and, say, the engineer artisan are too well known to require elucidation. We have all heard of the dustman's £4 a week and the skilled engineer's 58s., but what of the craftsmen employed not only in the same trade but in the same factory whose earnings vary enormously ? ' Mr. Pybus has no promising solution to offer. In his opinion ' the machinery of conciliation and wage settlement should be split into smaller groups '.

system of communism resembling that outlined in this book will become a national purpose.

We come, therefore, to the period when the country will have accepted the idea that a great economic change is inevitable, and that this will involve equality of incomes for all adult persons, the obligation of all to work for the public service, and the total abolition of private capitalism and profit-making activities. Convinced that the change to democratic communism is the only solution for the difficulties arising from the public operation of numerous industries on the basis of money economy, the nation will determine to prepare itself for the realization of communism, including the abolition of money, at an early date ; and intellectual energy will be devoted to the choice of ways and means of organizing the whole nation as a single economic unit.

The period of conscious preparation cannot be long, once the national determination has become obvious, for the simple reason that at this juncture private capitalism will cease to function in certain directions, since it will have no guarantee of continuance. Such capitalist profit-making enterprises as still remain—and they will probably be numerous in a variety of small industries—will not, of their own accord, make any further investments of capital in new plant ; and they will cease to renew plant which has worn out, because they will see no advantage likely to accrue to them from incurring capital expenditure when the State is about to take over at a stroke all the means of production without compensation.[1] To avoid the deterioration which must ensue from manufacturers failing to renew their plant, the Government will be forced, during this period of preparation, to take over one after another the small industries the efficiency of which is considered vital to the public interest either for direct operation or for lease to the former owners. An alternative method would be to provide the

---

[1] The question of compensation will be discussed later in this chapter ; but I may anticipate the conclusion by saying that in all probability there will be some compensation given to persons who choose to emigrate, but none to persons who elect to remain British citizens, for compensation could have no meaning for persons remaining in the country when all incomes must be equal.

requisite plant for such industries by means of permanent Government loans at fixed interest.

The general appreciation that the period of preparation must be short will lead, I think, to a great quickening of public activity. New ideas will be accepted and ideals formed with the rapidity characteristic of a revolutionary period. At present we are in a condition bordering on apathy. People nowadays are bewildered by great social changes which they find slowly taking place ; and, in the absence of any clear conception of an end to which social endeavour should be directed, they feel puzzled. They cannot be roused, and affairs proceed by mere drift.

The determination to realize communism will change this apathy into an enthusiastic purpose ; and all classes of the people will be interested in thinking out what the new form of society should be and what preparations should be made to realize it. There will, I think, be a general consensus of opinion that the main activities of the period of preparation must be in the direction of research and education.

The research would then be undertaken definitely at the order and expense of the State with a socialist government in power, for the express purpose of studying and preparing for the change to communism. I do not mean that the research necessarily will be bureaucratic and centrally organized ; though much of it which is purely technical will need to be, and it would be advantageous if some central body were to co-ordinate research carried on by private agencies. Public funds would, doubtless, be made available to universities and colleges and local or industrial research institutions which have undertaken to study questions connected with the transition. In the centres of higher learning there will be a great stimulus to studies in sociology in its many branches, in economics and statistics, and in all the applied sciences. All the secondary schools [1] by this time will have been brought under the management, or, at least, the supervision, of the State. Young people at the ages of seventeen to nineteen will have regular teaching in economics and civics, including town planning, so that they may understand the changes which have taken place and the proposed new system of communism.

[1] Including the so-called public schools, i.e. middle-class boarding schools.

Still more important will be the moral teaching in relation to civic duties. It will be realized with clearness that all children must be brought up with the idea that they have to work honestly and thoroughly for the good of the community in public service. Furthermore, they must be taught that they are to be the actual instruments for realizing the change to communism, and that they must be ready to take their place as loyal citizens when the change is made.

In the elementary and intermediate stages the teaching, although not so definitely directed to the understanding of communism, will be coloured by the impending change. It will be seen that the altruistic outlook must be developed and acquisitive tendencies discouraged. The importance of the teachers thoroughly appreciating and believing in the new system will be realized. Thus there will be a changed moral environment for the children. Not only in school, but in the homes, they will find new ideas as to what is good and what is bad. The schools will be expected to make the children conscious that if they act on the dictates of love, and loyally fulfil their duty in work in public affairs, they will always have guaranteed to them a comfortable livelihood.

It may be suggested that much research could be undertaken by psychologists along paths not yet entered which might prove fruitful of good results. For instance, it would be an advantage to find out what it is in education which makes some men take quickly to new ideas : some, for instance, to interest themselves in mechanical achievements, some to understand and advocate town planning, some to welcome socialism. The psychologist should discover what are the habits of thought wanted for the future state of society, and how best to promote the growth of them.

In practice, no doubt, the best of the school teachers who are enthusiastic for the change will find their own ways of developing the right attitude in their children. They will stimulate imagination in thought about the future : an interest in and belief in progress. Perhaps at this time in the secondary schools, no less than in the universities, ' Futurity ', that is to say, the study of the desirable progress of society in the future, and the means of achieving it, will become an accepted subject equal in importance to history.

THE FUNDAMENTAL LAWS

When a Government has come into power with a definite mandate from the country to establish the system of communism the necessary legislation will, of course, be carefully prepared. Doubtless, in preceding terms of office of a socialist government tentative Bills for bringing about the change will have been prepared and discussed in general terms. Hence, the lines on which the new laws should be modelled will have become clearly defined during the period of preparation ; and, probably, by way of concessions and promises of compensation, as much will have been done to meet the opposition of the privileged and capitalist classes as possible, short of sacrificing any of the fundamental principles involved.

The change to communism involves a revolution in property rights, and in the privileges and obligations of citizenship. A new code of civil law must be enacted ; the criminal law must be altered in certain respects, and changes of the Constitution must be made. Parliament doubtless will continue to modify the law from time to time after the adoption of communism in much the same manner as it does now—though, we may hope, with a clearer purpose and less of futile controversy ; but the framework of a completely new legal structure, based on the new principles of society, must be worked out carefully beforehand. The Act, or series of Acts, which will embody these new principles, and establish the new economic system, I propose to call ' the Fundamental Laws '. They will not, as I imagine them, attempt the impossible task of providing at one stroke all the law necessary for the working of communism. Rather, they will lay down the broad principles in regard to the definition of citizenship, the rights and duties of citizens, the control of property, and the powers of the new governing bodies to be placed in control of industries and distribution. I have assumed throughout this book that all parts of Great Britain will adopt communism at the same time, and form a national economic unit. It may be presumed that Ireland will follow suit at a somewhat later date and form a separate commonwealth, or possibly two at first, as economic conditions and interests differ widely in Northern Ireland and the Free State.

Let me now state briefly what I believe the chief provisions of the fundamental laws must necessarily be. As I envisage them there will be three Acts, or three principal parts of one Act, dealing respectively with : (1) the definition of citizenship, and the rights and duties of citizens ; (2) the rights of property and contract ; (3) constitutional changes, and the establishment of controlling authorities. It will be convenient to forecast the main provisions of each of these Acts in the order named.

The first or principal Act will begin by stating who are to be recognized as citizens, and to be entitled to the general allowance and all free services of the country. Probably citizenship will be granted to every person born in Great Britain who has continued normally to reside or maintain a home therein, and to such other persons as shall have been domiciled in Great Britain for at least twelve months before the passing of the Act and have been naturalized or are willing to become so. Foreigners who have been in the country less than twelve months will be liable to deportation, unless they have property to hand over to the State corresponding with the amount which will be demanded of immigrants according to age.[1] I do not think there will be any restriction as to the race and colour of persons who may become citizens, provided they fulfil the conditions imposed on all foreigners. There could not be any great number of foreigners resident in the country ; for, in order to avoid a wave of immigration from countries of low standard of living as soon as the adoption of communism seemed likely, an anti-immigration law, more stringent than the present Aliens Act, would have been adopted. It may be noted that the term ' British citizenship ' will mean citizenship of Great Britain : consequently it would be surrendered by permanent emigration. If the emigrant went to a British colony he would lose British citizenship, but retain British nationality.

The Act will doubtless require every person who was born in the country immediately to register himself or herself at a public general store, which normally should be the one nearest to his place of residence ; and all other persons, whether claiming British citizenship or not, to register themselves at the nearest police station and at a general store. The establishment of

---

[1] See Chapter XI, p. 218.

' travel bureaux ' would probably be provided for ; and these, when constituted, would take over the registration of foreigners.

The next fundamental provision will be that every citizen shall of right enjoy all the free services to be made available in any part of the country in which he may be, and shall be entitled to support by the State for the rest of his life, by having credited to his or her account at the store of registration a monthly allowance, the amount of the allowance to be determined from time to time (in practice annually) by the Council of National Economy, and to be equal for all adults. The right to receive this allowance will doubtless be made contingent upon the person having peaceably yielded possession of all his property to the State on the appointed day, on his being ready to work in the service of the State, or in any authorized occupation, until he reaches the retiring age, or is declared mentally or physically unfit, and on his not being convicted of any breach of the fundamental laws, or any serious crime.

The obligation of citizens of both sexes to work at an approved occupation will next be defined. It will probably read to the effect that from the appointed day every person over the age of eighteen and under fifty-eight must work regularly during normal hours as directed by the proper authority, and for this purpose must report himself or herself immediately, or on attaining the age of eighteen, to the registrar of occupations of the town or parish in which he resides.[1] The retiring age is not likely to be fixed at less than fifty-eight during the first five years for persons who were engaged in manual or administrative occupations, or were of independent means, before the passing of the Act, and at sixty for those engaged in professional and intellectual occupations ; and after the first five years probably at fifty-five and fifty-seven respectively. In the early stages of communism, when an immense amount of labour will be needed for the great reorganization of industries and improved housing, it will be desirable to keep in employment every person still capable of work. Light work could

---

[1] The use of the word ' directed ' seems to imply the regimenting of the whole population under a bureaucratic discipline. The use of such phraseology will be necessary in a legal enactment ; but it will be seen later in this chapter that people will, as a rule, be ' directed ' to work in the occupation of which they have had experience, or which they prefer, so far as practicable.

always be found for elderly people. Exemption from the obligation to work will be provided for women on the ground of motherhood, and for household duties, unless a substitute for domestic help be permitted, and for both sexes for attending a university or art school or course of technical training.

The Act relating to property will declare that, on its coming into force, all property in land and movable and immovable goods will vest in the State forthwith, and that rights of user will be subject to the laws and notifications of lawfully constituted authorities. All land and property suitable for agriculture outside municipal limits, excepting allotments, will be at the disposal of the Council of Agriculture, advised by county committees; and all land and property used in all other industries will be at the general disposal of the Council of Industries. Lands for communal use, such as roads, parks and playing-fields, and all lands used or reserved for residential purposes, will come under the control of town councils in urban areas and under county councils as regards planning and zoning in rural and semi-rural areas, and district councils as regards management, subject to laws to be enacted. Property such as personal belongings and household goods and furniture, although nominally transferred to the State, will in practice, for the most part, remain with the existing lawful users for life. The object of the proposed legal transfer to public ownership is twofold: to enable the public authorities to inquire what goods a person possesses in his house or houses with a view to requiring the rich to give up for the use of the poor articles not actually needed by the former; and to prevent accumulations of property of undue dimensions by inheritance or gift. It will be observed that I have written 'will remain with the existing lawful *users* for life', not lawful *owners*. A person living in a rented house furnished on the hire-purchase system would be the lawful user of both house and furniture; and it would be both expedient and just to give him the right to continue in occupation—at least until he should be removed for some other reason.

The same Act will also, I think, declare that all money ceases to be legal tender, and becomes the property of the State; and that all buying and selling for money is illegal. It will also prohibit all trade or traffic in goods or services, whether in exchange for other goods or services, or for credit at the public stores, if the object of any such exchange be the making of profit in goods or credit. No contract of exchange, nor any agreement for rendering services otherwise than to the State or a legally constituted public authority, will be recognized by the courts. The manner of dealing with property rights existing at the time of the establishment of communism will be considered presently.

The third of the fundamental Acts will make the necessary constitutional changes, give the necessary new powers to existing public authorities, and establish the new bodies needed to control industry and agriculture, home supply and foreign trade. No doubt the Act will provide for maintaining a suitable household for the Sovereign, and domestic assistance for members of the royal family, who might, as at present, undertake duties as officers in the Army or Navy, or in the public administration. The House of Lords, if not already fundamentally altered, could be changed into a Senate consisting perhaps mainly of representatives of professions, industries and associations, cultural and political. This Act would also establish the Supreme Economic Council, and all the important councils and controlling authorities, such as I have named in Chapter IX. It is probable that in some instances the prototypes of these bodies will have been called into existence many years previously ; and they will merely be continued with some alteration of constitution, and with new and enlarged powers. Provision will also be made for a great extension of local activities by the election of *ad hoc* committees, apart from the town councils, if the people of the locality so desire, for various purposes such as higher education, housing, the control of stores, the introduction of new industries, and so forth.

PROPERTY IN THE TRANSITION

The fundamental laws will relate to the permanent condition of affairs after the establishment of communism. A special Act will be required probably to regulate the transfer of property to the State, and to make all necessary provisions regarding the control of property during the transition, including the assignment to permanent emigrants of such sums as may be held to be due to them. It will provide doubtless that all persons and corporations shall furnish information as to their property used, or likely to be useful, in the production of any kind of goods, or in aiding any direct service ; and to submit to and assist in inventories being taken. The authorities will also be empowered to require information to be furnished as regards the houses, motor-cars, cycles, live stock, and certain other kinds of movable property in each person's use or possession. The export of property of all kinds, except by licence, will be prohibited. Particulars will also have to be furnished of ownership and destination of imports, that is, of all goods due to arrive by sea or air at British ports. All property rights of foreigners in Great Britain, and all investments abroad belonging to British citizens, will automatically vest in the British Government. This, however, is subject to an important proviso to be explained below.

It will probably be thought that fundamental laws on the lines above indicated are too uncompromising. An opportunist policy will probably be found expedient which will enable capitalists to remove themselves and a large part of their property from the country if they do not care for the prospects of the new régime. By some such concession it might be hoped to reduce the opposition of a number of property owners. The principle would be to allow any person within a limited period, say three months, to decide whether he would like to contract out of British citizenship and take his movable property with him. The law might provide also that any person who contracted out of citizenship and undertook permanently to reside outside Great Britain should be paid some percentage, probably not more than 60 per cent, of the value of his immovable property, situate in Great Britain, in any foreign currency which he might specify.[1] The amounts which might so become due to emigrants on account of property handed over to the· State would be paid by instalments over a series of years ; but any emigrant to whom such payments were being made would, of course, if he returned to the country, forfeit the right to

---

[1] The percentage retained might be graduated in accordance with the size of his fortune. The high rates at present levied for death duties on large estates would seem to indicate roughly the proportion of the individual's wealth which may be ascribed to the advantage of having lived and conducted his business in a highly organized community under British law.

receive the remaining instalments. He could not resume
British citizenship without either returning the amount paid
out to him, or securing payment of the interest thereon to the
British Government. Probably emigrants would also receive
a bonus calculated according to age on the plan described at
the end of Chapter XI.

Payment to emigrants of a part of the value of their immovable property would, of course, place a very considerable
burden on the country, if the number who elected to abandon
British citizenship were large ; but the State would be able to
set-off against this the monetary claims on foreign countries,
especially in respect of interest on the investments there of
the persons who elected to remain in this country as citizens.
If a balance due outwards remained, it would have to be
financed by an excess of exports over imports.

Were it not for the probability that emigrants will have to
be paid a proportion of the value of their immovable property,
companies and businesses might be taken over as going concerns
without the preparation of elaborate accounts and balance-
sheets. Inventories of the goods and plant taken over would
be sufficient for the information of the councils of industries ;
and knowledge of the monetary value of the property would
be required only approximately for purposes of cost accounts
in the future management of the industry. I think it will be
found necessary, however, if emigrants are to be credited with
a fraction of the value of their property, to prepare winding-up
accounts for every company and firm, with a detailed balance-
sheet as on the day preceding the appointed day. The prices
used for valuation will doubtless be those prevailing at some
previous date when markets were not affected by the proximity
of the change. The work of preparing inventories and winding-
up accounts would keep all professional accountants busy for
a year or more.

This leads us to an interesting question, namely : ' What will
happen to bank balances when money is abolished ? ' Will they
be simply wiped out, so that every one starts with a clean
slate on an equal footing ? This would seem to be the simplest
and fairest arrangement ; but a little consideration shows that
it would have its drawbacks. The change to communism, as
I conceive it, must be made on an appointed day ; but the

ideal would be so to organize the transition that business would run before and after the date as smoothly as it does now before and after New Year's Day. The transitional laws should be such, therefore, as will maintain in operation, so far as possible, the existing economic incentives up to the last moment. One deduction from this principle is that there should be no encouragement of wasteful expenditure on the part of the large class of the moderately well-to-do. Many of the latter, if bank balances were about to be wiped out entirely, might well think that they might as well spend what they had while they could. Indeed, it is probable that for months beforehand the State Bank (the sole and ubiquitous bank) would find nearly every one wanting to become its debtor, and suspension would be inevitable. I feel, therefore, that it would be necessary for all private bank balances, whether creditor or debtor, to be carried forward to some extent, in order to avoid over-consumption just before the transition. The law might be that credit balances could be carried forward to the amount of one or two months' general allowance, and that balances due to the bank would be carried forward *in toto*.[1] On the other hand, the working balances of business of all kinds, so far as they had not been divided already between partners or share-holders, would simply be merged in the general transfer of property to the State. For the sake of consistency, provable debts between private persons, not of a business character, might be deemed to have become at the appointed day debts respectively to and from the State Bank.

Property held abroad, that is to say, in any part of the world outside the Commonwealth of Great Britain, including money invested abroad, will be dealt with on a clearly defined principle. Every one will be required to declare the kind and value of any property which he holds abroad, and of any sums which will become due to him abroad, as, for example, for bills of exchange, for goods exported, or author's royalties on foreign

[1] In Chapter XII it was pointed out that prices in the new monetary unit will be arbitrary. It would be quite possible, therefore, for the State deliberately to depreciate the new £1 relatively to the old by an amount which was left uncertain before the change. The credit balance which could be carried forward would seem, therefore, before the change, likely to be large ; and so there would still persist some incentive to maintain fairly large credit balances. The depreciation of the currency unit would give some relief to debtors. In any case they would cease to pay interest.

sales. Property located abroad, if it belongs to foreigners resident in this country or to persons who have declared their intention of emigrating, will not be interfered with in any way ; but all the property held abroad by persons who elect to remain or become British citizens will be automatically transferred, like all home property, to the ownership of the British Government. The latter will probably establish agencies in foreign countries to manage it. To avoid the possible legal difficulty of a government holding land in a foreign country, real property might be sold, or else be transferred to a holding corporation (company, co-operative society or trust) formed under the laws of the country in which it was situate. In the case of a foreign country which had already adopted communism, no question of British citizens owning property there could arise, for any property previously owned by British citizens there would have been nationalized by that country with or without compensation.

I have tried to give in quasi-legal form the manner in which property might be treated on the introduction of communism. Briefly it may be said to amount to converting to national ownership all capital, in the two senses of producers' goods within the country and money invested abroad. Consumers' goods in the actual possession of consumers would be allowed to remain in their possession, for their use only ; but the State would have the right to interfere with the distribution of usable goods. Possibly it would do so in regard to the larger things, such as houses and motor-cars. Unnecessarily large houses of the wealthy would be taken over and be either divided up or assigned to some public purpose, the former occupants being given smaller but comfortable accommodation. In general, it may be anticipated that efforts would be made to restrict the interference with the normal course of private life to the minimum compatible with even justice to all classes.

ORGANIZING CONTINUITY OF PRODUCTION AND SERVICES

The fundamental laws must all be passed within a short period of time and be brought into force simultaneously : otherwise there would be a period of confusion in which people in control and direction of industry would have lost the right to control their property, and would cease work because the laws necessary for the reorganization of industry had not been passed. Some confusion during the change is inevitable ; but, if everything has been thought out carefully beforehand, the confusion should be less than that experienced during the general strike of 1926, and it need not last any longer.

The appointment of commissions of supply must be made beforehand in order to keep industries going and maintain the supply of goods for consumption ; and the organization of their business must be fully worked out before the appointed day. In selecting the commissioners and their staffs the choice must, of course, fall on persons having experience of the particular commodities for which they will be responsible. Many of the directors, officers and managers of the co-operative wholesale and retail societies would doubtless be chosen ; and a large number of merchants in the various trades, who indicate that they would elect to remain in the country, and their employees. I do not think there would be any difficulty in getting a sufficient number of experts acquainted with the details of each existing trade, considering how numerous are the merchants connected with every industry.

In order to prevent the occurrence of a period of disorganization of industries, one of the fundamental laws should make the necessary provisions to secure continuity of working. Obviously the essential provision would be one requiring every person to continue working on and after the appointed day at the occupation at which he was previously engaged. If everybody be compelled to do this there can be no serious cessation of work ; and an order to continue working as before can hardly be a hardship for any one—at any rate for a few weeks or months, until there has been time to ameliorate bad conditions of work, and put people into the occupations they most desire, as far as practicable. An essential condition that people shall be able to continue working as before in industries is that there shall be no cessation of the supply of the necessary raw materials and power. Hence every merchant and every producer, whether a company or an individual, would be required to continue delivering the goods he ordinarily sells to his usual customers in the quantities they require, unless otherwise instructed. At the same time, to facilitate and ensure this continuance of the supply of raw materials, all industrial establishments would be made responsible for keeping themselves going by indenting on their usual suppliers, or, if necessary, some other source, for the materials they require.

If there were any serious numbers of objectors to the change amongst the employers of an industry, such a mandate might not secure the continuity of production. Hence no reliance would be placed on voluntary continuance without supervision, except so far as might be necessary for minor and non-essential industries. In all probability a census of production would be taken some time before the appointed day ; and, on the basis of this, plans for production would be worked out beforehand. Thus all importers and producers of raw materials and partly manufactured goods would receive from the appropriate industrial council, through the commission of supply, the delivery orders which they must fulfil in the period immediately following the change. Makers of finished goods would, subject to the general scheme of the Council of Supply, receive orders direct from the local commission of supply for direct delivery ; and adjustments of surpluses or deficits would be made afterwards through the central office for the whole country. It is probable that the Government would have made itself responsible some time in advance for seeing that orders and finance are duly arranged to ensure the usual arrivals of raw materials and foodstuffs from overseas.

Professional and independent workers would be called on to organize themselves by appointing a council for the profession, if none were already in existence. I take it that the profession, whether of medicine, architecture, journalism, or any other, will work as a self-governing guild, constituted under a general Act, which will compel every person pursuing that occupation to belong to the guild, and conform to the orders of its council. The latter will appoint a supervisor or director of the profession in each county or regional division, the powers of such supervisor being not unlike those of a bishop over his diocese. In particular he would report to the council of the profession on the adequacy of the professional service in his area, and investigate complaints. In charge of the supervisors would be a Chief Supervisor, or Director-General, having statutory powers, appointed by the Council. Authors, artists, and other independent intellectual or manual workers, would be required to form their own professional organizations. Every person ordinarily occupied in such calling before the change would probably be allowed to go on working as before, subject to a certain amount of infrequent supervision—about as much as is exercised now by the Treasury over the staffs of universities and colleges which receive Government grants : that is, supervision or inspection sufficient to see that he is doing some sort of work which some group of citizens considers worth having done. A profession doubtless would be trusted to manage its work in the public interest ; but subject to criticism in the Press and in the councils of professions, the Council of Occupations, and ultimately, if necessary, in the Supreme Economic Council or the Legislative Assembly for Economic Affairs. In case things went wrong the composition of the council of the profession in question would probably be modified by outside interference, or other measures be taken to secure the necessary reform. Probably such interference would not be more frequent than present-day interferences of Government with our universities by royal commissions and legislation.

THE REDISTRIBUTION OF LABOUR

It is quite possible to form some idea of how the registration of people for the purpose of seeing that they work is likely to be carried out, and of how labour will be assigned where it is most required and the unemployed be set to work. As I envisage this vital stage of the change, whilst the commissions of supply and the industrial and professional councils are beginning work, and keeping production going, the registrars of occupations will be taking over the employment exchanges, proceeding greatly to expand their staffs, and establishing many new offices. A registrar of occupations will have been appointed for each ward of a town, and for each urban and rural district. The first duty of his office staff will be to compile a complete list of all the persons resident in the ward or district of working age ; probably using a folded card filing system. On each card will appear the name and residential address of the person, his (or her) store and registered number, former occupation, present occupation, place of work, and name

21

of employment manager, in the case of an office or industrial establishment, or of his supervisor, in the case of professional and individual services. As soon as possible a comparison will be made of the registers of occupations with the registers of the stores, in order to discover whether any persons are drawing supplies from a store without having registered an occupation or exemption. It might be practicable to make the store require of each person within seven days of his registering there a certificate from the registrar of occupations, failing which the store would be obliged to report to the registrar of the ward or district. The latter will, of course, in any case, take steps to verify the information which was supplied by persons when they registered. As soon as possible the permanent system will be introduced whereby employment managers and supervisors will be obliged to report to the registrar of occupations concerned the admissions and departures of persons from their charges.

At the appointed day there will be probably a very large number of persons fit for work unemployed—say three or four million men and women. These will naturally be given certificates of exemption until they can be absorbed into the industries and services which most urgently need expansion. Doctors, nurses and teachers will all be quickly at work. The building industry will start on a huge house-building program previously prepared. The clothing and footwear industries will soon absorb large numbers of women not gifted with artistic talent, organizing power or intellectual ability, and not required for housework or maternal duties. The various councils of industries and professions will send in requisitions for the numbers of workers they need, and men and women will be assigned immediately where labour is most required. It may be suggested that the first assignments of the unemployed will probably be made for periods not exceeding six months, and will be compulsory. During the six months there will be activity in arranging transfers, so that these people may be sorted out into the occupations in which they will be most efficient and which they prefer, so far as practicable.

An interesting and important question is what is to be done with the work-shy, the incompetent, and those who in resentment resort to sabotage. Direct refusal to register or to work

would doubtless be punished by imprisonment with hard labour
—of a useful kind. Blank refusals will not, I think, be numerous
in the face of a public opinion overwhelmingly in favour of the
new system ; but there might be a large number of men and
women who, though affecting to work, would be lazy or passively
disobedient. If we observe the types of men and women now
employed as petty shopkeepers and day labourers in our great
cities, we may well believe that there might be some millions of
objectors and lazy incompetents who would be a clog on any
industry to which they were assigned. As at least a generation
must pass before the appointed day arrives, we may hope that
the number of unemployables of the degenerated casual
worker and hawker type will have decreased substantially in
the meantime, as the result of measures based upon a study of
the problems which these classes of persons present. They
are to be pitied, not to be blamed ; for they are essentially the
product of our economic system—of the herding of thousands
in poverty-stricken working-class districts, and the desperate
uncertainty of their earnings. As a result of my observations
in many countries where I have travelled, I should say that
Great Britain has an unusually large proportion of this class,
due to more than a century of unregulated industrialism and
the growth of great port towns.

To admit such unemployables to the industries and services
staffed by the present manly skilled artisan and middle classes
would be fatal ; for it would destroy the *esprit de corps*, the
unanimity of desire for efficiency, which is vital for the success
of a society of equality. The lazy and incompetent, and the
less hopeless of the passive resisters, would have to be assigned
to special works and to labour colonies, where they would build
their own living accommodation and workshops, and be
supplied with modern machinery. For a few years they might
hardly earn the cost of their own board and lodging ; but they
would be liberally treated, and would be likely to improve in
new surroundings and with regular well-paid work, and so
would gradually be less of a charge on the rest of the community.
Educative measures carried on amongst the colonists might be
expected, in the course of a few years, effectively to reduce the
number of those who had still to be segregated from the
generality of workers. As a type they would die out, probably

in thirty or forty years at most ; and in any case the cost of supporting them would not be so great as the burden we now bear in supporting the idle rich, the police and lawyers required to protect their property, two millions or more of unemployed, our numerous indigent paupers, and the mentally defective. The rest of the community, far more efficiently organized and equipped for work than ever before, would soon find the burden light.

TEMPORARY COMPROMISE ARRANGEMENTS

It is to be hoped that some compromise arrangement, such as the undertaking to pay to emigrants a part of the value of their immovable property above described, would induce those property owners who were unwilling to co-operate in making the new commonwealth a success to leave the country peaceably. Other temporary concessions to persons of the well-to-do classes of fifty years of age or more might be expedient with a view to reconciling them to the changed conditions of life. For instance, should they elect to remain in the country, they might be allowed for a period of ten years, or perhaps for life, an increase of the general allowance, bearing some relation to the amount of property which they had peaceably surrendered to the State ; and they might be allowed to retain the services of one or two domestic servants each from amongst those who had been some years in their service. I think every Englishman will agree with me that any concessions which would secure a passive acceptance of the new order by the propertied classes, and which would entail no permanent violation of the principles of communism, would be abundantly justified.

The great majority of British socialists are anxious that their policy should be directed to realizing the social revolution without violence. The responsibility does not lie wholly with socialists and communists, however. Violent revolutions occur on account of the blind opposition of vested interests and conservatively-minded persons of the privileged and well-to-do classes. They refuse to recognize the march of progress—the inevitability of change. They foolishly believe themselves to be patriotic when they advocate denying to the ' lower classes ' progress to power and welfare ; and, at the least, they seek to put the clock back by a generation. The French and Russian revolutions are the great examples of the folly of gross selfishness and uncompromising hostility to the rights of the poor on the part of the landed and capitalist classes ; but there are many minor examples of thoughtless and selfish opposition having bred violence. I say, after the most thoughtful deliberation, that the onus of avoiding violence lies chiefly on the propertied and educated classes. Communism will come eventually, with or without their co-operation ; and in spite of their opposition, if unwisely they offer it. British socialists do not desire to molest persons of property and culture by physical force. They wish for their co-operation ; but demand at least their passive acquiescence in the enforcement of the will of the majority of the people. If the realization of communism is to be accompanied by serious disturbances or civil war it will be because of the attitude of the privileged and middle classes. In writing this, however, I am assuming that English socialists remain moderate in their policy and willing to offer reasonable compromises such as I have suggested.

It should be added that the doctrine of Marxian socialists and Russian communists, that the social revolution can be realized only through ' class war ', is based on the assumption that the landed and capitalist classes are inevitably grossly selfish and also stupid in their blind opposition to the advancement of the proletariat. The whole theory loses its validity if we assume the growth of true philanthropy and socialism amongst the middle class and a wise appreciation by the rich of the impossibility of resisting the ultimate loss of their privileged position.

WILLING EFFORT AND THE JOY OF ACHIEVEMENT

Personally I find it hard to believe that the transition will be accompanied by violence. There may be riots caused by the misleading of mobs of the poorest elements in some of our great port towns, or by ' patriotic ' organizations of young bloods in London suburbs ; but these should be easily suppressed. The change, worked out in detail beforehand, must have been accepted by an overwhelming majority of the people before the decision is reached to take the fateful step ; and once Parliament, by a substantial majority, has adopted the fundamental laws, the forces of law and order will be in operation to preserve peace during the transition. Everywhere the change will be hailed with vast enthusiasm, as ending for ever a long period of class hatred and industrial strife. The magnificent spirit of British officers in their relations with the rank and file in the trenches is proof, to my mind, that communism, once it is understood, will be accepted and can succeed in Britain.

It is but seldom that the British people becomes stirred to its depths. The last such occasion was the Great War. The realization of communism will be accompanied by an emotional upheaval probably surpassing any in the history of the nation. The conviction that long-deferred hope is about to be fulfilled will generate a revolutionary fervour hard for us, in our present apathy, to understand : a fervour, not for destruction, but for construction. There will be an immense quickening of the generous emotions—tolerance, a desire to see others happy, development of the team spirit and regard for self-sacrifice as the pre-eminent virtue. In certain spheres already we have abundantly the needed attitude of mind. We believe in social service ; and nothing is more typical of the Britisher than his ' sporting instinct '. The extension of these standards of judgment and action to all phases of life will carry the people through to success.

The great majority of citizens will be anxious and able to make an extraordinary effort to ensure the success of the new scheme of society. A man can endure long-sustained physical or mental exertion to attain some end on which he has set his heart ; and, if the achievement have in it an element of service to others, or call forth approval, the labour is greatly lightened. And, if a man working by himself is raised by his own volition to an abnormal effort, how much easier will be the labour, and greater the energy called forth, when all are filled with the same enthusiasm. Some inkling of what is possible may be gained by considering the huge increase of the productive power of the American people, and their willingness to endure sacrifices, once they had decided to come into the War. They threw themselves into it with an amazing energy : they rationed their food and coal supplies in order that distant

Europe might be the better supplied, and they established a co-operation amongst capitalists, and between employers and workers, which was a striking example to other belligerents.

So, when the change to communism occurs, there will be a general anxiety to see it through to success. An immense potential energy which now finds its outlet in sport and organized games will flow into the work of construction ; for every one will realize that great activity is inevitable during the first few years in order to raise substantially the standard of living. People will work willingly for long hours, because the result of the common effort will be something to be proud of. It will be no mean hunt for money, but a gigantic nation-building effort the like of which the world has not yet seen. The remodelling of Russian agriculture and industries, the reconstruction of Germany since 1919, and the enthusiasm and constructional achievements of Fascist Italy, afford suggestions of the far greater reorganization which may be accomplished by a well-organized people whose imagination has been fired.

If it may seem to some that I have stressed too strongly the need for harder work and the increase of production by the efficient reorganization of industries, let me say that I am by no means wholly in disagreement with Bertrand Russell, who maintained a few years ago that there is too great a tendency to regard a large volume of consumable goods as in itself a desirable end.[1] Increased production should be only the means to realizing a happier life by the right use of wealth and of increased leisure ; and, when a certain standard of living has been reached, it may well be questionable whether the pursuit of art, and many other beneficial activities, should not largely replace the effort for yet more physical wealth. This is one of the numerous questions which it is useless for us to try to decide for the future. A great increase of work and productive power will undoubtedly be necessary during the early years of communism ; and later on, when a permanently greater efficiency in production has been realized, the people will please themselves what hours they work and what proportion of the nation's labour they devote to increasing material wealth.

It is not to be thought that there will be uniform enthusiasm throughout the country for the new order of society. There

[1] *The Prospects of Industrial Civilization*, Chapter IX, p. 175.

is sure to be some hanging back : as, for example, in small towns, amongst the petty traders and professional men, and in rural districts, where the opinion of large farmers may prevail over others. Opposition *before* the transition can be overcome only by the persistent educative propaganda of an enthusiastic and united Socialist Party. Discontent and apathy existing in places *after* the change will demand the continuance of educative and persuasive methods. The Socialist Party will need to continue as a closely organized body of enthusiasts, taking the leadership in national and all manner of local affairs ; but the general allowance, its ample amount and its certainty, will doubtless soon persuade the whole of the working classes that the change is beneficial and must be permanent.

When things have settled down, when the new constitutional authorities and the reorganized industries are working smoothly and the hours of labour have been reduced, the change to communism will have been accomplished. The strain of realization over, the people will, I am sure, be filled with the joy of achievement. The ' reign of brotherly love ' will have been inaugurated ; every one will be anxious to do his share of the community's work, and ready to help every one else. But generosity will not supplant the ideal of justice between man and man, which is the essential basis of a society embracing many millions of persons. Society will protect itself by a new positive morality, and by laws and customs according therewith. Social discipline will be stringent, particularly so in regard to the relation of persons to their work ; but I feel sure that in some directions opinion will allow greater freedom than at present, as, for example, in dress, and in certain aspects of sex relations, and that customs and conventions which unnecessarily restrain behaviour and hamper art will fade away.

An active civic life will be aroused and stimulated by the acceptance of the new ideal, by the flow of new ideas and the uncommon energy of thought and work. People will, I think, find in their city, great or small, the proximate field for realizing their ideals ; and opportunity will not be wanting, as now so often, to any one who finds no outlet for enthusiasm in his daily work to labour for an ideal in his leisure time. Knowing the history of his city, contributing to its life in the present, and planning its future, the citizen will conceive it anew as an entity worthy of imaginative effort—an object of affection and of efforts for beautification. This civic awakening will itself react to inspire and augment the new energy and delight in work. And so, with their thoughts directed to the actualities of co-operative life and the potentialities of progress, many people will come to know more of their country as a whole ; will be anxious to make their contribution to the nation's life and to the guidance of its future. A passion for justice amongst nations, as amongst men at home, is certain then to arise and provide an active field for statesmanship, leading slowly perhaps, but with quickened pace, towards the total extinction of war.

APPENDIX I

MILL ON COMMUNISM [1]

NO reasonable person can doubt that a village community, composed of a few thousand inhabitants, cultivating in joint ownership the same extent of land which at present feeds that number of people, and producing by combined labour and the most improved processes the manufactured articles which they required, could raise an amount of productions sufficient to maintain them in comfort ; and would find the means of obtaining, and if need be, exacting, the quantity of labour necessary for this purpose, from every member of the association who was capable of work.

The objection ordinarily made to a system of community of property and equal distribution of the produce, that each person would be incessantly occupied in evading his fair share of the work, points, undoubtedly, to a real difficulty. But those who urge this objection forget to how great an extent the same difficulty exists under the system on which nine-tenths of the business of society is now conducted. The objection supposes, that honest and efficient labour is only to be had from those who are themselves individually to reap the benefit of their own exertions. But how small a part of all the labour performed in England, from the lowest-paid to the highest, is done by persons working for their own benefit. From the Irish reaper or hodman to the chief justice or the minister of state, nearly all the work of society is remunerated by day wages or fixed salaries. A factory operative has less personal interest in his work than a member of a Communist association, since he is not, like him, working for a partnership of which he is himself a member. It will no doubt be said, that though the labourers themselves have not, in most cases, a personal interest in their work, they are watched and superintended, and their labour directed, and the mental part of the labour performed, by persons who have. Even this, however, is far from being universally the fact. In all public, and many of the largest and most successful private undertakings, not only the labours of detail but the control and superintendence are entrusted to salaried officers. And though the ' master's eye ', when the master is vigilant and intelligent, is of

[1] Extract from the *Principles of Political Economy* by John Stuart Mill, Book II, Chap. I, § 3, the 4th and later editions.

proverbial value, it must be remembered that in a Socialist farm or manufactory, each labourer would be under the eye not of one master, but of the whole community. In the extreme case of obstinate perseverance in not performing the due share of work, the community would have the same resources which society now has for compelling conformity to the necessary conditions of the association. Dismissal, the only remedy at present, is no remedy when any other labourer who may be engaged does no better than his predecessor : the power of dismissal only enables an employer to obtain from his workmen the customary amount of labour, but that customary labour may be of any degree of inefficiency. Even the labourer who loses his employment by idleness or negligence, has nothing worse to suffer, in the most unfavourable case, than the discipline of a workhouse, and if the desire to avoid this be a sufficient motive in the one system, it would be sufficient in the other. I am not undervaluing the strength of the incitement given to labour when the whole of a large share of the benefit of extra exertion belongs to the labourer. But under the present system of industry this incitement, in the great majority of cases, does not exist. If Communistic labour might be less vigorous than that of a peasant proprietor, or a workman labouring on his own account, it would probably be more energetic than that of a labourer for hire, who has no personal interest in the matter at all. The neglect by the uneducated classes of labourers for hire of the duties which they engage to perform, is in the present state of society most flagrant. Now it is an admitted condition of the Communist scheme that all shall be educated : and this being supposed, the duties of the members of the association would doubtless be as diligently performed as those of the generality of salaried officers in the middle or higher classes ; who are not supposed to be necessarily unfaithful to their trust, because so long as they are not dismissed, their pay is the same in however lax a manner their duty is fulfilled. Undoubtedly, as a general rule, remuneration by fixed salaries does not in any class of functionaries produce the maximum of zeal : and this is as much as can be reasonably alleged against Communistic labour.

That even this inferiority would necessarily exist, is by no means so certain as is assumed by those who are little used to carry their minds beyond the state of things with which they are familiar. Mankind are capable of a far greater amount of public spirit than the present age is accustomed to suppose possible. History bears witness to the success with which large bodies of human beings may be trained to feel the public interest their own. And no soil could be more favourable to the growth of such a feeling, than a

Communist association, since all the ambition, and the bodily and mental activity, which are now exerted in the pursuit of separate and self-regarding interests, would require another sphere of employment, and would naturally find it in the pursuit of the general benefit of the community. The same cause, so often assigned in explanation of the devotion of the Catholic priest or monk to the interest of his order—that he has no interest apart from it—would, under Communism, attach the citizen to the community. And independently of the public motive, every member of the association would be amenable to the most universal, and one of the strongest, of personal motives, that of public opinion. The force of this motive in deterring from any act or omission positively reproved by the community, no one is likely to deny ; but the power also of emulation, in exciting to the most strenuous exertions for the sake of the approbation and admiration of others, is borne witness to by experience in every situation in which human beings publicly compete with one another, even if it be in things frivolous, or from which the public derive no benefit. A contest, who can do most for the common good, is not the kind of competition which Socialists repudiate. To what extent, therefore, the energy of labour would be diminished by Communism, or whether in the long run it would be diminished at all, must be considered for the present [1852] an undecided question.

Another of the objections to Communism is similar to that so often urged against poor laws : that if every member of the community were assured of subsistence for himself and any number of children, on the sole condition of willingness to work, prudential restraint on the multiplication of mankind would be at an end, and population would start forward at a rate which would reduce the community, through successive stages of increasing discomfort, to actual starvation. There would certainly be much ground for this apprehension if Communism provided no motives to restraint, equivalent to those which it would take away. But Communism is precisely the state of things in which opinion might be expected to declare itself with greatest intensity against this kind of selfish intemperance. Any augmentation of numbers which diminished the comfort or increased the toil of the mass, would then cause (which now it does not) immediate and unmistakable inconvenience to every individual in the association ; inconvenience which could not then be imputed to the avarice of employers, or the unjust privileges of the rich. In such altered circumstances opinion could not fail to reprobate, and if reprobation did not suffice, to repress by penalties of some description, this or any other culpable self-indulgence at the expense of the community. The Communistic scheme, instead of being peculiarly open to the objection drawn from danger of over-population, has the recommendation of tending in an especial degree to the prevention of that evil.

A more real difficulty is that of fairly apportioning the labour of the community among its members. There are many kinds of work, and by what standard are they to be measured one against another ? Who is to judge how much cotton spinning, or distributing goods from the stores, or bricklaying, or chimney sweeping, is equivalent to so much ploughing ? The difficulty of making the adjustment between different qualities of labour is so strongly felt by Communist writers, that they have usually thought it necessary to provide that all should work by turns at every description of useful labour : an arrangement which, by putting an end to the division of employments, would sacrifice so much of the advantage of co-operative production as greatly to diminish the productiveness of labour. Besides, even in the same kind of work, nominal equality of labour would be so great a real inequality, that the feeling of justice would revolt against its being enforced. All persons are not equally fit for all labour ; and the same quantity of labour is an unequal burthen on the weak and the strong, the hardy and the delicate, the quick and the slow, the dull and the intelligent.

But these difficulties, though real, are not necessarily insuperable. The apportionment of work to the strength and capacities of individuals, the mitigation of a general rule to provide for cases in which it would operate harshly, are not problems to which human intelligence, guided by a sense of justice, would be inadequate. And the worst and most unjust arrangement which could be made of these points, under a system aiming at equality, would be so far short of the inequality and injustice with which labour (not to speak of remuneration) is now apportioned, as to be scarcely worth counting in the comparison. We must remember too, that Communism, as a system of society, exists only in idea ; that its difficulties, at present, are much better understood than its resources ; and that the intellect of mankind is only beginning to contrive the means of organizing it in detail, so as to overcome the one and derive the greatest advantage from the other.

APPENDIX II

(A) RELATIVE INCREASE OF NON-PRODUCING WORKERS

(Reference from p. 186)

THE census figures, which group occupied persons in Great Britain by occupations or by industries, do not lend themselves to comparisons over a number of intercensal periods owing to changes of classification. Whilst extensive changes were made in 1911, the new classifications of 1921 by occupations and by industries marked a complete change of principle, so that few figures—even the totals of industries—are comparable with corresponding figures of any earlier census. At the present time (March 1933) the reports on occupations and industries as determined by the 1931 census have not been published. The best that can be done, therefore, is to select figures which are judged to be sufficiently comparable to illustrate the change which has taken place in the distribution of the occupied population between the producing and non-producing occupations during the past fifty years. The word ' producing ' is here used in the physical sense for those persons who extract, cultivate, work upon, or manufacture materials and foods.

It will be sufficient for the present purpose to take such figures as may be available for England and Wales. The Report on the Census of England and Wales, 1911, gives a table comparing numbers in the principal industries with the previous censuses from which the following table is extracted :

PERSONS IN ENGLAND AND WALES IN OCCUPATIONS BY GROUPS :
PROPORTION PER MILLION OF THE POPULATION AGED TEN
YEARS AND UPWARDS

Industry	1881	1891	1901	1911
		Per Million		
National Government	2,615	3,603	4,597	5,687
Local Government [1]	1,087	1,103	1,456	2,598

[1] Excluding police forces and commercial services such as tramways and gas undertakings.

Industry	1881	1891	1901	1911
		Per Million		
Professional Occupations [1]	21,674	23,029	23,940	25,146
Commercial Occupations [2]	16,413	18,879	23,323	27,706
Food, Tobacco, Drink, and Lodging [3]	36,849	41,609	42,403	48,677
Agriculture	70,058	58,273	47,304	45,486
Textile Industries [4]	46,089	43,124	35,041	34,559

[1] Including subordinate services.
[2] Including banking and insurance.
[3] Including all wholesale and retail dealers in food.
[4] Excluding dealers and drapers, and certain finishing traders.

The figures are not comparable exactly from census to census, as there were some changes in classification, especially in 1901 ; but these do not affect the broad changes illustrated by the above figures. The numbers employed in some other industries, such as engineering and coal-mining, were increasing during this period.

Changes since 1911 can only be partially illustrated. A rough comparison can be made as regards a few industries between the censuses of 1921 and 1911 and from them I have extracted the figures in the following table :

PERSONS IN ENGLAND AND WALES IN OCCUPATIONS BY GROUPS, AGED TEN YEARS AND UPWARDS

Employment	1911	1921
National Government	162,014	185,800
Local Government	74,000	300,000[1]
Professional Occupations and their Subordinate Services	717,140	861,090
Banking, Moneylending, and Insurance	144,000	214,000
Agriculture	1,297,000	1,124,000

[1] This figure is only a rough estimate to which I have been forced, because the census total apparently includes manual workers in trades, etc., classed elsewhere in 1911.

For the period subsequent to 1921 the only figures of any use are the Ministry of Labour returns of the number of persons insured against unemployment classified by industries. The following figures give an indication of the recent changes in numbers in the industries and employments which we have had under review :

Employment				1923	1932
National Government	..	..	..	181,170	121,840
Local Government ..	..	..	..	241.760	339,790
Professional Services	..	..	..	108,590	137,160
Commerce, Banking, Insurance, and Finance				226,660	243,130
Distributive Trades..	..	..	..	1,253,980	1,950,240
Hotel, Boarding-house, Restaurant, Public-					
house, etc.	..	..	..	258,960	381,930
Food, Drink, and Tobacco		..	..	499,990	535,810
Textile Trades	..	..	..	1,196,460	1,156,210

There have been minor changes of classification during the interval; but they do not affect the general trend of the changes observable. Figures for agricultural employees, who are not insured against unemployment, are given in the statistical summary issued annually by the Ministry of Agriculture. From 869,000 in 1921 the number of persons employed in agriculture fell to 716,607 in 1931. These figures (which exclude the occupier, his wife, and domestic servants) are not comparable with the census total of persons engaged in agriculture.

On comparing the above three tables it will be seen that they indicate a continuous increase from 1881 to the present time in the numbers employed in local government, in professional occupations, in commerce, banking, insurance, and finance, and in the food, drink, tobacco, and hotel and lodging-house trades, all of which are non-producing occupations in the physical sense of wealth production. It is impossible to give earlier figures of persons employed in the distributive trades because in the censuses before 1921 they were included in their corresponding industries.

(B) PRODUCTIVITY OF MODERN MACHINERY
(Reference from p. 192)

Interesting and important figures have been published recently regarding the extraordinary output per employee obtainable in America from recently invented labour-saving machines. A number of engineers and scientists, working in New York as a group under the direction of the eminent engineer Mr. Howard Scott, have been conducting an Energy Survey of North America. Some of the results have recently been made public in a series of articles by Mr. Wayne Parish in *The New Outlook*, and by Mr. Howard Scott in an article on ' Technocracy ' in *Harper's Magazine*.[1]

[1] *New Outlook*, Nov. and Dec., 1932 and Jan. 1933; *Harper's Magazine* Jan. 1933.

In the latter we read that in 1900 70 man-hours were required per ton of steel produced, while in 1929 only 13 man-hours per ton were necessary. ' In 1904 in the automobile industry 1,291 man-hours were required to produce one vehicle. In 1919 the industry manufactured approximately 1,600,000 vehicles requiring 606,409,000 total man-hours, or 313 man-hours per vehicle. In 1929 the industry reached its peak of production : 5,600,000 vehicles were made requiring 521,468,000 man-hours, or 92 man-hours per vehicle.'

These authors give a number of striking examples. In those which follow some of the comparisons are theirs, some are mine. One machine can make 500,000 needles a day ; and a new cigarette machine makes 2,500 cigarettes per man per minute against a maximum of 600 a few years ago. A modern American miner digs 20,000 tons of iron ore a year ; but a century ago could produce only 800 tons in the same time. Large blast furnaces in the United States produce 4,000 tons of pig iron per man per year against 25 tons 100 years ago. A big modern brick plant can produce 400,000 bricks per man per day. By the hand method which prevailed universally till the middle of the last century a daily average of 450 bricks per man was considered good. A farmer using the latest power-driven agricultural machinery can accomplish in one hour now as much as required 3,000 hours of labour a century ago. A modern shoe factory with 7,200 employees can produce 595,000 pairs in $5\frac{1}{2}$ days : that is, one pair per annum for every family in the United States. We may estimate that by the hand methods which prevailed till late in the nineteenth century, the same output would have required 200,000 skilled workmen. A modern flour mill will produce 30,000 barrels of good flour per man per day as against about 500 barrels per man per day in the small roller flour mill which was considered efficient 50 years ago.

In every industry, we may note, similar striking increases of the productivity of labour have been taking place, and many examples can be seen in England. Printers' type are now cast by a machine only requiring occasional attention hundreds of times as fast as skilled men yet alive used to do such casting by hand. In the Ford Motor Works at Dagenham may be seen many wonderful machines : e.g. a multiple spindle drill which at one operation in a few seconds drills 27 holes in the engine in three different directions with perfect accuracy, with only one man in charge, thus doing the work of about 120 men equipped with ordinary workshop drills. There is also a machine by which one man makes radiator tubes at the rate of 3,000 an hour, whereas by ordinary bench methods three men, dividing the work between them, could hardly produce 100 per hour. The great revolution in spinning and weaving resulting from invention and the application of power was well advanced 100 years ago ; but within the present century the output per worker in some modern mills, spinning coarse and medium counts and weaving plain goods, in certain countries, but not in England, has increased four- or fivefold from higher speeds, automatic stop and changing devices and numerous other improvements. I have failed to find a single industry, extractive or manufacturing, producing raw materials or finished goods in wide demand in which invention has not greatly increased the productivity of labour in recent years. The large steam-trawler, in constant touch with home markets by wireless telephone, is revolutionizing the fishing industry, and the harpoon gun and special lifting devices, and tanks for the oil, have greatly increased the output of whale oil per man ; and so on, from the mining of precious metals to manufacturing cheap jewellery or electric light bulbs.

APPENDIX III

BIBLIOGRAPHY

THIS Bibliography falls into two parts. The first gives a list of the well-known Utopias and plans for new systems of society with which readers of this book should have at least an acquaintance. The second part mentions the principal books (or works) which have assisted the writer in reaching and formulating his conclusions, or from which he has derived information, and of recent books and articles in English which have a close bearing on the subjects of economic equality, the study of consumption, a planned economic organization, and the realization of socialism or communism. Recognized theoretical and descriptive treatises on economics and sociology are omitted, though many of them have been used by the author at one time or another. A number of books have appeared in recent years suggesting new schemes of society, or the reorganization by the Government of currency and credit, or of industries, according to a plan which appears rational to its author. Most of these have been studied by the present writer for the sake of gleaning new ideas ; but, unless such books or pamphlets are based on a careful study of the existing structure of society and of present technical, social, and economic tendencies, they are worthless, and have therefore been excluded from the present list. It should be remembered that this Bibliography is intended merely for the guidance of English readers desiring to acquaint themselves with some of the best-known works on the foregoing subjects, and makes no attempt at a complete survey of the literature of the subjects which it includes. The order of statement in each class is chronological according to the date of first publication of the author's first book included in this Bibliography. A few books could not be regarded as confined to only one of the classes into which this Bibliography is divided and are mentioned in two classes, a cross reference being given.

PART I

1. *Utopias :*

PLATO : *The Republic.* Translated by Benj. Jowett. 3rd ed. 2 vols. Oxford Univ. Press, 1908. pp. 636. Also in one vol.

MORE, SIR THOMAS : *Utopia.*
Written in Latin and originally published at Louvain in 1516. The first translation into English by Raphe Robynson was published 1556. This has been reprinted frequently, both in the curious original spelling and with the English modernized. A good edition in the original spelling was edited, with introduction and notes, by J. Rawson Lumby, D.D., Camb. Univ. Press, London, 1913.
A new translation into modern English has been made by G. C. Richards. (Published by Blackwell, Oxford, 1923).
[All modern editions are expurgated, some observations not essential to the argument and now considered to be in bad taste, being omitted.]

BACON, FRANCIS : *The New Atlantis,* 1627.
[Describes the scientific methods and achievements of the people of this mythical country. The author failed to finish writing his ideas of their social organization.]

CAMPANELLA, TOMMASO : *Civitas Solis* or *City of the Sun,* 1637. [Fanciful, but interesting.]

MÉRCIER, LOUIS SEBASTIEN : *Memoirs of the Year 2500.* Translated from the French, 1772. New Edition corrected ; Liverpool, 1802.

SPENCE, THOS : *Description of Spensonia.* London, 1795.

SPENCE, THOS. : *Constitution of Spensonia.* London, 1798.
[Both reprinted privately with ' The Trial of Thos. Spence ' at the Courier Press, Leamington Spa, 1917.]

FOURIER, CHAS. F. M. : *Le Nouveau Monde Industriel.* Paris, 1829.

FOURIER, CHAS. F. M. : *Theory of Social Organisation.* (See below, Part II, § 5.)

DE GAMOND, MADAME GATTI : *The Phalanstery, or Attractive Industry and Moral Harmony.* London, 1841.
[Translation of a popular account of Fourier's theories of attraction and association as the basis of a new industrial order of society.]

CABET, ETIENNE : *Voyage en Icarie, roman philosophique et social.* Paris, 1842.

CABET, ETIENNE : *Le Populaire. Aux communiste Icariens.* Paris, 1848.

COMTE, I. AUGUSTE M.F.X. : *System of Positive Polity,* or *Treatise on Sociology* (4 vols.)—especially Vol. IV, entitled ' Synthetical Presentation of the Future of Man '. French original published 1851-54. Translation, London, 1875-9.
[The ' Positive Polity ' is part of Comte's great work, *The*

Republic of the West. Vol. IV of ' Positive Polity ' contains a reasoned anticipation of the course of evolution of Western civilization, and his conception of a practicable Utopia which might be realized by consciously organizing in accordance with the principles discovered by sociology. The ideal social organization, termed sociocracy, is based on the emergence of a patriciate, or class of leaders who attain power and fill all official positions, because actuated solely by the public interest ; and the ideal form of government is a dictatorship, functioning through a political triumvirate and an economic triumvirate. The growth of fascism appears almost to have been anticipated by Comte. The struggle between the positivists, who support the dictatorship, and the supporters of communism is clearly envisaged.]

BELLAMY, EDWARD : *Looking Backward.* Boston, 1888. Frequently reprinted in America and England in library and pocket editions.

BELLAMY, EDWARD : *Equality.* N.Y., 1897. Frequently reprinted in America and England in library and pocket editions. (Also classed II. 2.)

HERTZKA, THEODOR : *Freiland—Ein Soziales Zukunftsbild.* Vienna, 1889.

HERTZKA, THEODOR : *Freeland—A Social Anticipation.* Translation [of the foregoing] by Arthur Ransom. London, 1891. Pp. xxiv, 443.

HERTZKA, THEODOR : *A Visit to Freeland, or the New Paradise Regained.* Translated from the German and published by W. Reeves and the British Freeland Association. London, 1894. Pp. 155.

MORRIS, WILLIAM : *News from Nowhere.* First printed in *The Commonweal,* 1890 ; in book form Boston, U.S.A., 1890 ; London, 1891. Frequently reprinted in library and pocket editions and in Vol. XVI of the collected works of William Morris.

WELLS, H. G. : *A Modern Utopia.* London, 1905, etc.

2. Books about Utopias and new Social Schemes :

SARGANT, W. L. : *Social Innovators and their Schemes.* London, 1858.

KAUFMANN, REV. M. : *Utopias or Schemes of Social Improvement from Sir Thos. More to Karl Marx.* London, 1879. Pp. x, 267.

Morley, Henry: *Ideal Commonwealths.* (A volume of Morley's Universal Library.) London, 1885.

[This volume contains translations into modern English of the following : Plutarch's *Lycurgus* (an idealized account of the commonwealth of Sparta), More's *Utopia*, Bacon's *New Atlantis*, Campanella's *City of the Sun*, and a fragment of Hall's *Mundus Alter et Idem*, together with a brief introduction. In the British Museum and some other libraries this volume is not catalogued under Morley, but under the authors of the utopias it includes.]

Mumford, Lewis : *The Story of Utopias.* London, 1923.

PART II

1. *Books Describing Recent Changes in, and Analysing the Weaknesses of, the Capitalist-competitive System :*

Veblen, Thorstein : *Theory of the Leisure Class—An Economic Study of Institutions.* 1st ed. N.Y., 1899. Revised editions 1912, 1918. Frequently reprinted in U.S.A. and England.

Veblen, Thorstein : *The Theory of Business Enterprise.* N.Y. 1904. Pp. vi, 400.

Tawney, R. H. : *The Acquisitive Society.* London, 1922.

Webb, Sidney and Beatrice : *The Decay of Capitalist Civilization.* Published by the Fabian Society and Allen and Unwin. London, 1923. Pp. 182.

Russell, Bertrand (now Lord Russell) : *The Prospects of Industrial Civilization.* London, 1923. Pp. 283.

Chase, Stuart : *The Tragedy of Waste.* New York, 1925.

Brailsford, H. N. : *Socialism for To-day.* London (*The New Leader*), 1925. Pp. 142. (Also classed II. 3.)

Shaw, Bernard : *The Intelligent Woman's Guide to Socialism and Capitalism.* London, 1928. Pp. xxxvi, 495.

Meakin, W. : *The New Industrial Revolution.* London, 1928. [A study for the general reader of nationalization and of tendencies of capital and labour after the War.]

Hoyt, E. E. : *The Consumption of Wealth.* N.Y., 1928. Pp. xiv, 344.

Henderson, Fred : *The Economic Consequences of Power Production.* London, 1931.

Rationalization of German Industry. A study made and published by the National Industrial Conference Board, Inc., 247, Park Avenue, New York, 1931. Pp. 182. [Detailed account with financial and industrial statistics.]

HODGSON, JOHN L.: *Industrial and Communal Wastes.* Journ. Roy. Soc. of Arts, Vol. LXXX, pp. 331–75 (Feb. 19th), 1932.

WALKER, PROF. MILES : *The Call to the Engineer and Scientist.* Presidential Address to Section G of the British Association. Report of the Annual Meeting of the British Association at York, 1932.

[This, and the paper by J. L. Hodgson, give the views of thoughtful engineers. Both papers propose the establishment of a planned economic system on the basis of service, and not for private profit.]

PITKIN, WALTER B.: *The Consumer—His Nature and his Changing Habits.* New York, 1932. Pp. xiii, 421.

SILVERMAN, H. A.: *Economics of the Industrial System* (Pitman). London, 1931.

[This is a useful elementary text-book giving an outline of economic theory and some account of the modern structure of the industrial system. It does not analyse the weaknesses of the capitalist-competitive system, and is included here for the convenience of readers desiring to be acquainted with a reliable recent book on general economics.]

2. *Books on Economic Equality and the Principles of Communism (as the term is used amongst English authors not of the Marxian School) :*

GODWIN, WILLIAM : *Political Justice* (2 Vols.). London, 1793. A convenient edition was edited by H. S. Salt, and published Allen & Unwin. London, 1918.

THOMPSON, WILLIAM : *Practical Directions for the Speedy and Economical Establishment of Communities on the Principles of Mutual Co-operation, United Possessions and Equality of Exertions and of the Means of Enjoyment,* by Wm. Thompson (author of *An Enquiry into the Distribution of Wealth*). London, 1830.

[Contains, besides the Practical Directions, some discussion of the principles and methods of economic equality and of community of property.]

MORRIS, WILLIAM : *Communism.* An Address delivered in 1893 and first published in 1903 by the Fabian Society as Fabian Tract No. 113.

BELLAMY, EDWARD : *Equality.* (Also classed I. 1.)

TAWNEY, R. H.: *Equality.* London, 1931.

DENT, THOMAS : *Voluntary Socialism.* London, 1931. Obtainable from the Hon. Gen. Sec., Brit. Llano Circle. ' Llano ', Guildford Road, Farnham, Surrey.

3. *Modern Books on the Political and Economic Organization of a Socialist State or Proposing an Ideal Organization :*

KROPOTKIN, PRINCE : *Fields, Factories and Workshops.* London, 1898. Reprinted many times.

[This is included here for its discussion of the decentralization of industries and plan of rural life revivified by socially organized industrial production—an anticipation of what is now possible with the extension of electric power supply to many rural areas.]

HUGHES, W. R. (edited by) : *New Town, a Proposal in Agricultural, Industrial, Educational, Civic and Social Reconstruction.* Published for the New Town Council by J. M. Dent. London, 1919.

WEBB, SIDNEY and BEATRICE : *A Constitution for the Socialist Commonwealth of Great Britain.* London, 1920.

[A constructive work with proposals for political and economic organization based on development according to needs from existing institutions.]

WEBB, SIDNEY and BEATRICE : *The Consumers' Co-operative Movement.* London, 1921.

[The last chapter treats of the future of consumers and producers' co-operation and of their relations to municipal enterprise and the State in the formation of the co-operative commonwealth. The principles and organization of the commonwealth are sketched.]

REDFERN, PERCY : *The Consumers' Place in Society.* Co-operative Union, Ltd., Manchester, 1920. Pp. 107.

[The principles of voluntary consumers' co-operation can alone lead to a new economic order.]

POISSON, ERNEST : *The Co-operative Republic.* Translated from the French (published 1923) by H. J. May. Co-operative Union, Ltd., Manchester, 1925.

BRAILSFORD, H. N. : *Socialism for To-day.* London, 1925. (Also classed II. 1, *q.v.*)

SMITH, J. HALDANE : *Collectivist Economics.* London, 1925.

LASKI, H. J. : *Grammar of Politics.* London, 1925. Pp. 672. 2nd ed. 1930.

[Especially Chap. IX, ' Economic Institutions ', in which the organization and control of industries during the transition to socialism is considered.]

COLE, G. D. H. : *Essentials of Socialisation;* MITCHISON, G. R. : *Industrial Compensation;* and other pamphlets in course of publication by the New Fabian Research Bureau, 23, Abingdon Street, London, S.W. 1.

4. *Books and Articles on State Economic Planning (other than Russia) :*

Week End Review. A National Plan for Great Britain. Issued as a Supplement to the *Week End Review* (London). February 14th, 1931.

World Social Economic Planning—The Necessity for Planned Adjustment of Productive Capacity and Standards of Living. Report of the World Social Economic Congress held at Amsterdam, 1931, and volume of Addenda (documents). Published by the International Industrial Relations Institute, The Hague, Holland, and from Rm. 600, 130 East 22nd St., N.Y.

National and World Planning : a Collection of Papers on, at the 36th Annual Meeting. Annals of the American Academy of Political and Social Sciences, July 1932. Also *American Planning,* a compilation pubd. by the Academy.

[In the former, see especially a paper by H. S. Person on ' The Approach of Scientific Management to the Problem of National Planning '.]

BLACKETT, SIR BASIL P. : *Planned Money.* London, 1932. Part I, ' The Need for Planning '.

A Symposium on the Planning of Industries by SIR RAYMOND UNWIN, WM. RANDOLPH, BASIL CLYTHEROE, C. B. PURDOM, and others. *The Architect's Journal,* January 11th, 1933.

[The articles are theoretical and practical, and are illustrated by maps and diagrams.]

5. *A few Books on Sociology and Social Psychology :*

COMTE, AUGUSTE : *System of Positive Polity.* (See class I, 1.)

FOURIER, CHAS. : *Theory of Social Organisation.* Translated, with an introduction by A. BRISBANE (Sociological Series). New York, 1876.

FOURIER, CHAS. : *Selections from the Works of,* by Ch. GIDE, translated by JULIA FRANKLIN. London, 1901.

GIDDINGS, FRANKLIN H. : *Principles of Sociology.* New York, 1896, and pp. xvi, 476. 3rd ed., 1928.

GIDDINGS, FRANKLIN H. : *The Elements of Sociology.* New York, 1898 ; and later editions.

ROSS, ED. A. : *Social Control.* New York, 1901.

McDOUGALL, WM.: *Social Psychology.* London, 1908 ; and numerous later editions revised from time to time.

McDOUGALL, WM.: *The Group Mind.* Cambridge, at the Univ. Press, 1920 ; and later editions.

GEDDES, PATRICK and GILBERT SLATER: 'Ideas at War'. In *Making of the Future* Series. London, 1917.

ELLWOOD, C. A.: *Introduction to Social Psychology.* N.Y. 1917. Pp. xii, 343.

HARLAND, O. H.: *Some Implications of Social Psychology.* Published by Alfred A. Knopf, New York, 1928.

[The author is master at a high school in Leeds, Yorks.]

6. *Historical Accounts of Communistic Communities :*

NORDHOFF, CHAS.: *The Communistic Societies of the United States, from personal visit and observation.* London, 1875.

HINDS, W. A.: *American Communities.* Published by *The American Socialist,* Oneida, New York State, U.S.A. 1878.

BEER, M.: *Social Struggles of Antiquity.* London, 1922.

[Contains an account of communism in Sparta and amongst the early Christians and a chapter on communistic theories in Athens.]

WOOSTER, E. S.: *Communities of the Past and Present.* Printed and published at the Llano Co-operative Colony, New Llano, Louisiana, U.S.A., 1924. Pp. xi, 156. 5s.

The Gateway to Freedom : An illustrated pamphlet describing the Llano Co-operative Colony, New Llano, Louisiana, 1924. 1s. 3d. post free.

[Both the foregoing are obtainable from Llano publications, New Llano, La., U.S.A., or the Hon. Gen. Sec. British Llano Circle, ' Llano ', Guildford Road, Farnham, Surrey. The Colony issues a weekly periodical, *The Llano Colonist,* and other literature about its experiments and the system of integral co-operation.]

GIDE, CHAS.: *Communist and Co-operative Colonies.* Translated from the French original of 1928 by ERNEST F. ROW. London (Harrap), 1930. Pp. 223.

[This covers communistic states of society and experiments in co-operative colonies in all countries from the Middle Ages to recent years.]

INDEX

349

For Product Safety Concerns and Information please contact our EU
representative GPSR@taylorandfrancis.com
Taylor & Francis Verlag GmbH, Kaufingerstraße 24, 80331 München, Germany